Look Smarter Than You Are with Smart View and Essbase 11.1.2

(11.1.2.1.102 & 11.1.2.2)

An End User's Guide

Edward Roske
Tracy McMullen

2nd Edition

interRel Press, Arlington, Texas

Look Smarter Than You Are with Smart View and Essbase 11.1.2: An End User's Guide

Edward Roske
Tracy McMullen

Published by:

interRel Press
A Division of interRel Consulting Partners
Suite 304
1000 Ballpark Way
Arlington, TX 76011

Copyright © 2012-Present by Edward Roske and Tracy McMullen
1st edition
Printed in the United States of America

Library of Congress Cataloging-in-Publication Data
Roske, Edward, McMullen, Tracy
    Look Smarter Than You Are with Smart View and Essbase 11.1.2: An End User's Guide

Edward Roske, Tracy McMullen 2nd ed.
    p. 375 cm.
    Includes index.
    ISBN 978-1-105-56159-7

Trademarks

Various trademarked names appear throughout this book. Rather than list all the names and the companies/individuals that own those trademarks or try to insert a trademark symbol every time a trademarked name is mentioned, the author and publisher state that they are using the names only for editorial purposes and to the benefit of the trademark owner with no intention of trademark infringement.

This book is dedicated to our families. To our children who gave up many hours of "mom" and "dad" time and to our loving spouses for their eternal patience.

Edward Roske, Tracy McMullen

ABOUT THE AUTHORS

Edward Roske fell in love with Hyperion at first sight. In 1995, Edward was working for the Moore Business Forms printing facility in Mundelein, Illinois. While his official title was "Coordinator of Finance", his role focused on coordinating the linking of many, many Microsoft Excel sheets. When someone in his area deleted a row in a supporting workbook and #REF errors showed up in the summary workbook, Edward personally tracked them down cell-by-cell. When he saw his first demonstration of Arbor Essbase (as it was known at the time), he quit his job to become a full-time Essbase consultant (becoming in the process one of those rare individuals who quit stable jobs to consult on products for which they have absolutely no experience).

Edward is a pioneer. He was one of the first Essbase Certified consultants in the world. He was also one of the first people in the world to become certified in Hyperion Planning. While at Moore, he also obtained his first patent proving that there are still new ideas waiting to be discovered and exploited for financial gain.

In May of 1997, Edward left his senior consulting position with a Chicago-based firm to co-found interRel Consulting along with Eduardo Quiroz. Proving that being humble will get you nowhere, Edward helped write interRel's original motto: "Reaching for perfection, we deliver the impossible in record time." He has been the CEO of interRel Consulting since its inception growing them to be a multi-million dollar firm with offices from coast to coast.

Edward still keeps his Essbase skills sharp. He has overseen successful Hyperion implementations at over 100 companies. His optimizations have resulted in Essbase calculation improvements of more than 99.99%.

Continuing his quest to become the world's foremost Essbase-evangelist, Edward has been a regular speaker at annual Hyperion user conferences since 1995 and he is noted for his humorous slant to technically boring information. He is the chair of the Hyperion track for the Oracle Developer Users Group's (ODTUG) annual Kaleidoscope conference and an Oracle ACE Director. Visit Edward's blog at http://looksmarter.blogspot.com/.

Though it is not especially relevant, he also likes puppies.

ABOUT THE AUTHORS

Tracy McMullen, Oracle ACE Director, has been leading the development of Enterprise Performance Management and Data Warehousing applications for over 10 years. Her roles on projects have ranged from developer to architect and project manager on technologies from Hyperion and Business Objects to Cognos and Oracle. She's seen all of the business intelligence tools and Hyperion is her favorite.

Tracy started her career at Arthur Andersen Business Consulting on a project programming in RPG (fun stuff!). Thankfully, her next project introduced her to the world of multi-dimensional databases with a Cognos PowerPlay implementation for an oil and gas client (many years ago Tracy was certified in Cognos PowerPlay and Impromptu). Next, she helped clients from various industries revolutionize their information delivery with Hyperion and other technologies. After years of successful business intelligence implementations, a few shredded documents changed her career path from future Partner to eliminating cancer.

Tracy next joined The University of Texas M.D. Anderson Cancer Center where she lead the charge in implementing budget and planning solutions utilizing Hyperion Planning.

Fate stepped in once again with relocation to the South Texas Coast and Tracy found her new home with interRel Consulting as Director of Consulting and currently, Director of Special Projects (which really means she does a million different things from consulting to training to project management to sales).

Tracy is certified in Oracle Essbase, Hyperion Planning, Hyperion Financial Management and a Certified Project Management Professional (PMP). She is an Oracle ACE Director and the OAUG Planning Domain Lead. Tracy has been a regular instructor at interRel, user conferences and other professional seminars since 2000 on topics including information delivery, business intelligence, data warehousing, and Hyperion implementations. Her strong technical background is complimented by comprehensive practical experience in project management, a skill important not only on the job but at home as well where she manages her kids on a daily basis (ok, she attempts to manage with moderate success).

ABOUT INTERREL CONSULTING

Integrated solutions are key to providing our clients the timely information they need to make critical business decisions. Our philosophy, experience, and methodologies are integral components of our application development, project management, optimization and training. As a result of our experience and commitment to excellence, interRel has become one of the premier providers of analytical solutions using Oracle BI and Hyperion solutions.

interRel solves business problems by utilizing Business Intelligence (BI) and Enterprise Performance Management (EPM) technologies. Our EPM Assessment is designed to identify an organization's current performance management current state relative to the corporate strategy.

interRel has been in business since 1997, and we take pride in delivering our solutions with small teams composed of members with an average of over eight years of Oracle Hyperion and BI related tools, application and consulting experience.

Exclusive EPM/BI consultancy

- 100% of revenue is Oracle EPM / BI-Derived
- 100% of Consultants specialize in Oracle EPM System/Hyperion
- 100% of Senior Consultants are Hyperion Certified
- Senior Consultants have 8+ years of experience
- Junior Consultants have 5+ years of experience

Oracle Hyperion Community - Training, Free Webcasts, and More

Through our various outlets, our focus is always to interact and help others in the Oracle Hyperion community.

If you like this book, join us in person for a hands-on training class. interRel Consulting offers classroom education on a full spectrum of Oracle EPM solutions, including standard course offerings such as *Essbase and Planning Accelerated Fundamentals*, tailored for new Administrators as well as unique advanced courses like *Hyperion Calc Scripts for Mere Mortals*. All classes are taught by knowledgeable, certified trainers whose experience combines to an average of 8+ years. This interactive environment allows attendees the opportunity to master the skill set needed to implement, develop and manage Hyperion solutions successfully. All classes are held at headquarters in Dallas and offer CPE accreditation. interRel Consulting also provides custom training to clients.

interRel Consulting proudly offers free weekly webcasts. These webcasts include the full scope of Oracle BI and EPM System (Hyperion) products, including Essbase, Planning & HFM. Webcasts are primarily held every non-holiday week and twice in most weeks. Topics include 'Tips, Tricks & Best Practices,' which gives you an insider's guide to optimize the usage of your solution. The 'Administration' series focuses on making your job easier and giving a snapshot of the Accelerated Fundamentals course outline while the 'Overview' webcasts discuss the highlights of a solution and how it can be used effectively. All webcasts include interactive examples and demonstrations to see how the products really work.

Awards & Recognitions

- 2008 Oracle Titan Award winner for "EPM Solution" of the year
- 2008 Oracle Excellence Award winner with Pearson Education
- 2011 - interRel received honorable mentions in both the "Financial Management & EPM" and "Energy & Utilities Industry" categories
- Inc. magazine's 5000 fastest-growing private companies in the country (AKA: "Inc. 5000.") – 2008, 2009, 2010 and 2011
- The only Hyperion consulting partner with three Oracle ACE Directors

interRel's commitment to providing our customers with unsurpassed customer service and unmatched expertise make interRel the partner of choice for a large number of companies across the world. Learn more at www.interrel.com.

ACKNOWLEDGEMENTS

If we were to thank all of those who assisted us in the creation of this book, we would have to not only personally mention hundreds of people but also several companies and one or two federal agencies (though we will give a special shout-out to those wacky guys over at the Internal Revenue Service: keep it real, yo!). Suffice to say, if this book stands tall, it is only by balancing on the heads of giants.

We'd like to recognize Glenn Schwartzberg for contributing content to this book, though some of his actual submissions were later removed due to incorrectness, decency laws and the unanimous decision by the authors that delivery of technical information in sonata verse, though revolutionary, would not be acceptable to the audience of this book. Thanks also to Dyana Brune and Vanessa Roske for their proofing and editing skills under time and pressure.

Thank you to Matt Milella, Director of Development, Smart View at Oracle for writing the Foreword to this book. Matt has one of the best blogs on Smart View (http://essbaselabs.blogspot.com/)– don't miss it!

We are also grateful to Shubhomoy Bhattacharya, Principal Product Manager for Smart View at Oracle, for sharing an excerpt of his whitepaper on why you should move from the Excel Add-in to Smart View.

Edward also wants to say "thank you" to Melissa Vorhies Roske, Vanessa Roske, and Eliot Roske for giving up their time with him on evenings and weekends, so he could make his publishing deadline. On a related note, Edward would also like to thank in advance anyone who can figure out a way to get rid of publishing deadlines.

Tracy McMullen would like to thank her family for their never-ending support, patience and understanding.

We give our sincerest gratitude to all the people above, and we hope that they feel that this book is partly theirs as well (just without the fame, glory and most importantly, the royalties).

DISCLAIMER

This book supports versions 11.1.2.1.102 and 11.1.2.2. The version is important because in the 11.1.2.1.102 and the 11.1.2.2 releases of Smart View and Essbase, key features were added into Smart View that provides full parity (and then some) to the old Essbase Excel Add-in.

This book is designed to provide supporting information about the related subject matter. It is being sold to you and/or your company with the understanding that the author and the publisher are not engaged by you to provide legal, accounting, or any other professional services of any kind. If assistance is required (legal, expert, or otherwise), seek out the services of a competent professional such as a consultant.

It is not the purpose of this book to reprint all of the information that is already available on the subject at hand. The purpose of this book is to complement and supplement other texts already available to you. For more information (especially including technical reference information), please contact the software vendor directly or use your on-line help.

Great effort has been made to make this book as complete and accurate as possible. That said, there may be errors both typographic and in content. As such, use this book only as a general guide and not as the ultimate source for specific information on the software product. Further, this book contains information on the software that was generally available as of the publishing date.

The purpose of this book is to entertain while educating. The author and interRel Press shall have neither liability nor responsibility to any person living or dead or entity currently or previously in existence with respect to any loss or damage caused or alleged to be caused directly, indirectly, or otherwise by the information contained in this book.

If you do not wish to abide by all parts of the above disclaimer, please stop reading now and return this book to the publisher for a full refund.

TABLE OF CONTENTS

Foreword

Years ago when I was in the School of Finance I was just about the only person using Microsoft Excel; sort of the PC rebel. At the time it ran on Windows 3.0 and everyone else used and loved Lotus 123. Since then there have been many advances in technology and changes to the way people look at data. These changes continue, but the need for analysis and the power of the spreadsheet has not changed. Twenty plus years later I am a co-creator of the Smart View product (Toufic and Mike did all the hard work but I did help a bit) and run the Smart View development team at Oracle. Today I am still just as passionate about the end users' ability to analyze and present data. I am also passionate about end users having the tools and the information they need to leverage Smart View.

In this book Tracy and Edward show end users the key features of Smart View and how to use them while doing everyday work. The book will take you through real life scenarios that accountants, analysts, consultants, and others face every day while attempting to make sense of the vast amounts of data and sources of data found in their organization. The author's use of humor makes reading easy and you will truly relate to the scenarios that are presented. Trust me, making the topic of analyzing data in Office tools fun, relatable, and humorous is no easy task and deserves at least a mention if not a round of applause (OK maybe a golf clap if you are in the office).

The authors leverage their years of experience in the field to take you step by step through key pieces of functionality that will allow you to maximize the benefits of Smart View and work more effectively in Office applications (especially Excel). The book starts out with introductory features and logically moves on to more powerful features, making it an excellent resource for users at any level. The book is excellent for new Smart View users and as well as long time users who need to learn new features. This book is also an excellent choice for remaining Classic Add-in users that are still hanging on to the past but need to learn about Smart View.

Being responsible for Smart View, it is critically important for me make sure that end users have all the key information on how to correctly leverage the product. Given my experience working with end users in addition to being a former accountant and financial analyst myself (an end user just like you), trust me, the information in this book is invaluable to use as a Smart View user.

Matt Milella, Director of Development, Smart View

Chapter 1:
How I Almost Killed a Man

In the worst of times, desperate men can be driven to commit acts of madness. Case in point: I'm sitting in my cubicle at this moment, trying to figure out how to kill my boss with only the power of my thoughts. I've come to the conclusion that it would be much easier to kill him if 1) he was here at the office with me instead of home asleep in his bed; and 2) my brainwaves weren't reduced to brainripples since it is 3AM and the budget is due in six hours. I'll have to abandon the mental murder idea. On to Plan B: how to kill my boss using a partially consumed lukewarm Starbucks quad ten pump venti vanilla latte.

This isn't getting me anywhere. Murder probably isn't appropriate in a business situation and normally I wouldn't attack any of my coworkers with cold, milk-based drinks. How in the name of Thor did I end up like this? As best as my sleep-deprived memory can recall, it started with a phone call from my boss, Mr. Deadman. The phone rang; my heart sank.

"Sorry to bother you on such a lovely day," he said. I knew he was gazing at the sunset out his corner office window while I stared at my graying, windowless cubicle wall. At least I have that poster of a kitten clinging to a branch with the inspirational quote "Hang on... help is coming" to keep my morale up. I traded for it with the summer intern (he wanted the silver-plated pin with the company logo that I got for "5 years of dedicated service").

"No, no bother. Any questions on the consolidated budget? They're due tomorrow, so there *better* not be any questions. You know how I like to leave every day by 5." Since I hadn't left before 6 in this millennium, I laughed at my own semi-joke until I noticed that I was the only one laughing. He didn't say a word.

The silence stretched on like... something that stretches on for a really long time. As I stared at my kitten poster in hopes of salvation, he said, "Yeah...That's actually why I'm calling. I just need you to increase the IT hardware budget by 10%. Rising cost of servers, don't you know? No hurry, because I'm leaving for the day in just a couple of minutes. I won't even be able to look at the revised numbers until morning."

I could feel the anger rising as my morale sank. I threw a pencil at the stupid kitten picture. Through gritted teeth I managed to stammer "Sure... no... problem..." and in my head I continued 'you jerk.'

With the perky voice of someone about to leave at 5:05PM, he said, "Excellent, and since it's no problem, can you do me a favor and analyze the IT budget growth since last year? I'd do it myself but I have a doctor's appointment first thing in the morning and I won't be in until right before the budget review meeting."

I imagined that I was the one hanging from that kitten's little tree branch. He took my momentary pause in entirely the wrong way. "Oh, don't worry, it's nothing serious. It's just a routine checkup but I figured I'd do it before year end when things are going to get really hectic. Well, have a great one. Don't work too hard." He chuckled as he hung up the phone. Yes, he actually chuckled. I ripped the kitten poster off the wall and got back to work.

Updating the IT budget itself wasn't what took forever: it was consolidating all of our spreadsheets together. With over 200 Excel spreadsheets, I have to open up each one off the network share drive in exactly the right order, press F9, and then on to the next worksheet.

I ran into a frustrating situation around 11PM. After the initial submission of the budget sheets, someone had opened up his sheet and decided that his budget needed to be trimmed, so he deleted a column. My summary workbook, of course, wasn't smart enough to pick up on this change, so my formulas were adding in the wrong column. I noticed the issue around 11, but it took me until 3AM to find the source of the problem and correct it.

Now we're back to where our story began. Budgets have been consolidated, all errant formulas have been corrected, and I haven't even started on the analysis my boss requested. It's at this point that I realize that there's virtually no way to kill someone with a latte (even a really tasty and worth every dollar Starbucks latte) so I'd need to find a better plan. My eyes search my cubicle for implements of destruction.

My eyes wander past my red Swingline stapler and to my monitor where Excel is staring at me, mercilessly mocking me with its unnaturally straight gridlines. The numbers seem to be running across the screen and that's when I realize that I really need to take a nap. Wait. What is this menu item I see between Window and Help? Is this some salvation in the form of Essbase or is it just a mirage in the desert of my existence?

Choirs begin to sing as I realize that the key to my getting a few hours of sleep lies in the hands of a little Office add-in called Smart View and its good friend, Essbase.

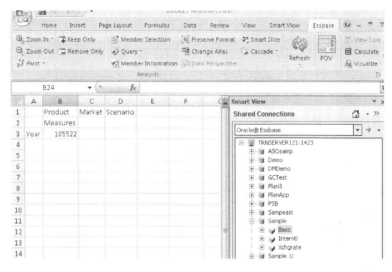

No, they aren't real choirs but rather my iPod playing Beethoven's Ninth, but surely this must be a sign. But will it work? You'll have to read this book to find out. (*Dramatic music* - duh-duh-duh)...

END OF THE CHAPTER QUICK REFERENCE – SUPPORTED SMART VIEW SOURCES

Per our publisher, each new chapter should start on an odd page. Since our chapters aren't quite "even", we'll share helpful highlight tables at the end of each chapter (at least those that end on an even page).

Smart View is a supported Office front end for the following EPM products:

	Smart View 11.1.2.2
Planning	Yes
Essbase	Yes
HFM	Yes
Hyperion Strategic Finance	Yes
Financial Close Management	Yes
Enterprise	Yes
HPCM	Yes
Financial Reporting	Yes
Interactive Reporting	Yes
Web Analysis	Yes

Chapter 2:
Smart View Basics

A traditional computer book would begin at the beginning, giving you the complete history of the topic at hand from when the product was a twinkle in the eye of its creator through all the various versions up to the current, cutting edge product. This book will do no such thing. While we will cover the history of Essbase, let's first grab a beverage and actually learn to do something (connect to Essbase via Smart View, retrieve data, learn about dimensions and members, analyze data, set options and more).

Imagine a company that sells soft drinks. The Beverage Company sells products across the United States and they want to find out which products and markets are profitable and which are losing money more quickly than their poorly named drink from 2001, "Diet Enron with Lemon."

To help with their analysis, they bought a product from Oracle called Essbase (which also includes its trusted Microsoft Office add-in, Smart View, as an end user interface to Essbase). They followed the more than 1,400 pages of instructions to get Essbase installed. During installation, they chose to install the sample applications and were pleasantly surprised to find that one of those applications was dedicated to analyzing The Beverage Company proving that Carson Daly and Earl were right about Karma.

Did you know Smart View is spelled "Smart View" and not "Smartview"?

Tip!

Let's say your name is Pete and you have the job of creating endless TPS reports full of financial and product analysis. To follow along as employee of TBC (The Beverage Company, *do* try to keep up), make sure that whoever installed Essbase at your company installed the sample applications. Until she's prepared the sample applications, you can either stop reading or follow along in your own mind instead of on the computer.

How you connect to EPM sources in Smart View will differ depending on your version. In this book, we'll show you how to connect in versions 11.1.2.1.102 and 11.1.2.2.

CONNECT TO ESSBASE WITH SMART VIEW

The Smart View Ribbon

Go ahead and launch Microsoft Excel. If you are in Excel 2007 or 2010, you should see the *Hyperion* ribbon appear on your menu bar (in Excel 2003, you will find it under *Add-in* menu). At this point, temporary TBC employee, you're probably faced with a blank Excel workbook and you have no idea where to begin. Luckily you have a book, so go up to the *Smart View* ribbon.

Some of you will be saying "Wait, I don't see a ribbon. I'm on Office 2003." Never fear, you will find all of the same options under the Smart View menu option. You'll use this menu for performing actions and should see all of the same commands like Zoom In and Refresh . For those of you on Office 2007 or Office 2010, you can also access the Smart View menu for the full list of functions. This Smart View menu is available under Add-ins ribbon.

The Smart View ribbon contains all of the common actions that you will perform across the Oracle Enterprise Performance Management (EPM) products. You'll see the Smart View ribbon even if you are not connected to an EPM source. When you are connected to Essbase, Planning, HFM, or the Reporting and Analysis framework, you will see and use the Smart View ribbon in addition to the connection specific ribbons.

Tip!

New in 11.1.2.2, extensions for Hyperion Strategic Finance and Predictive Planning are supported.

Before you connect to Essbase, though, notice some of the items in the *Smart View* ribbon that we'll be using later. For instance, one menu option is *Refresh*. Presumably, we'll be using this to refresh data from Essbase. When we need to send data back into Essbase (for budgeting, say), we'll use the *Submit Data* option:

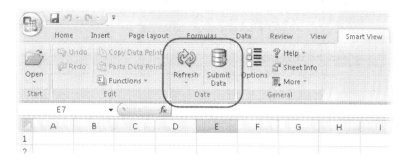

Note!   If you upgraded from an earlier version of Smart View, you may be wondering "Where is the *Zoom* option"? The 11.1.2 Smart View ribbon has undergone a makeover and you'll now find new connection specific ribbons that contain features like "Zoom". More on this as we make our way through the book.

Connect to Essbase with Smart View

If you are on version 11.1.2.1.102 (is anyone tired yet of reading this long version number? We are certainly tired of writing it), near the left side of the ribbon, you will see *Open*:

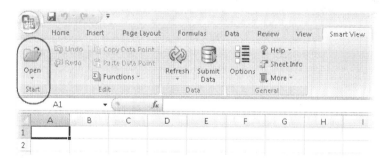

Before you begin to question whether or not you need this book if Essbase is going to be so darned easy to use, click *Open >> Smart View Panel*:

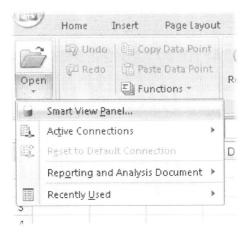

If you are on version 11.1.2.2, simply click on the Panel button on the Smart View ribbon:

The Smart View Panel is the hub of all Smart View activity. Here you will connect to data sources and create reports for Essbase sources. If you use Hyperion Planning or Hyperion Financial Management, you will use the Smart View panel to access task lists and data forms. If you are using Financial Reporting or Web Analysis, you can use Smart View to execute your reports and import them into Excel.

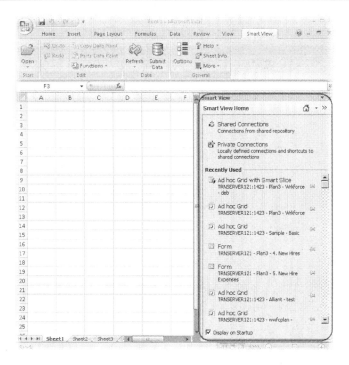

If this is the first time you've used the Smart View add-in you may need to specify the URL to connect to the common Shared Services.

Click the *Options* button on the Smart View ribbon:

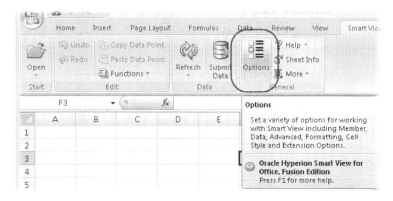

Choose *Advanced* option. Under the General section, type in the URL for the Shared Connections URL – something like http://*workspaceservername*:19000/workspace/SmartViewProviders (your administrator should be able to provide this to you):

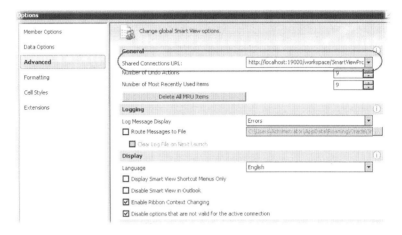

Click *OK*. Now you should see the Smart View panel.

The Smart View Home panel displays three main options:

- Shared Connections –available EPM connections set up by your Hyperion Administrator
- Private Connections –available EPM connections saved to your local computer and managed by you, the user, by entering the URL directly or saving a shared connection to your local computer; typically this is used for backward compatibility to sources on versions earlier than 11.1.2 (that are not available in the common Shared Services)
- Recently Used - list of recently used ad hoc grids or data forms and tasks lists (if you are using Hyperion Planning)

Select *Shared Connections*:

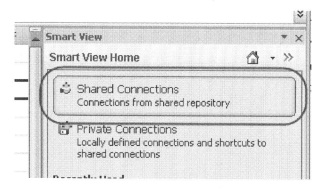

You should be prompted for an id and password. Before you continue, you need to know your Username and Password. Your login information controls access to various parts of the Essbase server. Depending on your Username, you might have access to the entire Essbase server, access to specific databases on the server, or no access at all (in which case, this book will be somewhat unhelpful to you).

For instance, at my company, I am an Essbase administrator. In this God-like state, I am master of all Essbase databases. For the servers that I supervise, there is not a database that I cannot see, not a setting that I cannot change, and not a user that I cannot delete. While this does make me feel really special, it also means that whenever anything goes wrong, I am probably going to get blamed.

Tip!

Only get Essbase access to what you need to do your regular job and avoid getting blamed for everything!

The Username and Password given to you by your Essbase Administrator (see "God-like administrator" above) will grant you access to only some of the databases.

Enter your Essbase ID and password. Click *Connect*:

Select the drop down list for the Shared Connections:

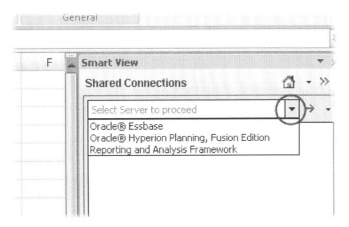

Three options are listed: Oracle Essbase, Oracle Hyperion Planning, and the Reporting and Analysis Framework. Select Oracle Essbase and you should see one or more Essbase servers (in the screen below, our Essbase server is called TRNSERVER121:

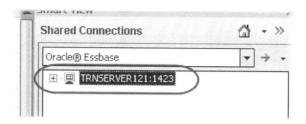

So what exactly is an Essbase server? Somewhere off in the basement of your company (or more likely, these days, in a server farm in Antarctica) is a really powerful machine that holds the Essbase software and all of the data for the Essbase databases we'll be using. The sample applications mentioned earlier are stored on this server.

Your computer (which in computer terms is called the "client") talks to this server. While all the data is stored on the server, all of the analysis happens on your client. Once we connect to the server, we can pull data back to the client and look at it in Excel. If we change the data we should send it back to the server so that everyone else in the company can look at the same set of numbers. You've probably heard the saying "everyone is looking at a single version of the truth."

Click the + sign next to your Essbase server (again, if you're not sure which one is the right server, give your handy Essbase admin a call.)

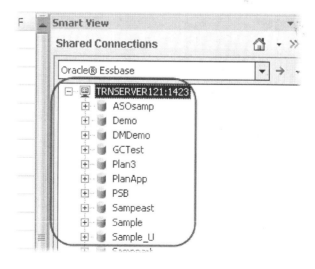

You will see a series of Applications appear in a list underneath the Essbase server (the cylinder icon denotes an application). If you click the plus sign next to the application, you will see the databases (the cube icon denotes Essbase databases or cubes).

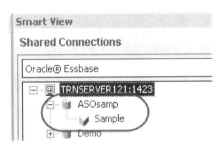

An Essbase application is a collection of one or more Essbase databases, but usually an application will contain only one database. In the image above, the ASOsamp application has one database, Sample. The Sample application has three databases within it: Basic, Interntl, and Xchgrate.

Note!

If your company uses Hyperion Planning, you should know the Essbase applications that support Planning often have more than one database and can have as many as five.

RETRIEVE ESSBASE DATA

The anticipation is overwhelming – you can't wait to start analyzing data. We'll be using the Basic database in the Sample application. We'll call it Sample.Basic, for short. First we need to connect the spreadsheet to *Sample.Basic*. Right click on the *Sample.Basic* database and choose *Connect*:

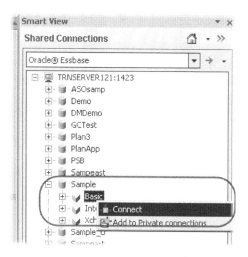

You are now connected to the database. Right click on Basic and you'll see you now have a number of options available to you. Select *Ad hoc Analysis*:

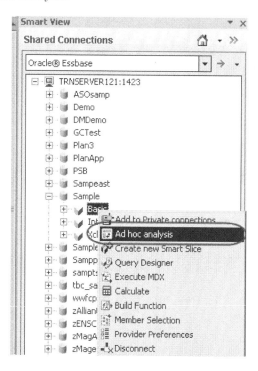

Your display in Smart View should have changed significantly.

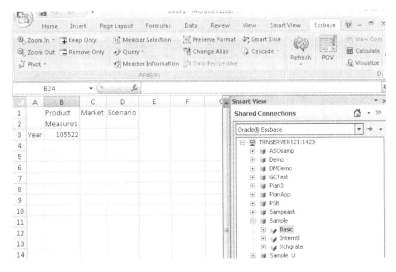

First notice that a new ribbon called Essbase now displays in Excel. A number of ribbon actions are available including Zoom In and Zoom Out, Keep Only and Remove Only, Refresh and POV:

The ribbon in 11.1.2.2 looks the same:

Second notice that data has been retrieved from the Essbase server and is displayed in the spreadsheet. You see the five dimensions in Sample.Basic along with a single data value.

If you don't see the above grid, let's troubleshoot (and even if you do see the above grid, read along because at some point you may see these issues). The first possible issue is that you might not see a number in cell B3. Instead of a number, there might be a dash or the word "#Missing" (more on that later). Or you also might see an error message:

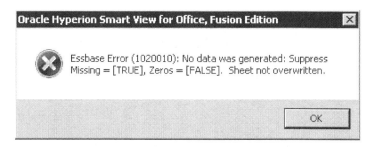

Quite simply, the Sample.Basic database doesn't have any data. Nicely ask your Essbase Administrator to load the Sample.Basic database, right click on Sample.Basic and select *Ad hoc Analysis* again, and you should see the spreadsheet grid shown above.

Before we start zooming and drilling (boy, Essbase sounds really exciting!), let's discuss connection information. The current spreadsheet tab in the current Excel workbook is the only one that's connected to Essbase. If you went from Sheet1 to Sheet2, Sheet2 wouldn't be connected. It is possible to click over to Sheet2 and connect it to Essbase, but at the moment, it's not.

This does bring up the interesting point that each sheet can be connected to a different Essbase database or no database at all. Sheet2 could be connected to Demo.Basic while Sheet1 is connected to Sample.Basic. Sheet 3 could be connected to both Sample.Basic and Demo.Basic at the same time. All this can get a bit confusing. To easily see which data source a worksheet is using, select the Smart View tab. Select the *Sheet Info* icon. All of the important connection information is displayed, including Server, Application, and Database (or Cube):

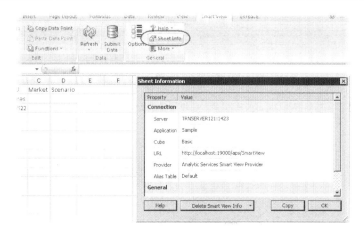

DIMENSIONALITY

Can we zoom now? Can we, can we? (My four year old just bounced into my head for a moment.) Not yet. First let's define "dimensions", something you need to know before zooming and drilling can commence. Remember our initial spreadsheet:

	A	B	C	D
1		Product	Market	Scenario
2		Measures		
3	Year	105522		

What is a Dimension?

Those two words at the top of the spreadsheet (Year and Measures) and the three words in the POV (Product, Market, and Scenario) are the dimensions of Sample.Basic. To oversimplify, a *dimension* is something that can be put into the rows or columns of your report (or it can apply to the whole page). Different databases have different dimensions, and Sample.Basic has the five just mentioned.

Let go of your mouse for a second, and have a look at this really simple Profit & Loss Statement:

	Actual	Budget
Sales	400,855	373,080
COGS	179,336	158,940
Margin	221,519	214,140
Total Expenses	115,997	84,760
Profit	**105,522**	**129,380**

It only has two dimensions. Down the rows, we have our "Measures" dimension (often called "Accounts"). Across the columns, we have our "Scenario" dimension. Some people like to call this dimension Category, Ledger, or Version. It is Essbase tradition to call the dimension that contains Actual, Budget, Forecast, and the like "Scenario," and we'll follow the tradition.

The only two dimensions so far are Scenario and Measures. The more detailed breakdowns of Measures (Sales, COGS, Margin, et al) are the members of the Measures dimension. Actual and Budget are members in the Scenario dimension. A *member* identifies a particular element within a dimension.

If we pivot the Measures up to the columns and the Scenario dimension over to the rows, our report will now look like this:

	Sales	COGS	**Margin**	Total Expenses	**Profit**
Actual	400,855	179,336	221,519	115,997	105,522
Budget	373,080	158,940	214,140	84,760	129,380

While it doesn't look very good, it does illustrate a couple of important points. First, a dimension can be placed into the rows, columns, or the POV (as we'll see in a second). If it's really a dimension (as Scenario and Measures both are), there are no restrictions on which dimensions can be down the side or across the top. Second, notice that the values in the second report are the same as the values in the first report. Actual Sales are 400,855 in both reports. Likewise, Budgeted Profit is 129,380 in both reports. This is not magic.

Note!   A dimension can only exist in one of rows, columns and POV at one time. You must have at least one dimension in the rows and one in the columns.

Three Dimensions

A spreadsheet is inherently two dimensional (as are most printed reports). It has rows and columns. This is great if your company only produces a Profit & Loss Statement one time, but most companies will tend to have profit (be it positive or negative) in every month. To represent this in Excel, we use the spreadsheet tabs (one for each month):

All Products and Markets.xls	Actual	Budget
Sales	31,538	29,480
COGS	14,160	12,630
Margin	17,378	16,850
Total Expenses	9,354	6,910
Profit	8,024	9,940

Jan / Feb / Mar / Apr / May / Jun / Jul / Aug / Sep / Oct / Nov / Dec /

We've now introduced a third dimension. Most people call it "Time" but Sample.Basic calls it "Year" just to be contrary. It could be across the columns (if you wanted to see a nice trend of twelve months of data) or down the rows, but we've put it in the pages (a new tab for each "page"). That is, if you click on the "Jan" tab, the whole report will be for January.

If you're looking for Actual Sales of 400,855, you won't find it now because that was the value for the whole year. We could get it by totaling the values of all twelve tabs onto a summary tab.

Four Dimensions and More

Right now, this spreadsheet is not broken down by product or market. Within Excel, it's problematic to represent more than three dimensions (since we've used the rows, columns, and tabs). One way is to have a separate file for each combination of product and market:

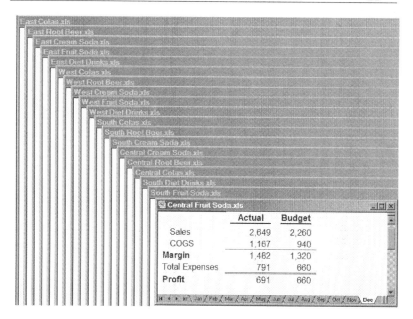

As you can see, this is getting ridiculous. What if we want to pivot our market dimension down to our columns so that we could compare profitability across different regions? To do this, we'd either have to have a series of linked spreadsheet formulas (which would break as soon as we added or deleted a new product or market) or we could hire a temporary employee to print out all the spreadsheets and type them in again with the markets now in the columns. While the latter method is obviously error-prone, the "rekeying" method is the one used by the majority of the companies in the world that do not own Essbase.

Since Market and Product are dimensions, it should be no more difficult to put them in the columns or rows than Scenario or Measures. As we'll discuss later, producing a report with markets down the side and products across the top is no more difficult than dragging-and-dropping:

	Actual	**Profit**	**Year**		
	Colas	Root Beer	Cream Soda	Fruit Soda	**Product**
East	12,656	2,534	2,627	6,344	**24,161**
West	3,549	9,727	10,731	5,854	**29,861**
South	4,773	6,115	2,350	–	**13,238**
Central	9,490	9,578	10,091	9,103	**38,262**
Market	**30,468**	**27,954**	**25,799**	**21,301**	105,522

In the bottom-right corner, you'll see our familiar actual profit for the year of 105,522. At the top of the report you'll see that we have to specify the three dimensions in our application that are not in our rows or columns, or Essbase wouldn't know which values to display. For instance, if we didn't specify "Profit", Essbase wouldn't know if we wanted Profit, Sales, Margin, or some random measure to be named later.

Tip!

Always specify a member from each dimension for each intersection. If Essbase doesn't know which member of a dimension to use for an intersection, it will use the topmost member of that dimension.

AD HOC ANALYSIS

Now that we understand that a dimension is anything that can be placed in the rows, columns, or the POV, let's get back to retrieving data and analyzing data.

Try It!

In case you weren't following along, go to a blank sheet in your workbook, connect to Essbase and then right click on Sample.Basic and select *Ad hoc Analysis*.

Try It!

Go to another blank sheet in your workbook and right click on Sample.Basic. Select *Ad hoc Analysis*.

You now have two spreadsheets that are connected to Essbase. Choose one and click on the cell that shows 105,522 and look at the formula bar just above the spreadsheet grid:

	B3			f_x	105522
	A	B	C	D	E
1		Product	Market	Scenario	
2		Measures			
3	Year	105522			

105,522 represents the total of all the months, products, and markets in our application. Notice, however, that the content of the cell is not an Excel formula summing up other values. The total is being calculated on the Essbase server and then returned back to us as a plain old number. This is one of the main reasons that Essbase is far faster than, say, a pivot table: all of the detail stays on the Essbase server and only the value we care about is returned to us.

You may also see a floating POV window in your spreadsheet. We'll review this component shortly.

Tip!   Since there are no formulas linking this spreadsheet to Essbase (only values), you can send this spreadsheet to people in your company who don't have access to the Essbase server.

Select the cell that contains *Measures* (cell B2 if you're following along). "Measures" tells us nothing, so go ahead and type the word "Profit" into that cell instead and press Enter. The numbers will not change, because you haven't told Essbase to re-retrieve your data yet. Choose *Refresh* from the ribbon:

	A	B	C	D
1		Product	Market	Scenario
2		Profit		
3	Year	105522		

Floating POV

Now let's turn our attention to the POV. In our current spreadsheet, the Point of View, commonly known as "POV", is "Product", "Market", and "Scenario". We are looking at the data value for total products, for total markets, and for a single scenario (likely actual, because this is how Essbase admins usually design their databases). If you prefer, you can toggle these POV dimensions to a floating POV window by clicking the POV icon on the Essbase ribbon:

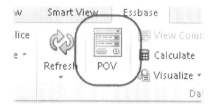

This toggles the POV window on:

	A	B	C	D	E
2		Profit			
3	Year	105522			
4					
5					
6					
7					

POV Sheet1_ ▼ ✕
Product ▼
Market ▼
Scenario ▼
Refresh ⓘ

This floating window pulls POV dimensions into a floating dialogue (really the clever developers have just hidden row 1). Some users love the floating POV. Others strongly dislike ("hate" is such a harsh word) the floating POV. In versions prior to 11.1.2.1.102 you could not turn off the floating window, but that changed in 11.1.2.1.102. Simply toggle off the POV using the POV button in the Essbase ribbon (new sheets start with the POV turned off).

Practice turning on and off the POV:

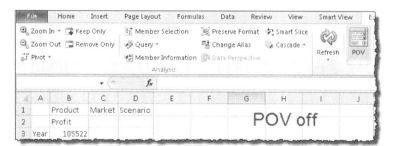

Notice the dimensions that were previously in the floating POV - Product, Market and Scenario - are now in the spreadsheet.

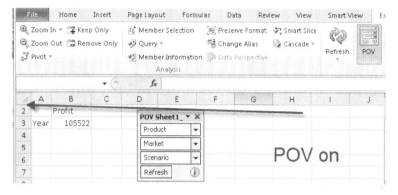

To switch back to the floating POV, choose the POV icon again. Notice row 1 is hidden. When the POV window is turned on, the members are actually still there, they're just hidden in the first row of the Excel spreadsheet. This allows you to print the POV on reports or use those hidden rows in formulas to create headings.

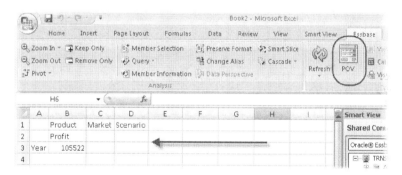

     Toggle the floating POV on and off.

Try It!

You can also easily move these dimensions from the floating POV to the spreadsheet and back again. To move the dimension, grab it by the drop down arrow. For example, select Scenario and drag it from the POV to the columns section of the spreadsheet, near Profit:

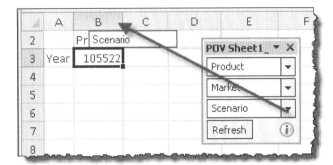

Scenario will be dropped into the grid either above or below profit depending on where you left your mouse:

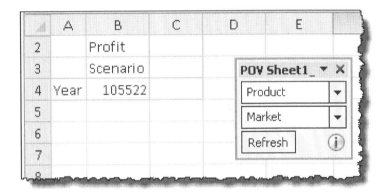

Next, let's update our analysis to focus on Budget. Type in "Budget" over Scenario and click *Refresh*:

◢	A	B	C	D	E
2		Profit			
3		Budget			
4	Year	129380			
5					
6					
7					

POV Sheet1_ ▼ ✕

Product	▼
Market	▼

Refresh ⓘ

If you spelled Profit or Budget wrong, Essbase will kindly put the dimension it thinks you didn't specify into the POV for you. Type "Budgets" over "Budget" in cell B1. Click *Refresh*:

◢	A	B	C	D	E
2		Profit			
3		Budgets			
4	Year	105522			
5					
6					
7					
8					

POV Sheet1_ ▼ ✕

Product	▼
Market	▼
Scenario	▼

Refresh ⓘ

Notice that cell B1 says "Budgets", so when we retrieved, Essbase put "Scenario" in the POV (thinking that we had forgotten a dimension). Essbase is very particular about spelling. It has no idea that "Budgets" and "Budget" means the same thing to you, so watch your spelling if you're going to be typing in the names of members.

Tip!

While spelling is important, members are not case-sensitive (unless the person setting up an Essbase application specified that it should be case-sensitive). Type in "BuDgEt" and Essbase will retrieve the data and replace your funky capitalization with "Budget".

You can also type member names directly in the floating POV. Type "Budget" over scenario in the POV window and click Refresh:

	A	B	C	D	E
2		Profit			
3		Budgets			
4	Year	129380			
5					
6					
7					
8					

POV Sheet1_ ▼ ✕
Product ▼
Market ▼
Budget| ▼
Refresh ⓘ

Let's go through one more scenario. Follow along with me. Open a new spreadsheet and type in the following:

	A	B	C
1		Actual	Budget
2	East		
3			
4			

Notice that we don't have a floating POV window and that we are not connected to a database. Right click *Sample.Basic* and select *Ad hoc Analysis*. Voila! Data is retrieved based on the member selections for the two dimensions displayed (Market and Scenario). The remaining dimensions are listed in the POV (either in the spreadsheet or floating POV, depending on what you have turned on):

	A	B	C	D
1		Year	Measures	Product
2		Actual	Budget	
3	East	24161	28390	

You might be prompted with the following message:

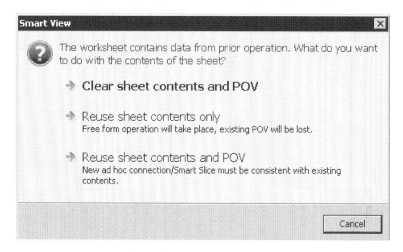

What Smart View is asking: Do you want to remove the contents of your spreadsheet and start with a blank spreadsheet? Or do you want to keep what you defined in the spreadsheet but remove the POV member selections? Or do you want to keep and reuse both the spreadsheet contents and the POV member selections?

If you want to start with a blank spreadsheet with the top level members of each dimension selected, choose *Clear sheet contents and POV.* The remaining two options will maintain the spreadsheet as you've defined it and apply the member selections/query to the connected source either with or without the POV.

We do not want to clear the contents of the sheet and we don't have a POV defined so we select *Reuse sheet contents only.* Now our spreadsheet is connected to the database and has retrieved values.

Go ahead and close this spreadsheet for now; we'll use the original query going forward. Are you ready to zoom?

ZOOM IN AND OUT

Your spreadsheet should look something like the following:

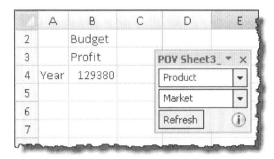

If so, select the cell that says Year (cell A4) and choose *Zoom In* from the Essbase ribbon:

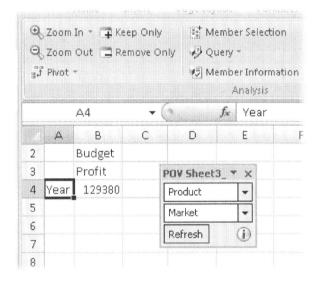

Though your report might not look exactly like this (depending on your current Essbase Options and Excel formatting), you should see the quarters that make up the total year:

◢	A	B	C	D	E
2		Budget			
3		Profit			
4	Qtr1	30580			
5	Qtr2	32870			
6	Qtr3	33980			
7	Qtr4	31950			
8	Year	129380			
9					
10					

POV Sheet3 ▼ ✕
Product ▼
Market ▼
Refresh ⓘ

Select the Qtr1 cell (cell A4) and again choose *Zoom In*. This will show you the three months that comprise Qtr1.

Tip!   There are also mouse shortcuts for zooming in and zooming out. To Zoom In using the mouse, double-click with the *left* mouse button on a member name. To Zoom Out, double-click with the *right* mouse button on a member name.

When we zoom in, we are navigating from the top of a dimension down the various levels, eventually getting to the bottom of the dimension. Zooming can also be known as drilling. In our example, we zoomed (or drilled) from Year to Quarter. Select Qtr1 and select *Zoom in* and we see the three months that make up quarter 1 – Jan, Feb, and Mar. We can zoom on any dimension in Essbase, quickly retrieving the data at various levels across the Essbase database (or for various member intersections within the database). For example, we've very quickly retrieved profit data for the three months that make up Qtr1 for all products and markets.

To go back up a dimension from bottom to top, you can either *Zoom Out* (or right double click on a member). Highlight any of those three months and choose *Zoom Out* from the *Essbase* ribbon. Select a quarter and choose *Zoom Out* again and we're back to where we started.

Change the Way You Zoom

Select the drop down arrow next to Zoom In. From the Essbase ribbon, you can choose how you want to zoom. Do you want to zoom in on the next level (default unless specified differently under the Options) or the bottom level? Simply select the desired option, though be careful with *All Levels* and *Bottom Level*. This could potentially bring back a LOT of members, which will slow performance and create run-away queries on the Essbase server.

Sometimes you will get a bit overexcited with your zooming and you will zoom one too many times (haven't we all been there?). If you need to "go back", Smart View provides Undo capabilities (that fortunately works excellently for undoing our actions in Smart View but unfortunately doesn't work anywhere else in our life).

Essbase Undo

To undo your last Essbase action, don't look under the *Edit* menu in Excel for Undo (and don't click the ![button] button on the Excel toolbar). Simply click the *Undo* button on the Smart View ribbon:

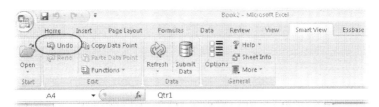

Note that you can also "Redo," which will reapply performed actions. How many times can you undo or redo? Well, it depends. Select the *Options* button from the Smart View ribbon. In the Advanced section, you can define how many "undos" you would like Smart View to perform:

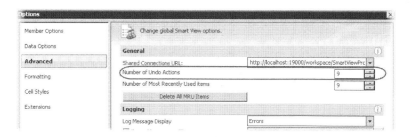

You can type in the number of undo actions you want to allow. Would you ever want to set this setting to 100? No, higher values can impact performance negatively. Keep the *Number of Undo Actions* to a lower number.

Try It!

Assuming that your report is back to looking like the one above with only the quarters and the year showing, click on Qtr1 and choose *Zoom Out*. Either *Undo* or *Zoom In* to display the quarters again.

KEEP ONLY / REMOVE ONLY

Let's say that you want to remove Year from the report. There are two ways to accomplish this. The first is by using the power of Excel: highlight row six and choose *Delete* from Excel's *Edit* menu. You can also use the power of Essbase by highlighting the Year cell and choosing *Remove Only* from the *Essbase* ribbon. Try it – *Remove Only* the member Year. *Keep Only* is the opposite of *Remove Only*. It will keep the members you have selected in the spreadsheet.

Keep Only / Remove Only works on multiple cells as well. Select the Qtr1 cell, hold down the control key, and then click the Qtr2 cell. Now select *Keep Only*. Your report should be reduced to two quarters:

⊿	A	B	C	D	E
2		Budget			
3		Profit			
4	Qtr1	30580			
5	Qtr2	32870			
6					
7					

POV Sheet2_ ▼ ✕

Product ▼

Market ▼

Refresh ⓘ

PIVOT

Since this report is fairly useless, click on Qtr1 and choose *Zoom Out* to return to the previous report. *Zoom In* again to display the quarters above the year. Let's drill down a second dimension. Highlight the Profit cell and choose *Zoom In*:

⊿	A	B	C	D	E	F
2		Budget	Budget	Budget		
3		Margin	Total Expenses	Profit		
4	Qtr1	51540	20960	30580		
5	Qtr2	54780	21910	32870		
6	Qtr3	56410	22430	33980		
7	Qtr4	51410	19460	31950		
8	Year	214140	84760	129380		
9						
10						

POV Sheet2_ ▼ ✕

Product ▼

Market ▼

Refresh ⓘ

Now select Margin and click *Pivot* from the Essbase ribbon. (Notice that you can just *Pivot*, which will pivot the selected dimension within the spreadsheet, or you can *Pivot to POV* which will move the dimension and selected members to the floating POV.) In this example, choose *Pivot>>Pivot*:

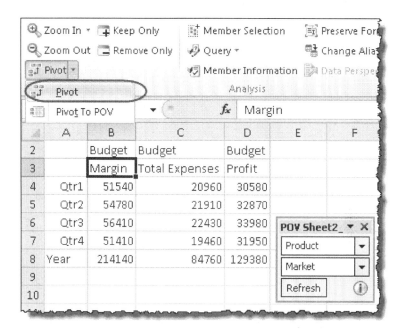

The result should look as follows:

◢	A	B	C	D	E	F
2			Budget			
3	Margin	Qtr1	51540			
4	Margin	Qtr2	54780			
5	Margin	Qtr3	56410			
6	Margin	Qtr4	51410			
7	Margin	Year	214140			
8	Total Expenses	Qtr1	20960			
9	Total Expenses	Qtr2	21910			
10	Total Expenses	Qtr3	22430			
11	Total Expenses	Qtr4	19460			
12	Total Expenses	Year	84760			
13	Profit	Qtr1	30580			
14	Profit	Qtr2	32870			
15	Profit	Qtr3	33980			
16	Profit	Qtr4	31950			
17	Profit	Year	129380			

POV Sheet2_ ▾ ✕
Product ▾
Market ▾
Refresh ⓘ

Tip!

Would you like to hide the repeating members for Margin, Total Expenses and Profit for each time period? Select the Smart View ribbon and choose *Options*. In the *Data Options* section, check *Repeated Members* under Suppress Rows:

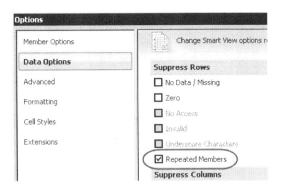

Click *Refresh* to update the spreadsheet.

We see how Smart View can show two dimensions on either the row or column axis at the same time. To get the quarters and years up to the columns, we could do that "hiring the temp to rekey" method we mentioned before, or we can do it the Essbase way. Highlight any of the member names in Year column, column B (Qtr1, say), and choose *Pivot*:

	A	B	C	D	E	F
2		Qtr1	Qtr2	Qtr3	Qtr4	Year
3		Budget	Budget	Budget	Budget	Budget
4	Margin	51540	54780	56410	51410	214140
5	Total Expenses	20960	21910	22430	19460	84760
6	Profit	30580	32870	33980	31950	129380
7						
8				POV Sheet1_ ▼ ✕		
9				Product ▼		
10				Market ▼		
11				Refresh ⓘ		
12						

Admit it: you're impressed. There is also a mouse shortcut for pivoting dimensions: it's called a "right drag-and-drop." Select the Qtr1 cell using your left mouse button. Now, with the mouse cursor over that cell, hold down the right mouse button. After a little while, a row of white member names should appear showing you what you're about to pivot. Don't let go of the right mouse button yet:

▲	A	B	C	D	E	F
2		Qtr1	Qtr2	Qtr3	Qtr4	Year
3		Budget	Budget	Budget	Budget	Budget
4	Year in	51540	54780	56410	51410	214140
5	Total Expenses	20960	21910	22430	19460	84760
6	Profit	30580	32870	33980	31950	129380
7						
8					POV Sheet1_ ▼ ✕	
9					Product ▼	
10					Market ▼	
11					Refresh ⓘ	

Move the white cells over to the cell where you want to pivot the dimension. In our case, drag the members over to cell A3. Okay, now let go of the right mouse button:

▲	A	B	C	D	E	F
2			Budget			
3	Qtr1	Margin	51540			
4	Qtr1	Total Expenses	20960			
5	Qtr1	Profit	30580			
6	Qtr2	Margin	54780			
7	Qtr2	Total Expenses	21910			
8	Qtr2	Profit	32870		POV Sheet1_ ▼ ✕	
9	Qtr3	Margin	56410		Product ▼	
10	Qtr3	Total Expenses	22430		Market ▼	
11	Qtr3	Profit	33980		Refresh ⓘ	
12	Qtr4	Margin	51410			
13	Qtr4	Total Expenses	19460			
14	Qtr4	Profit	31950			
15	Year	Margin	214140			
16	Year	Total Expenses	84760			
17	Year	Profit	129380			

While you're back to having two dimensions on the rows, you've changed the orientation of the two dimensions to show each measure by each time period. If all we wanted to show for each time period was Profit, we could use the *Keep Only* function. Select one of the Profit cells (cell B5, say), and choose *Keep Only*. This will remove all the instances of Margin and Total Expenses (alternatively, we could also have used *Remove Only* on the other two members).

	A	B	C	D	E	F
2			Budget			
3	Qtr1	Profit	30580			
4	Qtr2	Profit	32870		POV Sheet1_ ▼ ✕	
5	Qtr3	Profit	33980		Product ▼	
6	Qtr4	Profit	31950		Market ▼	
7	Year	Profit	129380		Refresh ⓘ	
8						

This method is much more efficient than simply adding and deleting rows in Excel.

To clean up the report (since it looks a bit silly showing the same member repeatedly in the rows), again select one of the Profit cells and choose *Pivot*. Since there is only one member to be pivoted, Essbase will assume that you want the member to be pivoted up to the page instead of the columns.

Try It!

At this point we're letting the reins go. Continue to play around with the features we've just illustrated. Try zooming in, zooming out, and pivoting the five dimensions of Sample.Basic. Test toggling on and off the floating POV.

While you can make a very ugly report (no offense, but you *can*), you can't harm the data in any way: it's safely stored on the Essbase server.

Remember – "Where is Row 1 in my Excel spreadsheet"?

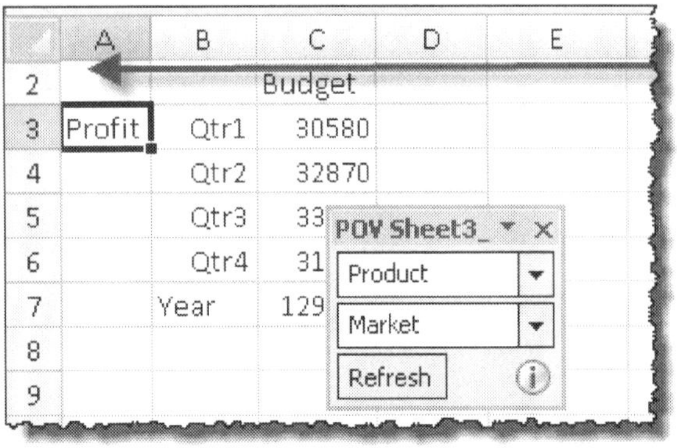

	A	B	C	D	E
2			Budget		
3	Profit	Qtr1	30580		
4		Qtr2	32870		
5		Qtr3	33		
6		Qtr4	31		
7		Year	129		
8					
9					

POV Sheet3_ ▼ ✕

Product ▼

Market ▼

Refresh ⓘ

This is where Smart View is storing the POV members. Toggle off the floating POV and Row 1 appears like magic!

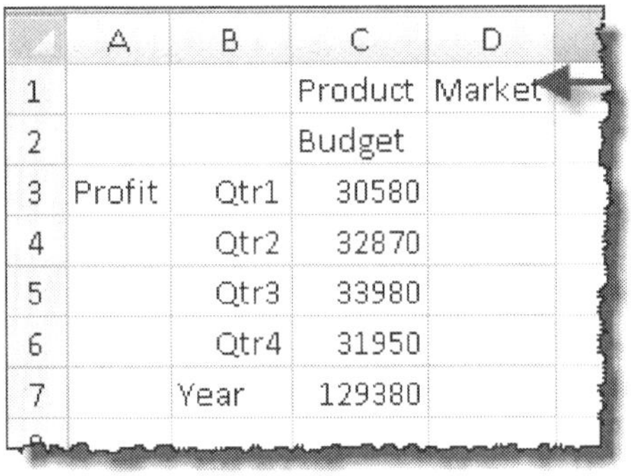

	A	B	C	D
1			Product	Market
2			Budget	
3	Profit	Qtr1	30580	
4		Qtr2	32870	
5		Qtr3	33980	
6		Qtr4	31950	
7		Year	129380	

Multi Member Zoom

Beginning in Smart View 11.1.2.1.102 you can zoom on more than one member (or more than one dimension) at the same time. Create the following query, changing "Budget" to "Actual". Select Qtr1 and Qtr2 so it is highlighted in the spreadsheet:

	A	B	C	D
1			Product	Market
2			Actual	
3	Profit	Qtr1	24703	
4		Qtr2	27107	
5		Qtr3	27912	
6		Qtr4	25800	
7		Year	105522	

Click *Zoom In* from the Essbase ribbon. Both Qtr1 and Qtr2 drilled to the next level:

	A	B	C	D
1			Product	Market
2			Actual	
3	Profit	Jan	8024	
4		Feb	8346	
5		Mar	8333	
6		Qtr1	24703	
7		Apr	8644	
8		May	8929	
9		Jun	9534	
10		Qtr2	27107	
11		Qtr3	27912	
12		Qtr4	25800	
13		Year	105522	

(Old die hard Excel Add-in folks are cheering. Can you hear them?)

REFRESH THE DATA

You can refresh the data in a spreadsheet at any time. To refresh the data to the current values in Essbase, select the *Refresh* button:

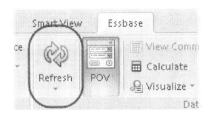

You can also refresh all worksheets by choosing the drop down arrow and selecting *Refresh All Worksheets*. Refresh All will refresh all worksheets in a workbook for the database connection.

This is really helpful in instances when you've created a workbook of reports that you run regularly. For example, you create and update your monthly reporting package each month. With one menu item, you can refresh the data for all reports within your workbook.

ALIASES

Using your new Essbase knowledge, create the following query with the floating POV turned off:

	A	B	C	D	E	F	G
1			Budget	Market			
2			Qtr1	Qtr2	Qtr3	Qtr4	Year
3	Product	Margin	51540	54780	56410	51410	214140
4		Total Expenses	20960	21910	22430	19460	84760
5		Profit	30580	32870	33980	31950	129380
6							

Zoom in on Product:

	A	B	C	D	E	F	G
1			Budget	Market			
2			Qtr1	Qtr2	Qtr3	Qtr4	Year
3	100	Margin	15670	16890	17770	15540	65870
4		Total Expenses	5880	6230	6330	5490	23930
5		Profit	9790	10660	11440	10050	41940
6	200	Margin	14920	15390	15580	15450	61340
7		Total Expenses	6440	6550	6750	5650	25390
8		Profit	8480	8840	8830	9800	35950
9	300	Margin	11580	12620	12850	11650	48700
10		Total Expenses	4610	4940	5140	4650	19340
11		Profit	6970	7680	7710	7000	29360
12	400	Margin	9370	9880	10210	8770	38230
13		Total Expenses	4030	4190	4210	3670	16100
14		Profit	5340	5690	6000	5100	22130
15	Diet	Margin	14340	14910	15180	14250	58680
16		Total Expenses	5430	5690	5800	5040	21960
17		Profit	8910	9220	9380	9210	36720
18	Product	Margin	51540	54780	56410	51410	214140
19		Total Expenses	20960	21910	22430	19460	84760
20		Profit	30580	32870	33980	31950	129380
21							

Note! Product does not equal the sum of the products underneath this, but it does equal the sum of products 100, 200, 300, and 400. Diet Drinks is a custom total that includes select products from the other product groupings. This is called an alternate hierarchy (discussed in detail in a later section).

Product 100 is doing very well this year, especially compared to product 400. "100" is the member name of a specific Product member. Member names are the short "computer-like" way of referencing things and are completely unintuitive to the average user. Essbase allows member names to have longer, more user-friendly descriptions for members called "Aliases." For instance, the alias for "100" is "Cola". So how do we change the display from member names to aliases? On the Essbase ribbon, choose Change Alias.

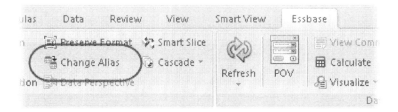

A list of available Alias tables for the connected Essbase database will display (alias tables are created and managed by the Essbase Administrator).

Select the *Default* alias table and click OK:

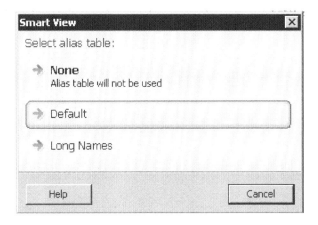

The spreadsheet will refresh with the aliases:

	A	B	C	D	E	F	G
			Budget	Market			
1			Qtr1	Qtr2	Qtr3	Qtr4	Year
2							
3	Colas	Margin	15670	16890	17770	15540	65870
4		Total Expenses	5880	6230	6330	5490	23930
5		Profit	9790	10660	11440	10050	41940
6	Root Beer	Margin	14920	15390	15580	15450	61340
7		Total Expenses	6440	6550	6750	5650	25390
8		Profit	8480	8840	8830	9800	35950
9	Cream Soda	Margin	11580	12620	12850	11650	48700
10		Total Expenses	4610	4940	5140	4650	19340
11		Profit	6970	7680	7710	7000	29360
12	Fruit Soda	Margin	9370	9880	10210	8770	38230
13		Total Expenses	4030	4190	4210	3670	16100
14		Profit	5340	5690	6000	5100	22130
15	Diet Drinks	Margin	14340	14910	15180	14250	58680
16		Total Expenses	5430	5690	5800	5040	21960
17		Profit	8910	9220	9380	9210	36720
18	Product	Margin	51540	54780	56410	51410	214140
19		Total Expenses	20960	21910	22430	19460	84760
20		Profit	30580	32870	33980	31950	129380

If you type in a member, you can type in either the member name or the alias and Essbase will be able to find it. For instance, below the cell with Product, type in the word "100-20" (without the quotes). "100-20" is the actual product member name. Re-retrieve your data and you'll see that Essbase replaced "100-20" with "Diet Cola". "Diet Cola" is the alias name.

Tip! To type in a member name that Essbase could confuse with a number (like "100"), type in a single apostrophe before the member name. For "100", you would type in: '100. This tells Essbase (and Excel) that this is text and not a number.

Since some companies have multiple ways of referring to the same items (for instance, product 100 might be called "Cola" in the Northeast and "pop" in the Northwest), Essbase allows up to 32 different aliases for each member. Right now you're using the "Default" alias, but if your application has other descriptions for members beyond the defaults (called "alternate alias tables"), you can choose a different alias table in the *Change Alias* option on the Essbase Ribbon.

Note!

Sample.Basic comes with another alias table, called Long Names, in addition to Default.

MEMBER AND DATA OPTIONS

As mentioned before, your report might not look identical to the pictures in this book. The most common reason for this is that your Options have been changed. Options are tab-specific settings that control how Essbase operates. All of these settings are found by selecting the *Options* icon on the *Smart View* ribbon.

Some of the options are Global, which means they apply to all workbooks and any future workbooks and worksheets. The Global options are those under Advanced, Extensions and Cell Styles.

Sheet level options are those that are specific to each worksheet. New worksheets will use the default options until a change is made. Changes in options for one worksheet will not impact other worksheets and workbooks. Sheet level options are those under the Member Options, Data Options and Formatting sections.

Set Default Options

As we discussed, sheet level Smart View options will use default settings. Each new spreadsheet will use the default options unless specifically changed by the user. Once the sheet level settings are changed for a worksheet, those settings will be remembered for that worksheet.

If you don't like the default options, you can change them! Update the settings under Member, Data and Formatting sections to your preference. Then simply select the drop down on the *OK* button and choose *Save As Default Options*:

To reset the default options to those that are set during the installation and configuration, click *"Reset"* on the Options window.

Follow along to see how this works. On the Smart View ribbon, select Options. Under the Data Options section, make sure *Repeated Members* is checked.

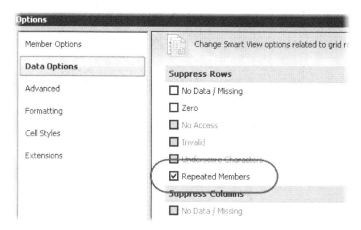

Select the drop down arrow next to OK. Choose Save as Default Options:

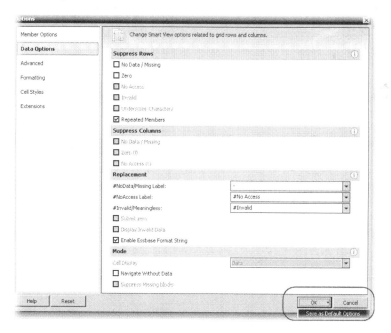

Open a new worksheet. Right click on Sample.Basic and select *Ad hoc Analysis*. Double click on Year to zoom into it. Double click on Product to zoom in on that. Notice that the product members are not repeated for each quarter.

	A	B	C	D
1			Market	Scenario
2			Measures	
3	Colas	Qtr1	7048	
4		Qtr2	7872	
5		Qtr3	8511	
6		Qtr4	7037	
7		Year	30468	
8	Root Beer	Qtr1	6721	
9		Qtr2	7030	
10		Qtr3	7005	
11		Qtr4	7198	
12		Year	27954	
13	Cream Soda	Qtr1	5929	
14		Qtr2	6769	
15		Qtr3	6698	
16		Qtr4	6403	
17		Year	25799	
18	Fruit Soda	Qtr1	5005	
19		Qtr2	5436	

For this worksheet, go back to Options on the Smart View ribbon. Under the Data Options section, uncheck *Repeated Members* under Suppression.

Click OK (not the Save as Default option; just OK). Then Refresh. Your spreadsheet should now have repeated product members for each quarter.

	A	B	C	D
1			Market	Scenario
2			Measures	
3	Colas	Qtr1	7048	
4	Colas	Qtr2	7872	
5	Colas	Qtr3	8511	
6	Colas	Qtr4	7037	
7	Colas	Year	30468	
8	Root Beer	Qtr1	6721	
9	Root Beer	Qtr2	7030	
10	Root Beer	Qtr3	7005	
11	Root Beer	Qtr4	7198	
12	Root Beer	Year	27954	
13	Cream Soda	Qtr1	5929	
14	Cream Soda	Qtr2	6769	
15	Cream Soda	Qtr3	6690	

Finally, open a new worksheet. Right click on Sample.Basic and select *Ad hoc Analysis*. Double click on Year to zoom into it. Double click on Product to zoom in on that. Notice that the product members are not repeated for each quarter, using the original default settings defined. You can even close and open the workbook. The worksheet specific settings will remain.

Now that we have a good understanding of how options are applied to worksheets, let's review the different option settings. The options in 11.1.2 are categorized into six groups: Member Options, Data Options, Advanced, Cell Styles and Extensions:

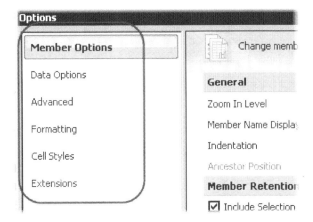

Member Options - Zoom In Level

When you zoom in, you tend to want to see the members that comprise the current member. When you *Zoom In* on Year, you most likely want to see the quarters. Likewise, a *Zoom In* on Qtr1 should show the first three months of the year. Some impatient people don't like passing through the levels in the middle on the way to the bottom-level of a dimension. To control how far Essbase drills with each zoom, go to Member Options section. Under General, you can choose the Zoom In level:

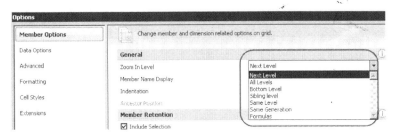

Right now, Zoom In is set to *Next Level* (the default for the sheet). This means that when you drill into Year, you see the quarters. You can override this default by changing the Zoom In Level selection. If, when you drill into Year, you want to see every single member in the Year dimension, set your Zoom In to *All Levels*. If you were to then drill on Year, you'd see every month and every quarter. If you want to jump from the Year down to showing all the months without showing any of the quarters, select *Bottom Level*.

Try It!

Change your Zoom In level and then try zooming in and out on several dimensions. You can make a very large spreadsheet very quickly, and Essbase remains extremely fast.

Tip!

Before you drill into a dimension that has thousands of members, make sure that your Zoom level is not set to *All Levels* or *Bottom Level*. Sample.Basic has no dimension with more than 25 members, so you're safe for the moment.

The Member Retention options are related to the Zoom In setting:

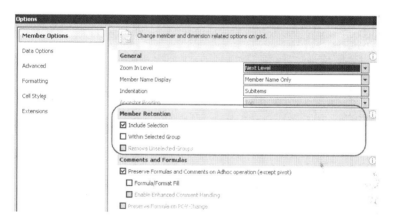

This option allows you to define what happens to the member that you drill on – do you want to keep it as part of the grid or remove it? If *Include Selection* is checked and you zoom in on Year, Year will still remain. If you uncheck this option, when you zoom in on Year you will only see the children of Year. The *Within Selected Group* option will perform ad hoc operations like Zoom, Keep Only and Remove Only on a selected range of cells, excluding any unselected cells. *Remove Unselected Groups* will remove all dimensions and members except for the selected member and retrieved members when zooming.

Member Options – Member Name Display

The default option for Member Name Display is *Member Name Only* (which is a little confusing because you can toggle between member name and alias). Basically this option allows you to either view the member name or the alias but not both at the same time.

The option *Member Name and Alias* allows you to view both at the same time. This much anticipated feature of 11.1.2 allows users to see both the member name and alias:

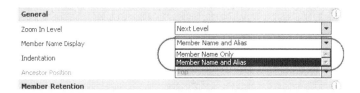

By choosing member name and alias, an additional column is added to the spreadsheet.

	A	B	C	D	E	F
1					Market	Scenario
2					Measures	
3	100	Colas	Qtr1	Qtr1	7048	
4			Qtr2	Qtr2	7872	
5			Qtr3	Qtr3	8511	
6			Qtr4	Qtr4	7037	
7			Year	Year	30468	
8	200	Root Beer	Qtr1	Qtr1	6721	
9			Qtr2	Qtr2	7030	
10			Qtr3	Qtr3	7005	
11			Qtr4	Qtr4	7198	
12			Year	Year	27954	
13	300	Cream Soda	Qtr1	Qtr1	5929	
14			Qtr2	Qtr2	6769	
15			Qtr3	Qtr3	6698	
16			Qtr4	Qtr4	6403	

Display Member Name and Alias will apply to all dimensions in the rows of a grid.

Member Options - Indentation

Notice that in the grid below, the detail beneath each member (for example, the quarters underneath the Year member) is indented.

	A	B	C	D
1			Market	Scenario
2			Measures	
3	Colas	Qtr1	7048	
4	Colas	Qtr2	7872	
5	Colas	Qtr3	8511	
6	Colas	Qtr4	7037	
7	Colas	Year	30468	
8	Root Beer	Qtr1	6721	
9	Root Beer	Qtr2	7030	
10	Root Beer	Qtr3	7005	
11	Root Beer	Qtr4	7198	
12	Root Beer	Year	27954	
13	Cream Soda	Qtr1	5929	
14	Cream Soda	Qtr2	6769	

For those who went to accounting school prior to 1990, it might seem better to indent the totals. On the *Indentation* section under Member Options, you can switch the indentation from *Subitems* to *Totals* (or *None*):

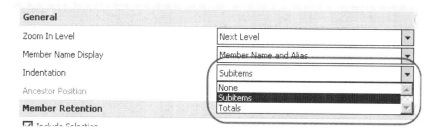

The next time you retrieve your data, each summary-level of totals will be further indented. See the example below where Year is further indented from the quarters:

	A	B	C	D	E	
1			Market	Scenario		
2			Profit	Inventory	Ratios	N
3	Colas	Qtr1	7048	29448	57.40178857	
4		Qtr2	7872	29860	57.28473167	
5		Qtr3	8511	36461	57.39589978	
6		Qtr4	7037	35811	56.99467561	
7		Year	30468	29448	57.27288145	
8	Root Beer	Qtr1	6721	33000	55.38738874	
9		Qtr2	7030	31361	55.49797453	
10		Qtr3	7005	35253	55.06764011	
11		Qtr4	7198	32760	56.21773123	
12		Year	27954	33000	55.53966595	
13	Cream Soda	Qtr1	5929	28865	54.11926491	

To turn off indentation entirely, choose *None* under Indentation. We'll cover the Formulas options later in this book when we get more advanced in our analysis and report creation.

Data Options – Suppress Rows

Under Options in the Data Options section, review the available suppression alternatives for Suppress Rows: suppress no data/missing data, zeros, and Repeated Members. Uncheck the box for *No Data/#Missing*:

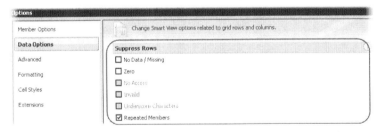

The Suppress Rows options No Access, Invalid, and Underscore Characters are supported for Hyperion Financial Management only. (The Essbase admin can configure suppress no access in the Essbase.cfg file with the SUPPNA setting.)

Under Replacement section, notice the #NoData/Missing Label (or change it to match the screen below):

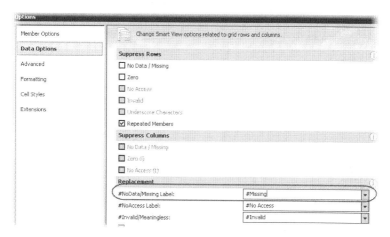

Click *OK*. Create the following spreadsheet.

▲	A	B	C	D
1		Year	Market	Scenario
2		Profit		
3	Product	105522		

Zoom into the next level for Product. Zoom into the next level for Market. Notice that Fruit Sodas for the South Region does not have any data and is showing a '#MISSING':

	A	B	C	D	
1			Year	Scenario	
2			Profit		
3	East	Colas	12656		
4		Root Beer	2534		
5		Cream Soda	2627		
6		Fruit Soda	6344		
7		Diet Drinks	2408		
8		Product	24161		
9	West	Colas	3549		
10		Root Beer	9727		
11		Cream Soda	10731		
12		Fruit Soda	5854		
13		Diet Drinks	8087		
14		Product	29861		
15	South	Colas	4773		
16		Root Beer	6115		
17		Cream Soda	2350		
18		Fruit Soda	#Missing		
19		Diet Drinks	4912		
20		Product	13238		

Notice that the South is not a big fan of Fruit Soda. Data is missing (denoted by Essbase with the term "#Missing"). A missing value to Essbase is very different from a value of zero. A profit of zero means that your sales were cancelled out exactly by your expenses. A profit of #Missing means that we have neither sales nor expenses at this particular combination. Data for South Fruit Soda Profit for the year simply does not exist.

If you don't want to see #Missing on your reports, you can replace it with a label that makes more sense to you. Go to your Display options and in the box next to "#Missing Label", fill in something that makes sense to you:

Under Options >> Data Options >> Replacement section, change the #NoData/Missing Label to "-":

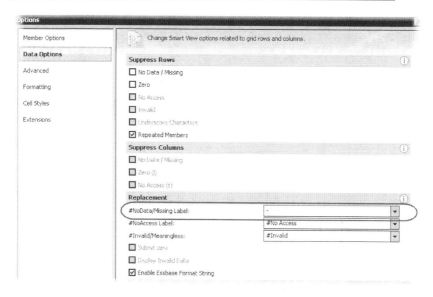

Click *OK*.

	A	B	C	D
1			Year	Scenario
2			Profit	
3	East	Colas	12656	
4		Root Beer	2534	
5		Cream Soda	2627	
6		Fruit Soda	6344	
7		Diet Drinks	2408	
8		Product	24161	
9	West	Colas	3549	
10		Root Beer	9727	
11		Cream Soda	10731	
12		Fruit Soda	5854	
13		Diet Drinks	8087	
14		Product	29861	
15	South	Colas	4773	
16		Root Beer	6115	
17		Cream Soda	2350	
18		Fruit Soda	-	
19		Diet Drinks	4912	
20		Product	13238	
21	Central	Colas	9490	

Tip!

The most common #Missing labels are: N/A, #numericzero (0), -, and a space.

In general, there will be lots of intersections of data in your applications that don't exist, and retrieving them into a report takes unnecessary time. If you have 100,000 products and 5,000 stores, as few as 2,000 products might be sold each day at each store. Do you really want to see a report that's 98% empty? If you don't, check the box next to suppress *No Data/#Missing* on the Ad hoc tab:

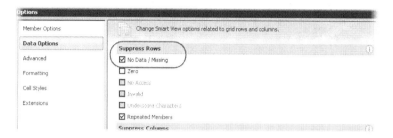

This will suppress any rows where the data all the way across the row is #Missing. If a single column has a real number, the row will not be suppressed.

If you also don't want to see intersections where all the values in the row are zero, check the box to suppress *Zero* as well. You can also suppress rows for which you have no access (No Access check box) or rows that are invalid (used for Varying Attributes; more on this later in the book).

Notice that under Data Options you can also suppress columns based on similar criteria. This would be a great feature if only it were supported for Essbase connections (it is currently supported for HFM only).

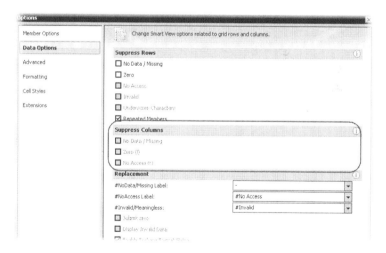

Data Options - Mode

Navigate without data under the Mode section allows you to set up your spreadsheet, defining the layout without the added time of retrieving data. This can shorten report creation time as you don't have to wait for Essbase to send the data:

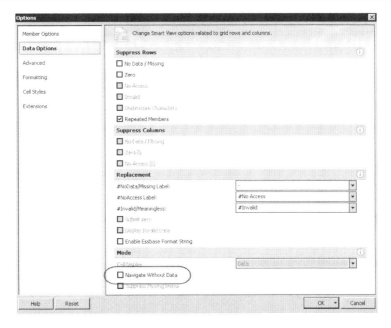

We'll cover a number of the other Essbase options throughout the rest of the book.

CHANGE DATA

Submit Data

So far, all of your work with the add-in has been for reporting and analysis. One of the major uses of Essbase is for budgeting (or planning or forecasting or whatever you call putting information back into Essbase instead of just taking it out).

Using the techniques you've learned to this point, create a new report that looks like the following:

	A	B	C
1		Cola	Jan
2		Actual	Budget
3		Sales	Sales
4	New York	678	640
5	Massachusetts	494	460
6	Florida	210	190
7	Connecticut	310	290
8	New Hampshire	120	110
9	East	1812	1690

Tip!

To make a quick report, you can always type the member names into a blank spreadsheet. Click *Refresh*. Make sure that each intersection is represented by all dimensions.

The budget for cola sales in New York is looking a little light, so let's up it to 700. Type 700 into cell C4 (or wherever your report has the intersection of New York and Budget). Note the cell color changes to a yellow, highlighting an adjusted number:

	A	B	C	D
1		Cola	Jan	
2		Actual	Budget	Variance
3		Sales	Sales	Sales
4	New York	678	700	-22
5	Massachusetts	494	460	34
6	Florida	210	190	20
7	Connecticut	310	290	20
8	New Hampshire	120	110	10
9	East	1812	1690	122

Choose *Submit* on the Smart View ribbon:

Or the Essbase ribbon:

The data will automatically refresh, showing you the saved 700 data value. Now type in "Variance" next to Budget in cell D2. Click *Refresh*:

	A	B	C	D
1		Cola	Jan	
2		Actual	Budget	Variance
3		Sales	Sales	Sales
4	New York	678	700	-22
5	Massachusetts	494	460	34
6	Florida	210	190	20
7	Connecticut	310	290	20
8	New Hampshire	120	110	10
9	East	1812	1690	122

This isn't going to make any sense, but we want to show you a possible scenario that you could run into in your application. Type 50 in cell D4 (you're saying "what in the ..." but trust us). The cell shading will change to yellow.

	A	B	C	D
1		Cola	Jan	
2		Actual	Budget	Variance
3		Sales	Sales	Sales
4	New York	678	700	50
5	Massachusetts	494	460	34
6	Florida	210	190	20
7	Connecticut	310	290	20
8	New Hampshire	120	110	10
9	East	1812	1690	122

Now select *Submit Data* on the Smart View or Essbase ribbon. Was the data saved to Essbase? Nope. Depending on the Essbase and security design, there will be some data points where you can't save data. In the case of Variance, this member is a dynamically calculated member and never stores any data. The other common causes are insufficient rights to edit those numbers and sending numbers into summary members (also called upper-level members).

Adjusting Data

One cool feature we want to illustrate along with Submit Data is the Adjust feature. In Smart View, you can select a cell or cells and click the *Adjust* button.

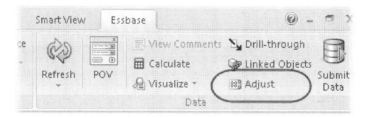

A window will display with some built in financial calculations to adjust the data set you've selected. Options include: Add a Fixed Value, Subtract a Fixed Value, Multiply Selected Cells by a Fixed Value, Divide Selected Cells by a Fixed Value, and Increase/Decrease Selected Cells by a Percentage:

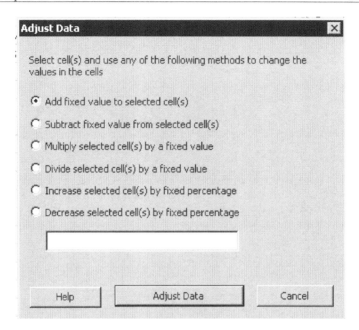

When you've adjusted the data, it has not been submitted to the server. You have to click *Submit Data* to commit the changes back to the Essbase database.

Note!

When using Adjust, you must have Write security for the appropriate dimensions and intersections of data.

Try It!

Adjust the budget for New York Cola for January by 5%.

Running Calculations

If we submit 735 over the budgeted 700 value, math wizards in the audience will immediately note that 735+460+190+290+110 does not equal 1,690. It's actually 95 short, because we haven't told the Essbase server to recalculate the totals. Depending on the type of Essbase database, you may need to run an additional calculation to aggregate data to all levels of the Essbase database. If your database is a block storage database, many of the summary members in an Essbase application are "stored," meaning that Essbase stores the pre-calculated totals to speed retrieval. This faligns with the common Essbase belief that analysis tends to start at the top of the hierarchy and then drill down.

Note!

One of the major differences between Essbase and a relational database is that relational databases assume that you want to look at detail (so displaying totals is much slower) and Essbase assumes that you want to look at summaries (though detailed data is not any slower).

Other members may be "dynamically calculated" (though the cool kids say "dynamic calc"), meaning that Essbase calculates those members at the time the user requests them. While some members in Sample.Basic are dynamically calculated (the upper-level Measures, for instance), it's always best to assume that you should recalculate the database after submitting data to a block storage database.

Assuming that you have access to recalculate the database, choose *Calculate* from the Essbase ribbon:

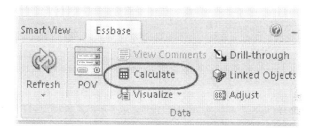

This will pull up a list of calc scripts for which you have access. You can filter this list by database. Select the calc script you wish to run and click *Launch*. In this example, choose Default for the Basic cube (basically means "calculate everything in the database that needs to be recalculated.")

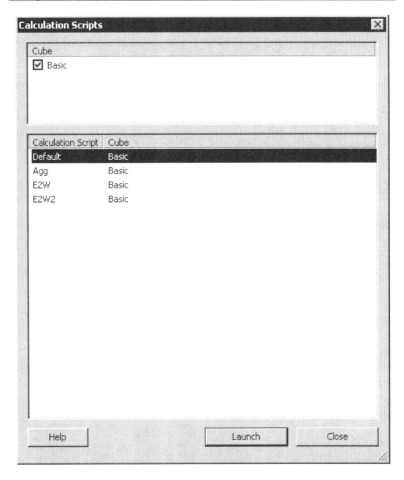

Smart View will check with the Essbase server every few seconds to see if the calculation has completed yet. You can always continue to work in Excel in the meantime, just don't work with this Essbase database unless you're okay with potentially erroneous results.

While the default calculation for Sample.Basic will always take just a few seconds, complex calculations against large databases can take several minutes or even hours. For instance, if your company had a multi-step allocation process that allocated corporate expenses by thousands of stores for thousands of products (to get a complete Income Statement by location by SKU), it would take a whole lot longer than five seconds. Be patient, and Smart View will let you know when the calculation is finished.

Once you get the calculation message, click *Refresh* to re-retrieve your data and you should see the correct value for East with the additional 95 in it:

	A	B	C	D
1		Cola	Jan	
2		Actual	Budget	Variance
3		Sales	Sales	Sales
4	New York	678	700	-22
5	Massachusetts	494	460	34
6	Florida	210	190	20
7	Connecticut	310	290	20
8	New Hampshire	120	110	10
9	East	1812	1750	62

Logging Off

You can disconnect from a spreadsheet if you choose. Simply right click on the Essbase database and select *Disconnect*. You can also just close the spreadsheet and this will end your connection to the active Essbase database for the spreadsheet.

Can you believe it? You're already pretty sufficient in retrieving and analyzing data in Essbase. You successfully connected to an Essbase data source, zoomed and pivoted, and set a number of options for analysis. Congratulations! But we're not done yet. Put down your mouse as we take a trip through history and also review some important fundamental concepts of Essbase and Smart View.

END OF THE CHAPTER QUICK REFERENCE – SUPPORTED OFFICE PRODUCTS

Smart View is the common Microsoft Office interface. The following Office products are supported by Smart View.

	Smart View 11.1.2.2
Excel	Yes
Word	Yes
PowerPoint	Yes
Outlook	Yes

Chapter 3:
What Does Essbase Stand For?

Essbase is currently produced by a company named Oracle. Prior to the earthshaking acquisition by Oracle, Essbase was produced by a company named Hyperion Solutions Corporation. Although Hyperion was founded in 1981, the Essbase product came along in the early 1990's compliments of a company whose only product was Essbase: Arbor Software. Up until 1998 when Hyperion and Arbor "merged", the two companies were fierce competitors who were just as likely to spit on each other in waiting rooms as work together. (We are kidding, but only slightly.)

Arbor Software was founded in 1991 by Jim Dorrian and Bob Earle. They noticed at the time that companies were beginning to use spreadsheets not just for presentation of information but as a place to store data and business logic. Often, multiple sources of data were being consolidated together in spreadsheets and they were even seeing companies begin to release analysis to the public based on data in spreadsheets.

Jim/Bob wanted to build a database for spreadsheets. Essbase actually stands for <u>S</u>pread <u>S</u>heet data<u>base</u> (the "e" was added to help folks pronounce the name correctly). Thanks to some creativity and some venture capital (of course) from Hummer Winblad, they released the first version of Essbase in 1992 (originally shown as eSSbase). This original release of the product garnered three whole paragraphs of press coverage in Software Magazine on May 15, 1992. Here it is in all its "babe in the woods waiting to be eaten by bears" naiveté:

DATA SERVER "FEEDS" 1-2-3 OR EXCEL

Arbor Software Corp.'s Essbase data server
Software Magazine; May 15, 1992

Following a three-year development effort, start-up Arbor Software Corp., Santa Clara, Calif., has built a data server that "feeds" popular desktop offerings, including 1-2-3 from Lotus Development Corp., and Excel from Microsoft Corp., on client machines.

"We conceded the front end to [widely installed] spreadsheets," said James Dorrian, president and co-founder. "We built the product with two assumptions: that people knew their spreadsheets and that people knew their jobs."

According to Marketing Vice President Michael Florio, the OS/2-based $22,000 Essbase offers users in client/server environments simultaneous access to large volumes of multidimensional spreadsheet data.

Notice that it was originally developed to run on OS/2 and its claim to fame was that it fed spreadsheets. Also, notice that you could get a copy for only $22,000 which sort of goes to show you that technology doesn't always get cheaper over time.

The first version of the product wasn't nearly as user friendly as it is today. Ignoring the Herculean steps required to actually build an Essbase database, retrieving data into Excel (or Lotus, at the time) required writing requests to Essbase in a language known as "Essbase Report Scripting."

	A
1	<PAGE (Measures, Product, Market)
2	Profit
3	Product
4	Market
5	<COLUMN (Scenario)
6	<CHILD Scenario
7	<ROW (Year)
8	<ICHILD Year
9	!
10	

But with time we came to know and love the Essbase Spreadsheet Add-in for Excel. When you chose *Essbase >> Retrieve*, you'd see a much friendlier interface:

	A	B	C	D	E
1			Profit	Product	Market
2		Actual	Budget	Variance	Variance %
3	Qtr1	24703	30580	-5877	-19.21844343
4	Qtr2	27107	32870	-5763	-17.53270459
5	Qtr3	27912	33980	-6068	-17.85756327
6	Qtr4	25800	31950	-6150	-19.24882629
7	Year	105522	129380	-23858	-18.44025352
8					

The Essbase Add-in was everything we thought we needed for Essbase until Smart View came along.

INTRODUCTION TO SMART VIEW

What is Smart View? This may be a silly question because you used Smart View in the entire last chapter. But in case you missed it, Smart View is THE Office Add-in for all of the Oracle EPM System (formerly known as Hyperion) products, including Essbase, Planning, Financial Management, Hyperion Profitability and Cost Management, Crystal Ball, Financial Reporting and (soon) Oracle Business Intelligence Server, Hyperion Strategic Finance and Predictive Planning. It's Oracle's version of the Swiss army knife and that makes you MacGyver.

Many of you old Essbase users might think you're completely satisfied with the Essbase Spreadsheet Add-In for Excel (the old school add-in for analyzing Essbase data). Per Oracle, you are wrong. They do have a point: among other things, the Essbase Add-In only works in Excel. What if you want to pull some Essbase data into a Word document? What if you need to make PowerPoint presentations with tables that automatically update from Essbase? Well, your problems are solved by the Smart View Add-In.

When used in Excel, Smart View has similar functionality to the Essbase Add-In. Yes: two different tools to do the same thing. The navigation is a bit different in Smart View but you can drill down, swap rows and columns, etc. Why do we need two tools? Since there is a world-wide problem of starving computer programmers, one might speculate that Oracle is doing their part by keeping two development teams gainfully employed. But is there another reason?

Smart View takes Essbase reporting and analysis to another level above the Excel Add-in. With Smart View you can create reports in Word or PowerPoint with live data from Essbase sources. Features like Report Designer, Query Designer, and Cascade (report bursting) give end users powerful reporting capabilities in the tools they know and love: Excel, Word and PowerPoint (beat that, Excel Add-in).

Smart View also brings Add-In functionality for all of the Oracle EPM products that need an Add-In. Smart View provides a single Excel interface for Financial Management and Planning, replacing the old Planning Spreadsheet Add-In and HFM Spreadsheet Add-In. For Hyperion Planning, end users have full functionality in Smart View so, if they choose to skip the web, they can perform all Planning end user tasks in Smart View. You can import Reporting and Analysis documents as images into Microsoft Word or PowerPoint. You can import query ready or fully formatted grids into Microsoft Excel. Is there anyone at this point that doesn't want to toss the Essbase Add-In on the 8-track tape trash heap of obsolescence?

This book focuses on how the Smart View Add-In works with Essbase, showing you how to perform ad hoc analysis in Excel and how to pull Essbase data into Word and PowerPoint. We'll also include information on how to import Financial Reporting documents into Excel and PowerPoint via the Reporting and Analysis Framework connection. While we will not show you how to scramble an egg while it's still inside its shell, Smart View probably could do that too.

OLAP AND OTHER TERMS

When Essbase was first released, no one was quite sure what it was. Was it some sort of spreadsheet on steroids? Was it a temporary employee who was really good at typing? Was it a database? If so, why didn't it have records and fields and most importantly, why didn't it let IT geeks write SQL to access it?

Everyone was pretty sure what it wasn't: a typical relational database. The creators originally called it a "data server." Shortly after Essbase was created, they commissioned a study by the late Dr. E.F. Codd (the same Ph.D. who came up with the original rules for what constituted a true relational database) to determine what the heck Essbase was.

Dr. Codd was definitely impressed. He felt that this wasn't a relational database yet it was definitely a database and a very important new type to boot. He called it an "OLAP" database to separate it from every other database up to that point.

To put it simply, all databases prior to Essbase were built for the purpose of storing transactions. The goal for these systems was to get individual records into the database as quickly as possible and to get those same records back out again as quickly as possible. A side goal was to store that data in as small a space as possible, because those were the days when hard drive space cost as much as a good mule. Summarization of these types of databases was possible, but definitely not the objective of the database design. Dr. Codd classified traditional relational databases "OLTP" (On-Line Transaction Processing).

He knew that Essbase was the first database designed purely to support analysis. Knowing that this was going to be The Next Big Thing, he created a term to describe these databases: OLAP (On-Line Analytical Processing). There were several features that Essbase offered that no previous database could handle.

Multi-Dimensional Databases

First of all, Essbase was a multi-dimensional database (MDDB or MDB, for short). What did the good doctor mean when he said Essbase was multi-dimensional? Simply that any of the dimensions set up in a database could be put in the rows or the columns (or applied to the whole page/report).

All databases up to this point were two-dimensional: records and fields. Essbase had no theoretical dimension limit (though there was certainly a practical limit). The Sample.Basic database we were accessing above has five base dimensions: Year, Measures, Product, Market, and Scenario. (It actually has five more "attribute" dimensions that we haven't even seen yet: Caffeinated, Ounces, Pkg Type, Population, and Intro Date.) The ASOSamp.Basic database is a sample Aggregate Storage database with 14 dimensions. The largest database we've ever seen had over 100 dimensions, but we think they were just trying to show off. In general, Essbase databases have five to ten base dimensions. By base dimension, we mean dimensions that show up all the time (like the five mentioned above in Sample.Basic).

While any relational database can be set up to give the appearance of having multiple dimensions, it takes a lot of up front work by developers. Essbase and other OLAP databases have dimensionality built-in.

Optimized for Retrieval

Essbase databases were also optimized for retrieval at any level of the hierarchy, even the very topmost number that might represent every dollar the company has ever made in its history.

OLTP databases (relational databases) were nicely optimized for retrieval of detailed records but definitely not hierarchical information. By pre-saving summarized information, Essbase allows analysis to happen from the top down with no decrease in performance.

For OLAP databases, the hierarchy is native to the database itself. This is far different from relational databases that store the data in one table and then have one or more other tables that can be joined in to view data in a rolled-up fashion. For Essbase, the hierarchy is the database. When you change the hierarchy logic in Essbase as to how a product is grouped or a market rolls-up, you actually change where the data is stored.

Because hierarchy is inherent to OLAP databases, drill-down (sometimes known as "slicing and dicing" but never known as "making julienne data") is inherent as well. Essbase is great at doing Ad hoc analysis (see Chapter 2) because it knows that when a user double-clicks on Qtr1, she wants to see Jan, Feb, and Mar. This is because the roll-up of months to quarters is pre-defined back on the server.

Dr. Codd came up with ten rules for defining OLAP databases. Some of them (such as the ability to write-back data) were more interesting than others. While some other databases at the time met one or more of the qualifications, the only OLAP database to meet all ten was Arbor Software's Essbase. (Remember that Arbor is the company that commissioned the study.)

DSS, EIS, BI, BPM, EPM…

For the first few years, everyone called Essbase (and its competitors like Cognos and Business Objects) either an MDDB or OLAP database. The problem was that this was very difficult to explain to a casual user. Since casual users (CEOs, COOs, CFOs, etc.) are the ones who tend to sign checks at most companies, this produced a marketing problem of the highest order. What is the actual purpose of these OLAP databases?

The overarching belief was that OLAP/MDDB databases "helped users make decisions and then provided them the information they needed to support those decisions." Since HUMDATPTTITNTSTD makes for a lousy acronym, the term DSS was created and thus the "Decision Support Systems" term was coined.

Since 1992 when Essbase was released, other terms have been bandied about at various times including EIS (either "Executive Information Systems" or "Enterprise Information Systems" depending on whom you ask) and BI (Business

Intelligence). Business Intelligence is still used fairly frequently (thanks to a well funded marketing campaign by IBM in the late 90's), but its popularity is quickly being overtaken by BPM.

BPM (Business Performance Management) and more recently EPM (Enterprise Performance Management) is meant to include BI and expand it to also include any information a user needs to manage the performance of her company. Nowadays, this goes well beyond just a database and includes applications such as scorecarding, planning, and financial consolidation. If there is a number that needs to be manipulated, rolled-up, sliced, or diced, BPM should be able to handle it whether the original number is in an OLAP or OLTP database.

Historically, Essbase (and pretty much every other product Hyperion made) has been seen as a financial tool. The reason for this is two-fold. First, financial minds tend to understand Essbase really well. Financial analysis is inherently multi-dimensional. Income Statements tend to have accounts, time periods, scenarios, organizations, departments, companies and years on them. Since relational databases do a poor job at multi-dimensional data, finance types started using spreadsheets. Since Essbase was a database for spreadsheets, it made it really easy to explain the value to CFOs, Controllers, VPs of Planning, and the like.

The second reason for Essbase's traditional stereotyping as "something the bean counters use" has to do with sales and marketing. Since Essbase was so easy to explain to end users in accounting and finance, that's the group that the Essbase sales representatives tended to call on. The sad part about this is that the IT organization often felt left out and turned to inferior products from competing vendors because those vendors were seen as developing products that were more "IT-centric."

As for the current market, Oracle is generally accepted to be the market leader in the EPM space. They should be since they created the term in the first place in the early 21st century. EPM is quite the hot software niche these days thanks in no small part to Sarbanes-Oxley bringing compliance and management of data to the forefront. Simply put, Sarbanes-Oxley can put you in jail, and EPM can help keep you out.

Tip!

Putting Essbase, Hyperion, and EPM on your resume may very well get you a 10% boost in salary at your next job. Feel free to share half of that with the authors of this book.

ESSBASE TERMINOLOGY

We managed to make it all the way through the last chapter without learning a lot of Essbase terminology, but to truly succeed in the world of Essbase, there are some handy terms to pick up. Some of them we've already learned.

A "dimension" defines different categories for your data. A dimension can be located on the rows, columns, or pages of your queries. A "member name" is the short, computery name for the member of an Essbase dimension (like "100-10"). An "alias" is the longer, more descriptive name for a member (like "Cola"). All of the dimensions in a database make up the "outline."

Here is a portion of Sample.Basic outline:

```
Outline: Basic (Active Alias Table: Defau
⊟·Year
   ⊟·Qtr1 (+)
       ─Jan (+)
       ─Feb (+)
       └Mar (+)
   ⊞·Qtr2 (+)
   ⊞·Qtr3 (+)
   ⊞·Qtr4 (+)
⊟·Measures
   ⊟·Profit (+)
       ⊟·Margin (+)
          ─Sales (+)
          └COGS (-)
       ⊞·Total Expenses (-)
   ⊞·Inventory (~)
   ⊞·Ratios (~)
⊟·Product
   ⊞·100 (+) (Alias: Colas)
   ⊞·200 (+) (Alias: Root Beer)
   ⊞·300 (+) (Alias: Cream Soda)
   ⊞·400 (+) (Alias: Fruit Soda)
   ⊞·Diet (~) (Alias: Diet Drinks)
⊞·Market
   Scenario
```

Family Tree Relationships

The most common way to refer to members in an outline relative to each other is by using "family tree" relationships. The members directly below a member are called its children. For instance, the Product dimension has five children: Colas, Root Beer, Cream Soda, Fruit Soda, and Diet Drinks. If we ever wanted to refer to those members on a report without hard coding them, we could say "give us all the children of Product."

The advantage to this aside from the saving in typing is that if a new product line were to be added (say, "Water"), we wouldn't have to modify our reports. Any report designed to display the children of Product would pick up the new "Water" product and add it to the list automatically.

If Colas, Root Beer, and the other rug rats are all the children of Product, what relation is Product to its children? Assuming you didn't fail "Birds and the Bees 101," you'll know that Product must be the *parent* of Colas, Root Beer, and the rest. In other words, the parent of any member is the one into which the member rolls-up. Qtr2 is the parent of May. Year is the parent of Qtr2.

Since Colas and Root Beer are both children of Product, Colas and Root Beer are siblings. This is simple, but what relationship do January and May have? Well, their parents are siblings so that makes them... cousins. Correct, but "cousins" while technically correct isn't used that often. In general, people say that January and May are at the "same level."

What if you want to refer to all the members into which May rolls (not just the one right above)? Well, those are its ancestors which in this case would be Qtr2 and Year. Correspondingly, the descendants of Year would include all four quarters and all twelve months.

Note that there are members that don't have any children. In the picture above, May is childless. We refer to childless members as being "level-0". If you ever want all of the bottom, child-less members of a dimension, just ask for the level-0 members. For example, the level-0 members of the Year dimension are the months and the level-0 members of the Market dimension are the states.

Level-0 members are sometimes also referred to as "leaves," because they're at the edges of the family tree. Edward sometimes refers to level-0 members as "the ones who aren't allowed to sit at the main table on Thanksgiving," but we think he is the only one.

All of the parents of the level-0 members are referred to as level-1. Since the level-0 members of the Year dimension are the months, the level-1 members are the quarters. For the Market dimension, the level-1 members are the regions: East, West, South, and Central.

Just as the parents of the level-0 members are level-1 members, the parents of level-1 members are level-2 members. Their parents are level-3 members and so on up the hierarchy. There are many places in Essbase that you can specify, for example, "All the level-2 members of the Product dimension," so remember that levels count up from the bottom of a dimension starting at 0.

If you want to count down the hierarchy, use generations instead of levels. The dimension itself is considered generation-1 (or "gen1," for short). Its children are gen2. For the Year dimension, the gen2 members are the quarters. The children of gen2 members are gen3 and so on down the hierarchy.

Yes, the quarters are both level-2 and generation-2. Why do we need both levels and generations? Well, in some dimensions with many, many levels in the hierarchy, you'll want to count up from the bottom or down from the top depending on which you're closer to. We've seen a dimension with 17 levels in the hierarchy, and it definitely was nice to have both options available.

Note!
Why do generations start counting from 1 and levels from 0? It's because generation 0 is considered to be the outline itself making its children, the dimensions, generation 1.

While counting with generations is pretty straight-forward, levels can sometimes be a bit tricky. Look at this portion of the Measures dimension from Sample.Basic:

For this dimension, Gen1 is Measures. Gen2 is Profit and Inventory. Gen3 is Margin, Total Expenses, Opening Inventory, Additions, and Ending Inventory.

So far this is looking pretty easy, but let's switch our focus to the levels. The level-0 members are Sales, COGS, Marketing, Payroll, Misc, Opening Inventory, Additions, and Ending Inventory. The level-1 members are Margin, Total Expenses, and Inventory. What are the level-2 members? Profit (because it's the parent of level-1 members Margin and Total Expenses) and Measures (because it's the parent of level-1 member Inventory).

Measures
⊟ **Profit**
  ⊟ **Margin**
    ├ **Sales**
    └ **COGS**
  ⊟ **Total Expenses**
    ├ **Marketing**
    ├ **Payroll**
    └ **Misc**
⊟ **Inventory**
  ├ **Opening Inventory**
  ├ **Additions**
  └ **Ending Inventory**

The trickiness is that Measures is *also* a level-3 member because it's the parent of Profit, a level-2 member. This means that if you ask Essbase for level-2 members, you'll get Measures, but you'll also get Measures if you ask for level-3 members. Notice that this counting oddity does not occur with generations.

Note!

This instance of a dimension is also known as a ragged hierarchy.

Time to pick up your mouse and get moving again. Let's work those Essbase muscles and learn the skills we need, like member selection and data points, to become a power Essbase user.

END OF THE CHAPTER QUICK REFERENCE – HELPFUL SMART VIEW BLOGS

You'll find great information at these Hyperion / EPM blogs by the experts.

Blog	Link
Glenn Schwartzberg's Essbase Blog	http://glennschwartzbergs-essbase-blog.blogspot.com/
Look Smarter Than You Are by Edward Roske	http://looksmarter.blogspot.com/
Essbase Labs	http://essbaselabs.blogspot.com/
Tim Tow's Hyperion Blog	http://timtows-hyperion-blog.blogspot.com/
More to Life Than This...	http://john-goodwin.blogspot.com/

Chapter 4:
Become a Power User

Up to this point, we've primarily been navigating our way to data by zooming in or out, using keep/remove only, or just typing members into our spreadsheet. In this chapter, we'll introduce you to member selection capabilities, the Smart View Query Designer, the POV Manager and more: all tools that will help you get the information you need faster and easier.

What if your boss, let's call him Lumberght, requested a detailed market report analyzing financials by state just as you were about to duck out for the weekend. Despite your attempts to avoid him at the end of the day on Friday (one can only hide in the copy room for so long), he catches you with an "I'm gonna need you to go ahead and come into tomorrow" to get the state analysis done.

You could create this sheet by opening up a blank spreadsheet, typing Measures into cell B1, Product into C1, Scenario into D1, all the months into B2:B13, and all the states into the cells starting at A3.

	A	B	C	D	E	F	G	H	I	J	K	L	M	N	O	P
1		Jan	Feb	Mar	Apr	May	Jun	Jul	Aug	Sep	Oct	Nov	Dec			
2	New York	512	601	543	731	720	912	857	570	516	766	721	753			
3	Massachusetts	519	498	515	534	548	668	688	685	563	477	499	518			
4	Florida	336	361	373	408	440	491	545	529	421	373	337	415			
5	Connecticut	321	309	290	272	253	212	198	175	231	260	310	262			
6	New Hampshire	44	74	84	86	99	125	139	136	93	81	75	89			
7	California	1034	1047	1048	1010	1093	1185	1202	1269	1122	1053	923	978			
8	Oregon	444	417	416	416	400	402	414	412	409	421	467	444			
9	Washington	405	412	395	368	378	372	372	392	394	397	385	371			
10	Utah	237	251	256	277	262	246	276	248	217	269	309	307			
11	Nevada	219	267	289	330	365	411	493	451	268	317	281	348			
12	Texas	504	547	531	507	547	556	556	595	552	531	497	502			
13	Oklahoma	241	234	243	277	279	306	335	338	292	284	309	353			
14	Louisiana	259	263	251	228	231	227	202	253	262	302	279	235			
15	New Mexico	-7	2	9	28	38	43	78	48	4	13	23	51			
16	Illinois	912	963	980	1036	1102	1160	1237	1191	1025	1017	915	1039			
17	Ohio	384	362	357	370	359	363	378	347	352	330	395	387			
18	Wisconsin	297	307	309	287	303	310	315	334	307	284	247	247			
19	Missouri	125	132	142	151	133	104	135	80	79	101	139	145			
20	Iowa	653	677	706	734	781	821	854	871	786	739	662	777			
21	Colorado	585	622	596	594	598	620	604	621	596	638	594	559			
22	New York	512	601	543	731	720	912	857	570	516	766	721	753			
23	Massachusetts	519	498	515	534	548	668	688	685	563	477	499	518			
24	Florida	336	361	373	408	440	491	545	529	421	373	337	415			
25	Connecticut	321	309	290	272	253	212	198	175	231	260	310	262			
26	New Hampshire	44	74	84	86	99	125	139	136	93	81	75	89			
27	California	1034	1047	1048	1010	1093	1185	1202	1269	1122	1053	923	978			
28	Oregon	444	417	416	416	400	402	414	412	409	421	467	444			

POV Sheet3 ▼ ×
Measures ▼
Product ▼
Scenario ▼
Refresh

This, however, would mean coming in on Saturday. Is there another way to get this done and save your plans for organizing the sock drawer? Yes! You can use a previously ignored menu item called *Member Selection*.

MEMBER SELECTION

Member Selection Basics

Member Selection is like your own personalized temp typist. Let's see how handy he can be at generating spreadsheets like the one above. First, we'll make Member Selection (often shortened to Member Select) type in our states for us.

In a blank worksheet, right click on Sample.Basic and select *Ad hoc Analysis*. Drag the Market dimension to rows and the Year dimension to the column. Move Measures back to the POV. Your spreadsheet should look something like this:

On your default query, select cell A3 and then choose the *Member Selection* button:

The Member Selection window will display:

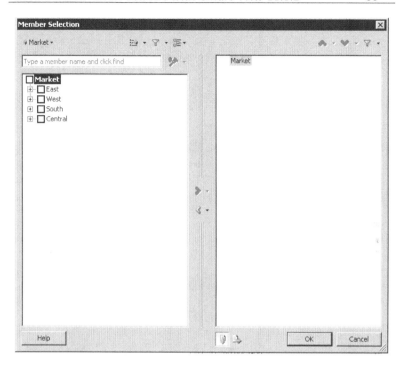

Notice that the dimension that comes up is Market. Smart View will retrieve the dimension you want to use for picking members based on what's in the cell you currently have selected. Select a blank cell and try clicking *Member Selection.* What do you see?

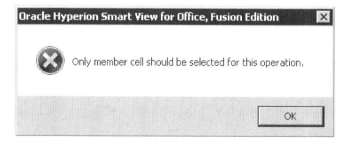

You could also see a Dimension Name Resolution screen which allows you to pick the desired dimension and the desired orientation for the spreadsheet (e.g. vertical position to list members down the page). As you can see, layout is very important when defining queries and using member selection.

Back to the task at hand, let us take a closer look at the Member Selection window.

The upper left hand corner shows the current dimension selected:

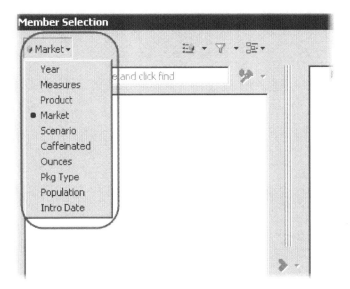

Notice the full list of dimensions is listed. You could, if you had a hankering to, change the dimension for the selected cell (e.g. Market to Product). Let's assume we don't have a hankering and keep the Market dimension for the current cell. The members in the left box should list for the Market dimension. Click the plus sign next to East and it will expand to show you the states in the East.

Notice that we are viewing this dimension by "Hierarchy":

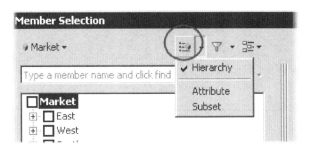

We could also choose to view the members of the Market dimension by Attribute or Subset. For now we'll leave the selection as Hierarchy.

Click the check box for all of the East states:

Now click the *-> arrow* button. You should now see five of the fifty most important states in the USA appear in the box to the right under Selection. Use this same method to add the states under West, South, and Central to the list on the right. You should now be looking at the following:

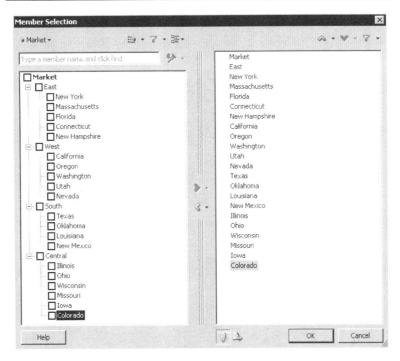

If you're an obsessive-compulsive type and want to manually alphabetize your state names before entering them into the sheet, highlight the state you want to rearrange in the list and then click either the *Move Item Up* or *Move Item Down* buttons. If you want to jump a member all the way to the top, select the drop down arrow and choose *Move to Top*:

If you accidentally add any member more than once, highlight the member to remove and choose the <- *arrow* icon. To clear the whole list, select the drop down arrow and choose *Remove All*:

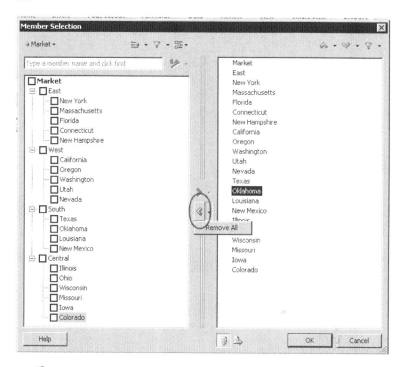

 Try to shift+click or control+click to select multiple members. Unfortunately it doesn't work, but don't worry, Note! we'll show you more tips for selecting members.

Assuming your list is complete (and alphabetized if that's how you roll), click *OK* and you'll be able to watch while Essbase enters the states down the left side of your spreadsheet.

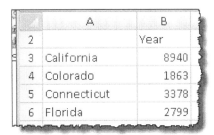

 After you use Member Selection to type in your members, you will need to choose *Refresh* yourself. Member Selection Note! does not do a retrieve on its own.

Let's use a slightly different method to type in the months. Select cell B2 and choose *Member Selection*. The Year dimension should appear.

Be default, you are viewing the Year hierarchy in the member selection window by Hierarchy:

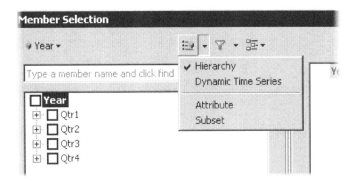

Click the Filter icon and choose *Level* (notice the default is set to None):

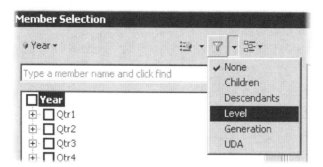

The Filter icon allows you to search for a specific set of members in a hierarchy. For any member in the selected dimension, you could easily select the member itself ("None"), its children, its descendants, members at the same level or generation of the selected member, or members for specific user defined attribute (UDA).

Remember for our example that the months are level-0 since they don't have any children (through no lack of trying, mind you). Enter the level number in this case, 0:

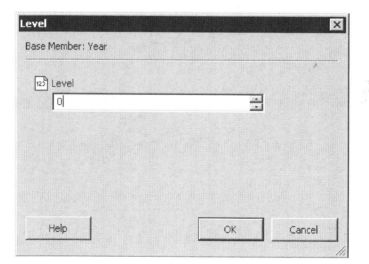

Tip!

You could also use the arrow keys to select the available levels for the selected dimension.

Click *OK* and you will see the level zero months are available in the Members section. Note they haven't been selected yet. We've only filtered them in the Members section:

Click the *Check mark* drop down box (just right of the Filter icon) to select *Check Base Members* (much easier than having to manually check month by month):

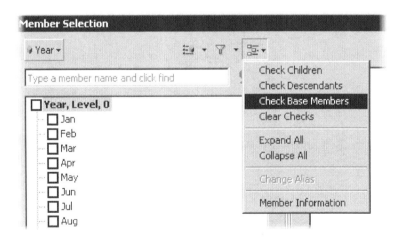

You can also choose to *Check Children* or *Check Descendants* of filtered members, providing a faster way to make your selection. If you want to clear all check marks, select *Clear Checks*.

Now move the months over to the Selection section by clicking the right arrow icon. Notice the two small icons at the bottom of the Member Selection window. Because the Year dimension is in the columns, the selected members will be inserted horizontally by default. You could change this to list down the rows:

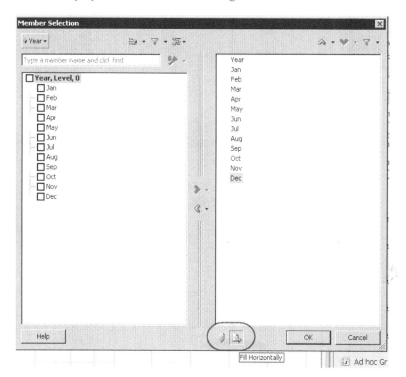

Leave the default for horizontal placement of members. Click *OK* and the months are placed across the columns in your spreadsheet:

	A	B	C	D	E	F	G	H	I	J	K	L	M	N
2		Year	Jan	Feb	Mar	Apr	May	Jun	Jul	Aug	Sep	Oct	Nov	Dec
3	California	8940												
4			POV Sheet1_ ▾ ×											
5			Sales ▾											
6			Cola ▾											
7														

Remember to click Refresh to see the data.

Tip! Member selection just selects members from the source dimensions. It may not create a usable report. For example, if you selected to put months Fill vertical in the example above, Smart View would add the members vertically in column B, creating a problematic resulting format.

More Member Selection Options

What about changing the members that are displayed in my floating POV? Remember in the first chapter we could change the selected member by just typing a member name over the current name in the floating POV window. We can also use Member Selection, following a similar process. Before we get there, let's do one thing. If necessary, select *Change Alias* from the Essbase ribbon and select Default. Remember, this is the way you toggle back and forth between member names and aliases in Smart View.

Tip! While you can select multiple members in the floating POV, Smart View will only display data for a single member from each POV dimension.

Select the drop down arrow next to Product and choose the ellipses (...).

The Member Selection window is launched:

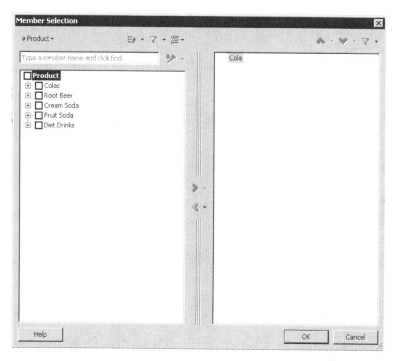

Let's say we want to perform analysis on the Diet Drinks. Remove any other selections that currently exist. Check the Diet Drinks check box and then select children under the right arrow icon:

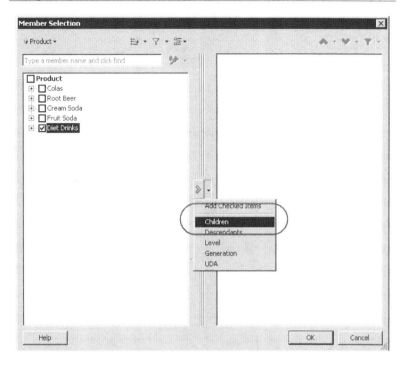

The children of Diet Drinks are automatically added to the Selection section:

Click *OK*:

Now in the Product drop down, all selected members are available:

Change the selection from Product to Diet Drinks and click *Refresh* to see the new data.

Go back to the Member Selection for product. Choose the drop down option for Dimension and note you can select the members for all of the dimensions in the POV. Go ahead and select the Scenario dimension:

Select the *Check Base Members* of Scenario and move them into the Selection section:

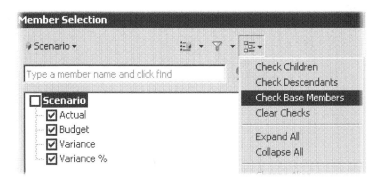

Next choose the Measures dimension:

Type in sal* in the text box next to the flashlight icon to search for the member beginning with the letters "sal*":

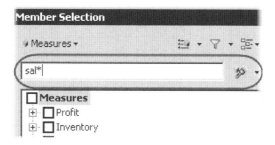

In the drop down next to the flashlight, choose *Check All Found*. This option will find all matches to the search criteria and check them (so they are easily moved to the selection panel of the Member Selection window).

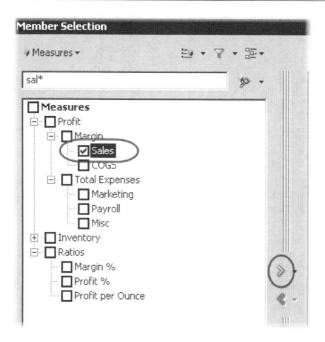

Note that you can also find the next or previous member in the hierarchy from the selected member that matches the search criteria.

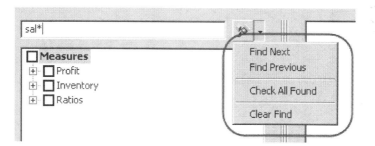

Tip!

Use the * as a wildcard when searching in Member Selection.. Wildcards only work as trailing wildcards.

Move the Sales member over to the Selection section.

Lastly, let's go back to the Product dimension. In the Filter drop down, select *Generation*:

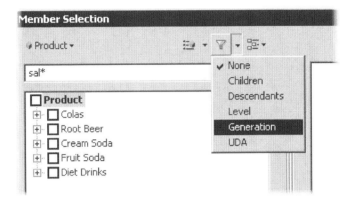

Type in or select *2* as the Generation and click OK.

Move the Gen2 products into the Selection section. Click OK to finally close the Member Selection window:

Check out your new member selection selections in the floating POV:

Let's walk through one more use case for member selection. We want to create a report that just pulls in the level zero members under the East region. Follow along to learn the easiest way to build this query.

Create the following starting point query using your growing Smart View skills:

	A	B	C	D	E	F	G	H	I	
2		Year	Jan	Feb	Mar	Apr	May	Jun	Jul	A
3	California	7151	546	545	567	587	612	634	678	6
4				POV Sheet1_ ▼ ×						
5				Sales ▼						
6				Diet Root Beer ▼						
7				Actual ▼						
8				Refresh ⓘ						
9										

Select cell A3 and choose Member Selection from the Essbase ribbon. In the Member Selection window, remove the selection for California. Check the box next to East. In the drop down arrow key to move over the selected member, choose *Level*:

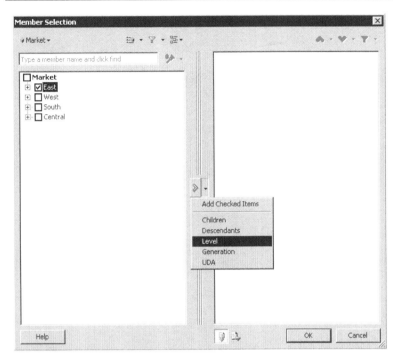

Enter zero:

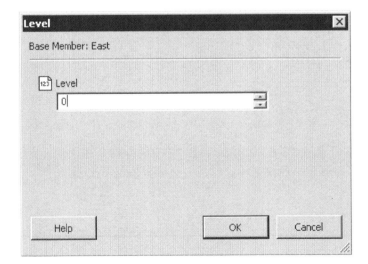

Click OK. The level zero members under East are added to the selection panel:

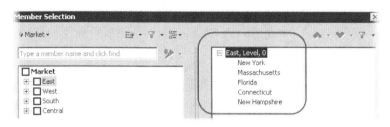

Click OK and you are off and running.

So in summary, there are many ways to filter members in your dimensions for reporting and analysis. Remembering your Essbase terminology and knowing the hierarchies will be important in effectively using Member Selection. When searching for members to add to your analysis, you can filter the dimension by:

- Children
- Descendants
- Level
- Generation
- Attribute
- UDA
- Subset (which is really just another way to filter by attribute)
- Search using wildcards

You can then "one-click" check desired members for your analysis by using Check Children, Check Descendants or Check Base Members.

DYNAMIC TIME SERIES

Lumberght has a new request: while we have data for the entire year, he wants a report with sales through May along with a year to date total at the end. Create the following starting point query:

	A	B	C	D
1		Sales	Diet Root Beer	Actual
2		Year		
3	East	3777		

Use Member Selection to select the months January to May. Next we want to add a year to date column. How could we accomplish that? We could add an Excel total column to the right of column F to sum the values in January through May, but if your Essbase administrator has turned on Dynamic Time Series, all you have to do is retrieve this information. (Oh right, time can now be spent actually analyzing the data versus getting and calculating the data.) Dynamic Time Series will be based on your Periods or Year dimension and is not applicable to other dimensions.

Dynamic Time Series means that Essbase will take and dynamically add up time periods up to whatever period you specify just as if that member was stored in the outline. For instance, if you ask for Q-T-D (Q-T-D is short for Quarter-To-Date) through May, Essbase will total the data for April and May (since those are the months in the quarter containing May) and put them into a Q-T-D member. This member can then be pivoted and for the most part treated just like a stored member.

Sample.Basic has two Dynamic Time Series members (often abbreviated as "DTS members"): Q-T-D and H-T-D. H-T-D stands for History-To-Date. Other common DTS members include Y-T-D (Year-To-Date), M-T-D (Month-To-Date), W-T-D (Week-To-Date), S-T-D (No not a disease but Season-To-Date), P-T-D (Period-To-Date) and . D-T-D (Day-To-Date).

Since we want January through May to be totaled for us, select H-T-D and add it to the right side of our starting point query. Select cell G2 in your spreadsheet (to the right of May). Type in "H-T-D(May)" and click *Refresh*.

	A	B	C	D	E	F	G
1		Sales	Diet Root Beer	Actual			
2		Jan	Feb	Mar	Apr	May	H-T-D(May)
3	East	310	310	312	314	317	1563

The year to date value (named H-T-D or History-To=Date in Sample.Basic's example) is returned with no further calculation.

You can also select dynamic time series members via Member Selection. Select cell G2 and click *Member Selection*.

Change the member view selection ⊞▾ from Hierarchy to Dynamic Time Series:

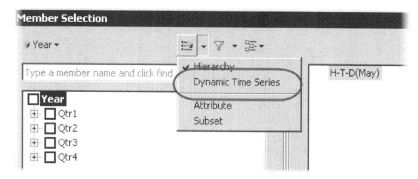

Check the Q-T-D option and click the > arrow to move it to the right panel:

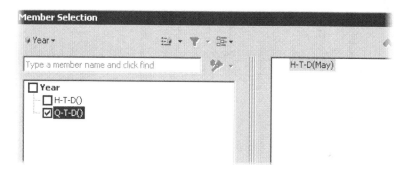

When prompted select the Month that should be used as the basis for the quarter to date calculation. In our example, choose May:

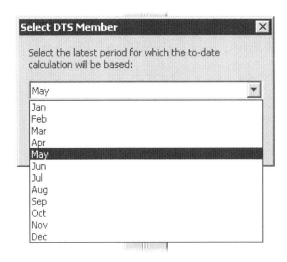

Click *OK* twice to complete the member selection steps which should now have both H-T-D and Q-T-D. Once you are back in the spreadsheet, click *Refresh* and the values are retrieved:

	A	B	C	D	E	F	G	H
1		Sales	Diet Root Beer	Actual				
2		Jan	Feb	Mar	Apr	May	H-T-D(May)	Q-T-D(May)
3	East	310		310	312	314	317	1563	631

Note!

You can also type in DTS members directly. To specify a specific month, put it in parentheses after the member. For instance to get Q-T-D through March, type in Q-T-D(Mar). There is no space between the member and the parenthesis. The member entered must always be the level zero members of the time dimension

Note!

Your Essbase administrator enables D-T-S.

SUBSTITUTION VARIABLES

Another retrieval alternative available to you, if your administrator has defined them, is substitution variables. These objects are created and managed by the Essbase administrator to help in Essbase maintenance as well as reporting (that's the part you care about). The variable is a holding place for information that changes on a periodic basis and used in a number of places. Current month, current year, and prior year are all examples of common substitution variables. Beginning in 11.1.1.1, Smart View supports Substitution Variables. To use a substitution variable, simply type an ampersand ("&") in front of the variable name in the spreadsheet where you'd like to display the member:

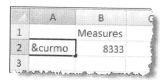

Click *Refresh* and the member assigned to the variable will display. So now when Lumberght requests that TPS report, you can type in the substitution variable and immediately refresh the report. Greaaaaatttttt.

Tip! Even better, using the function =hsgetvariable("HSActive","CurrMth") will return the value of the sub var, but keep the formula so the value will be updated each time you retrieve.

ATTRIBUTE DIMENSIONS

All the analysis of Sample.Basic up to this point has been done using five dimensions. There are five other dimensions in Sample.Basic that we could be using but to this point, we've been ignoring them. These dimensions are known as "Attribute Dimensions," and they are alternate ways of summarizing our base (sometimes called "standard" or "stored") dimensions. You don't see Attribute dimensions unless you specifically reference them in an analysis.

Thankfully we are covering these dimensions now because since you wow'ed Lumberght with the detailed state analysis he has just requested an additional analysis by Caffeinated products. He is sure this will require work over the weekend. "I'm also going to need you to come in on Sunday too."

Note!

Unlike base dimensions, the totals for attribute dimensions are not pre-calculated in Essbase. As such, retrieval of attribute dimensions will often be slower as Essbase dynamically calculates the results. Also watch out for instances where dynamically calculated member values are off due to the use of Attribute dimensions. Hopefully your Essbase administrator caught these but let her know if you see any calculation issues with Attributes.

Sample.Basic has five attribute dimensions: Caffeinated, Ounces, Pkg Type, Intro Date, and Population. The first four of these are alternate ways of rolling up the Product dimension. Population is an alternate way of rolling up the Market dimension. As an example, let's limit the report we just made to only caffeinated drinks for all products.

First type in cell C1 "Products" replacing the member reference for "Diet Root Beer". Click *Refresh*.

Type "Caffeinated" in the cell E1. Click *Refresh* and Caffeinated attribute dimension is now referenced in the query:

	A	B	C	D	E	F	G	H
1		Sales	Product	Actual	Caffeinated			
2		Jan	Feb	Mar	Apr	May	H-T-D(May)	Q-T-D(May)
3	East	6780	6920	6921		7213	7341	35175	14554

Since we haven't been getting much sleep lately, let's focus just on Caffeinated products. *Zoom in* to Caffeinated and you should see the data broken up by Caffeinated True and Caffeinated False:

	A	B	C	D	E	F	G	H	I
1			Sales	Product	Actual				
2			Jan	Feb	Mar	Apr	May	H-T-D(May)	Q-T-D(May)
3	Caffeinated_True	East	4578	4559	4641	4871	4980	23629	9851
4	Caffeinated_False	East	2202	2361	2280	2342	2361	11546	4703
5	Caffeinated	East	6780	6920	6921	7213	7341	35175	14554

One last tip for using Attributes in ad hoc analysis. What do you think is the fastest way to find which products are Caffeinated? You might think zooming in on Product, which will certainly work, but depending on how you zoom you may have to step through two or more levels. The super-fast method to pull up this list is to zoom in on Caffeinated_True. Try it now and you'll see your query displays the list with a single double click:

	A	B	C	D	E
1				Year	Actual
2				Sales	
3	Massachusetts	Caffeinated_True	Cola	6518	
4			Diet Cola	-	
5			Old Fashioned	1370	
6			Diet Root Beer	-	
7			Dark Cream	1418	
8			Vanilla Cream	-	
9			Diet Cream	-	
10		Caffeinated_False	Product	5351	
11		Caffeinated	Product	14657	

Attributes and Member Selection

Can you use Member Selection with Attribute dimensions? Absolutely, but you need to first add the attribute to the spreadsheet (just as we did with the Caffeinated attribute dimension). Let's create another analysis, this time with the Population attribute dimension. You just know that Lumberght is going to want to see sales broken down by Population. So create the following starting point query:

	A	B	C	D	E
1		Year	Market	Product	Actual
2		Sales			
3	Population	400855			

By typing Population into cell A3, we can now use Member Selection to pick and choose our desired members. (We could also Zoom In and Keep Only too but we'd like to show you the interface for selecting attribute members).

Select cell A3 and choose *Member Selection*. All of the same member selection options are available for Attribute dimensions (that are applicable; e.g. UDAs and Attributes are not available for attribute dimensions).

Select the Filter icon and filter the Population hierarchy for Level 1 members:

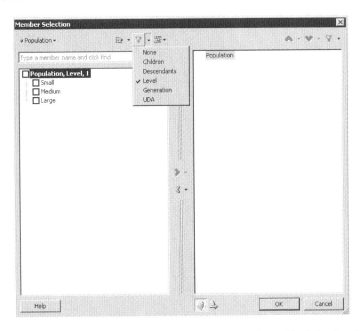

Select Check Base Members option to select all of the level 1 members. Use the > arrow key to select the members and click *OK*. Click *Refresh*.

	A	B	C	D	E
1		Year	Market	Product	Actual
2		Sales			
3	Population	400855			
4	Small	216321			
5	Medium	84091			
6	Large	100443			

Let's walk through one more analysis example using attributes. This time we are going to filter members in the Product dimension using attribute dimensions (this is really just another way to get to the same answer but in some cases this member selection method can be more efficient). Create the following starting point query:

	A	B	C	D
1		Year	Market	Actual
2		Sales		
3	Product	400855		

Select cell A3 ("Product") and choose *Member Selection*. From the 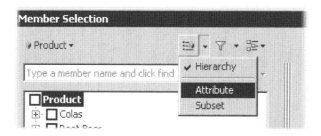 icon, select Attribute:

A new window will display. Click the magnifying glass icon; this will launch another window. Choose "Intro Date" attribute dimension:

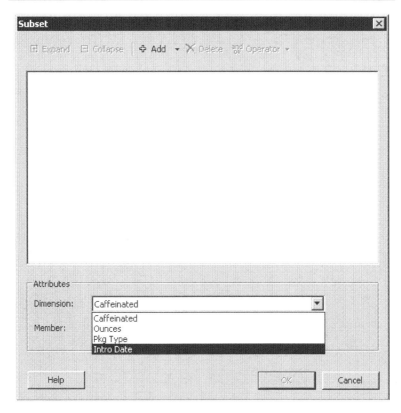

Then select the member "Intro Date 3-25-1996" and click *Add*. The Member is added to the subset:

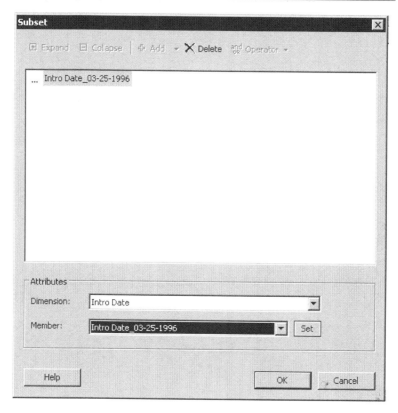

If we mistakenly selected the wrong date, we could choose the correct date and select *Set* to confirm the date. Click *OK* twice.

The members listed in member selection are those that have an introduction date of 3-25-1995. You can then use your check options to select the members.

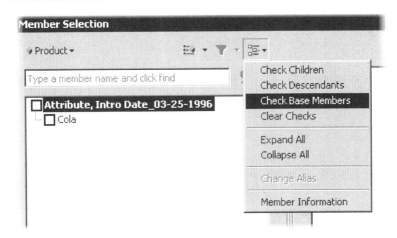

The resulting spreadsheet displays the filtered Product members. Note that the attribute member itself does not display; we simply used this method to quickly filter the product members:

	A	B	C	D
1		Year	Market	Actual
2		Sales		
3	Product	400855		
4	Cola	62824		

Tip!

Another way to perform analysis on attribute dimensions: insert a column before column A and either type the Attribute dimension name (e.g. "Ounces") into A3 or use member selection, select the attribute dimension members. Click *Refresh*:

A3		× ✓ ƒx	Ounces		
	A	B	C	D	E	F
1			Year	Market	Actual	
2			Sales			
3	Ounces	Product	400855			
4						

Now that we've covered the regular attributes, let's discuss varying attributes.

VARYING ATTRIBUTE DIMENSIONS

Did you get the memo? As of version 11.1.1 Essbase can now handle varying attributes (attributes that may vary over one or more dimensions). For example, your administrator may have created an attribute for Job Status assigned to the Employee dimension. An employee may change their status over the course of the year (e.g. Active to Sabbatical). In a regular attribute dimension when we try to report on the job status, we only see the current assigned status assigned to the employee. So it looks like the employee has spent the whole year on sabbatical when in reality he was active for the first three months of the year. Varying attributes allow you to analyze based on "reality" or based on a historical point in time.

Oh no. Lumbereght is back with a new report requirement. "Yeah. The Board of Directors is coming tomorrow. I'm going to need a sales report by Sales Manager so we can understand everyone's performance." Thankfully your Essbase administrator set up the Sales Manager attribute as a varying attribute dimension because the products managed can vary over time. You want to get this right; peoples jobs are at risk!

Note! The following examples use a modified version of Sample.Basic which includes varying attributes. (The installed samples do not include varying attributes.) To obtain a copy of this outline and sample data, please email info@interrel.com. Your administrator can take these objects and create another sample application for you.

In this example, a Sales Manager has been assigned to each product. By using all of the techniques we've covered so far, create the following worksheet (Bob and Larry are level 0 members of the Sales Manager varying attribute dimension):

	A	B	C	D	E	F	G	H	I	J	K	L	M	N	O
1			Sales	Market	Actual										
2			Jan	Feb	Mar	Apr	May	Jun	Jul	Aug	Sep	Oct	Nov	Dec	Year
3	100-10	Larry	#Invalid	#Invalid	#Invalid	#Invalid	5252	5748	5959	6014	5325	4902	4817	5174	43191
4		Bob	4860	4821	4904	5048	#Invalid	#Invalid	#Invalid	#Invalid	#Invalid	#Invalid	#Invalid	#Invalid	19633
5		Sales Manager	4860	4821	4904	5048	5252	5748	5959	6014	5325	4902	4817	5174	62824
6	100-20	Larry	#Invalid	#Invalid	#Invalid	#Invalid	#Invalid	#Invalid	#Invalid	#Invalid	#Invalid	#Invalid	2311	2503	4814
7		Bob	2372	2433	2471	2588	2628	2741	2929	2724	2404	2365	#Invalid	#Invalid	25655
8		Sales Manager	2372	2433	2471	2588	2628	2741	2929	2724	2404	2365	2311	2503	30469

In a matter of seconds, you create the report Lumberght requests. You can see that Bob managed product 100-10 from January through April and then Larry took over product sales in May. For product 100-20, Bob managed from January through October and Larry managed from November through the end of the year. By default, you are viewing reality.

Now pretend you are Bob and you've had two products taken away from you over the year. You're worried about the consultants and want to find out what your sales would have been had you continued to manage product 100-10 and 100-20 through the end of the year. This will help you to decide whether or not to throw the venti latte in your hand at Larry.

So to change your "perspective" on the data select *Data Perspective* from the Essbase ribbon. Choose the *Custom* radio button and select March for the Year dimension (how Sales Manager can vary).

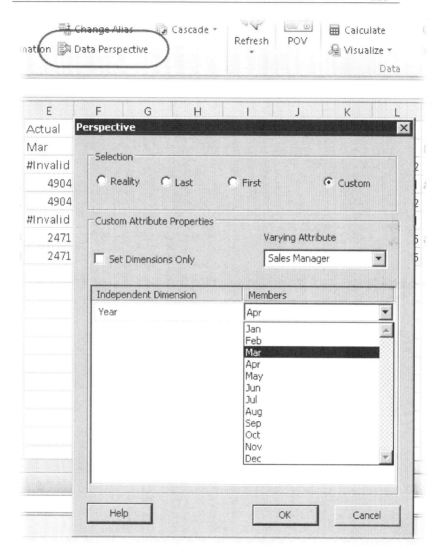

Click *OK* and refresh the data. The view will now display Bob as the Sales Manager for the full year as if it were March (back when life was good and full of cola products to manage). Still pretending that you are Bob, you grab your venti-latte and start looking for Larry.

	A	B	C	D	E	F	G	H	I	J	K	L	M	N	
1			Jan	Feb	Mar	Apr	May	Jun	Jul	Aug	Sep	Oct	Nov	Dec	Year
2			Sales	Sales	Sales	Sales	Sales	Sales	Sales	Sales	Sales	Sales	Sales	Sales	Sales
3	100-10	Bob	4860	4821	4904	5048	5252	5748	5959	6014	5325	4902	4817	5174	6363
4	100-20	Bob	2372	2433	2471	2588	2628	2741	2929	2724	2404	2365	2311	2593	3066
5															

You can also use varying attributes for member selection as well. For example, Bob wants to pull in a list of all products that he has ever managed using the Member Selection Varying Attribute option. This will only display if you have varying attributes defined for the selected dimension.

Select the Member Selection for the Product dimension if necessary. Under Filter, select *Varying Attribute*:

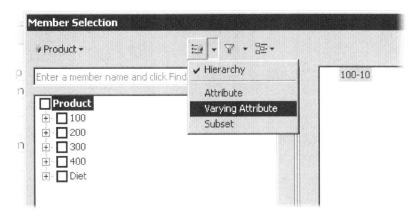

Click the magnifying glass to select the attribute. Choose the ellipsis button to choose the varying attribute dimension:

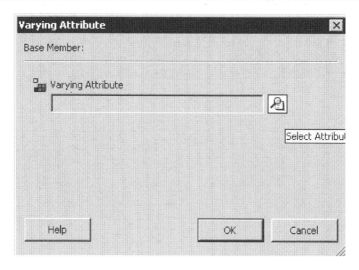

Select the Sales Manager attribute dimension (bottom of the dialog box), choose Bob and finally click the *Add* button:

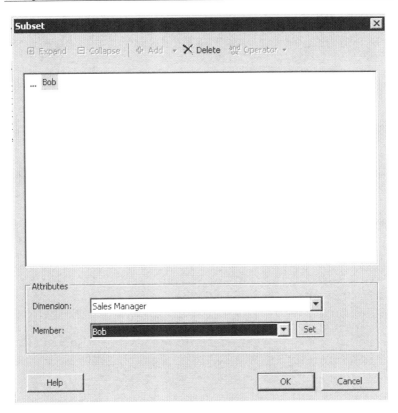

Note!

Notice how we jump from top to bottom to top in the Attribute/Subset window.

Click OK.

Choose Range to define the range of members. Optionally, you could have chosen Snapshot (filter for a specific member). In this example of the worried employee, choose Jan as the start tuple and Dec as the end tuple. This allows us to see any products that Bob has managed in the months January through December.

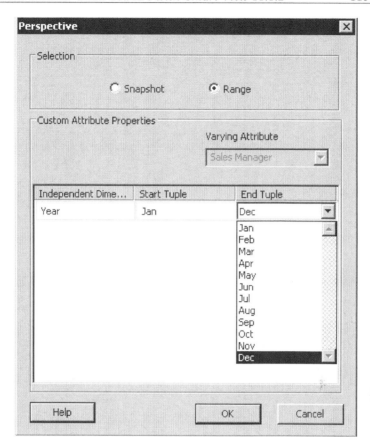

Once you click OK, you should see the following:

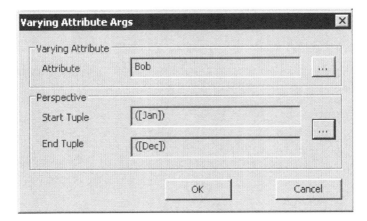

Click OK again (are we ever going to get there?):

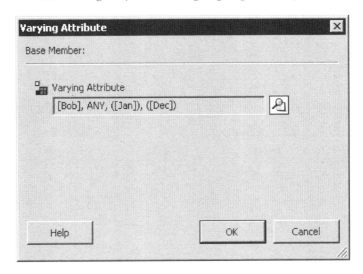

Finally, we see the member list filtering Products that Bob managed throughout the year, even those managed for just a few months.

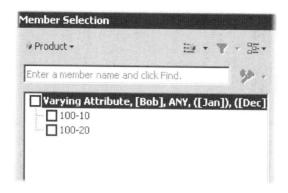

Now you and Bob are fully prepared for the performance review with the consultants. You've pulled the good, the bad, and the ugly for each and every sales manager, using the new Essbase 11 feature varying attributes, to fully understand how sales varied over other Essbase dimensions. Before we move on, let's test your skills using Smart View to find data.

ANALYSIS, ANALYSIS, ANALYSIS

Lumberght has just made a new list of information requests (he is bound and determined to keep you working late tonight). Answer the questions below and see if you'll be working this weekend.

 Try It!

- How many different caffeinated products are sold in Massachusetts for the year?
- What were the sales for Actual Cola for the East Region for Jan, Feb, Mar?
- What were Actual, Budget and Variance for the Margin on the Cola products for Q1 for the West region?
- What were the top selling products for the year for all markets?
- What were the product codes for the top selling products for the year for all markets?
- Which product had the highest negative Actual to Budget variance for Sales for all regions?
- For that product, what two regions had the most impact on the negative variance?

- Which region had the highest total expenses as a percent to total sales?
- What were the bottom three performing states for Profit, total Products, for the year?
- What size population (small, medium, large) are those three states?
- Which packaging type sold more in Small Populations?
- What were the two top selling months for diet products for all regions for the year?
- What two states purchased the most diet products for the Q2?
- What state beginning with the letter C had the top sales for the year for all products?

 The Answers!

- How many different caffeinated products are sold in Massachusetts for the year?
    - o 4 different caffeinated products are sold in MA
- What were the sales for Actual Cola for the East Region for Jan, Feb, Mar?
    - o $1812 $1754 $1805
- What were Actual, Budget and Variance for the Margin on the Cola products for Q1 for the West region?
    - o $2065 $2570 ($505)
- What were the top selling products for the year for all markets?
    - o Cola, Dark Cream, Old Fashioned
- What were the product codes for the top selling products for the year for all markets?
    - o 100-10, 300-10, 200-10
- Which product had the highest negative Actual to Budget variance for Sales for all product?
    - o 100-10
- What regions had the most impact on the negative variance?
    - o West, South
- Which region had the highest total expenses as a percent to total sales?
    - o South
- What were the bottom three performing states for Profit, total Products, for the year?
    - o New Mexico, New Hampshire, Missouri

- What size population are those three states?
  - ○ Small, small, small
- Which packaging type sold more in Small Populations?
  - ○ Bottle
- What were the two top selling months for diet products for all regions for the year?
  - ○ July and August
- What two states purchased the most diet products for the Q2?
  - ○ California and Illinois
- What state beginning with the letter C had the top sales for the year for all products?
- California

If we've been doing our job in this book, you should NOT have to work the weekend. At this point you might think you're done, but we still have a ways to go. Hold tight; it will be worth it. Next let's review an Essbase 11.1.1 feature – support for text and dates.

TEXT AND DATE LISTS

At the beginning of this book, you were probably one of those people who often said, "I uh, I don't like my job, and, uh, I don't think I'm gonna go anymore. Not going to quit. I'm just gonna stop going." Now that Essbase has entered your life, things are different now. No working on the weekends for Lumberght. Plenty of time to organize the sock drawer. Just wait... it gets better. Beginning in 11.1.1.1 Essbase now supports text and date list values (whoo hoo!! Yes. We are certified geeks). It's still not free form text, but we finally have the ability to present and analyze non-numeric data:

The text and date values are created and managed by your administrator. How do you analyze this information? The exact same way that we've been analyzing the numeric data. If you have write access to the text or date list, you can also choose a value from the drop down list and submit it back to the server:

FORMATSTRING

Formatstring is another new feature in Essbase 11.1.1.1 that provides the administrator the ability to format data on the Essbase server. They can add prefixes or suffixes to data values (e.g. adding parentheses for negative values) or convert numbers to text based on defined criteria (e.g. see Variance Level in column G; variance has been translated to a text based value):

	A	B	C	D	E	F	G
1					Market		
2					Sales		
3			Actual	Budget	Variance	Variance %	Variance level
4	100-10	Year	62824	67190	-4366	-6.50	Low
5	100-20	Year	30469	33520	-3051	-9.10	Low
6	100-30	Year	12841	13600	-759	-5.58	Low
7	100	Year	106134	114310	-8176	-7.15	Low
8	200-10	Year	41537	42300	-763	-1.80	Low
9	200-20	Year	38240	37860	380	1.00	Low
10	200-30	Year	17559	15270	2289	14.99	High
11	200-40	Year	11750	11310	440	3.89	Low
12	200	Year	109086	106740	2346	2.20	Low
13	300-10	Year	46956	39150	7806	19.94	Very High
14	300-20	Year	17480	14160	3320	23.45	Very High
15	300-30	Year	36969	31920	5049	15.82	Very High
16	300	Year	101405	85230	16175	18.98	Very High
17	400	Year	84230	66800	17430	26.09	Very High
18	Diet	Year	105678	103300	2378	2.30	Low
19	Product	Year	400855	373080	27775	7.44	Medium level

In order to see the Formatstring values, make sure to check the option *Enable Format String* under *Data Options:*

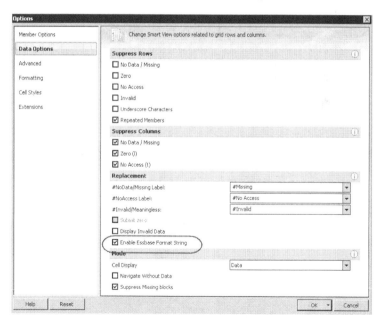

Click *OK* and you are now ready to view the formatstring data. If you'd like to see the underlying numbers that support the formatstring logic, simply uncheck this box.

Report and analysis requests are now overflowing from Lumberght. Despite his repeated question "Is this good for the company", you are sure he is just trying to somehow make you work the weekend. But with Essbase at your side, you are an invincible analyzing machine and we'll show you more tools to quickly create queries: Query Designer, Point of Views and Copy/Paste Data Points.

QUERY DESIGNER

In addition to ad hoc queries and "zooming," Smart View provides a Query Designer to help users create queries against Essbase. This feature is helpful when you already know the layout for your report, as you define the layout in one single step (vs. drilling, zooming, and member selecting). You create a cross dimensional layout for the query and then add filters for properties like UDAs, attributes or filters for data.

Another nice feature of Query designer is the dynamic nature of the results. For example, you have a regular retrieval and have listed the products listed down the rows of your spreadsheet. If a new product is added, you either have to remember to add into the spreadsheet or zoom out and then back in on products to get the complete list from the Essbase outline. Using Query Designer, you can specify level zero products (using functions or family relationships) and Query Designer will dynamically create the list of products based on the outline every time you refresh the query.

You can also execute free form MDX query in the Smart View Query Designer.

Some restrictions should be considered during the design of queries in Query Designer:
- Formulas are not supported
- Asymmetric reports are not supported
- Comments are not supported on the query sheet; only member names are supported
- Blank rows or columns are not supported
- Alias tables cannot be changed
- Ad Hoc actions, such as zoom in and out, keep and remove only, and double-click are not supported

However, after design is complete and you've run the query, these features are available for use.

On a new worksheet connect to *Sample.Basic*. Click the *Query >> Query Designer* option on the Essbase ribbon:

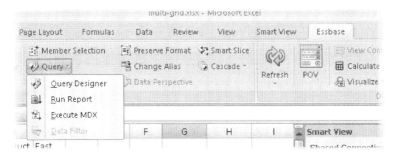

The Query Designer will display:

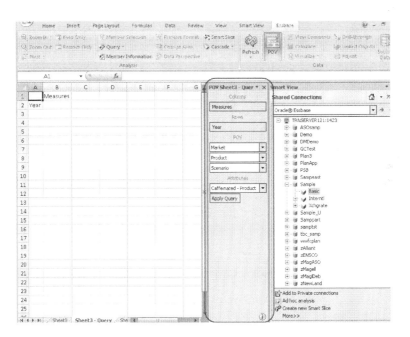

Using the Query Designer, first organize your layout by dragging dimensions to the desired rows, columns and POVs. Next use member selection to select the specific members for each dimension just as you learned in the previous section (double click on the dimensions in the rows and columns section to launch

Member Selection). Don't forget that in the Member Selection window, you can add member filters by the following:

- Children
- Descendants
- Level
- Generation
- UDA
- Attribute
- Subset of attribute dimensions to create conditional expressions

In this example, let's define the layout for our query with the four quarters across our columns, children of Margin and Margin in the rows, and Actual, Markets, "100" in the POV:

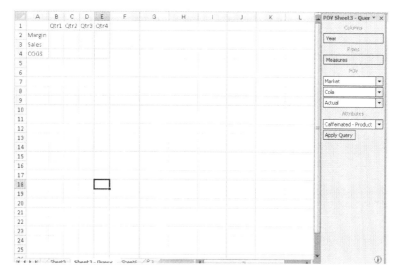

Click *Query>>Run Report* from the Essbase ribbon or *Apply Query* from the Query Designer:

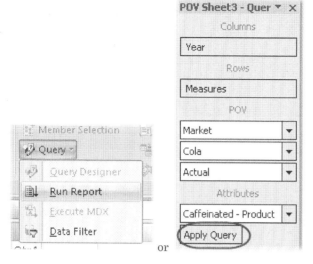

The query will process and display:

	A	B	C	D	E
1		Market	Cola	Actual	
2		Qtr1	Qtr2	Qtr3	Qtr4
3	Margin	8904	9912	10735	9075
4	Sales	14585	16048	17298	14893
5	COGS	5681	6136	6563	5818

You can toggle back to the query designer by selecting the *Query >> Query Designer* button.

If you want to extract a query from an existing report so that you can more easily modify its definition or apply a data filter, simply select the *Query Designer* button and modify the query as needed. Select *Run Report* or *Apply Query* after the modifications have been made.

Create your own query using Query Designer for Sample.Basic. Show it to all of your friends (if you still have friends).

Try It!

To save a query, simply save the Excel spreadsheet. You can share the Excel spreadsheet and the query design with other users.

Tip!

Did you know that you can pick up and move around the Query Designer and the Data Source Manager windows? Try it! Select the Window title and move it to another place in the spreadsheet. Then move it back to the right side of your screen.

APPLY A DATA FILTER

As mentioned earlier, one benefit of the Query Designer is that you can apply data filters. You'll first want to set up the base query with the appropriate members in the rows or columns (e.g. if you want to see the top 5 products, the Products dimension should be in your rows). Modify your query design to look like the following:

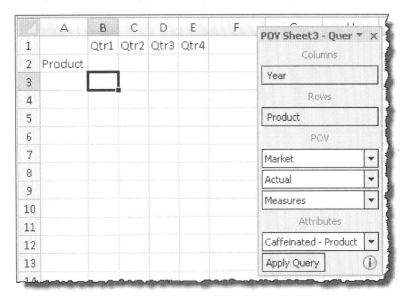

To apply a data filter, select *Query >> Data Filter* from the Essbase ribbon (you must be in Query Designer to see this option):

Under Count, select Top or Bottom and specify a number. We'll choose Top and 5:

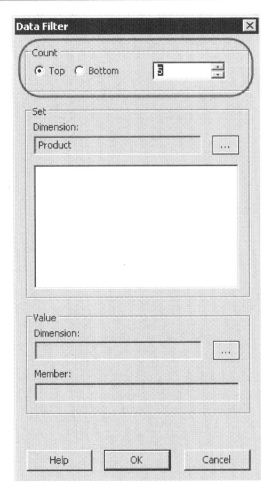

Under Set, select the Dimension (Product in this example). Click the ... icon to launch the Member Selection. Here you want to identify the member set that should be ranked. You can use the normal member selection capabilities to identify the members (e.g. manually picking or using functions like level or children). In the Member Selection dialog box, select a row member for ranking and click *OK* to return to the Data Filter dialog box.

For our example choose the Filter icon and select Level:

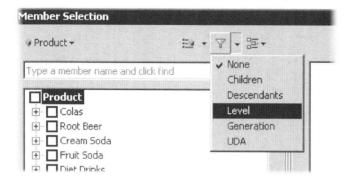

Enter 0 when prompted as we want to pull in the top 4 products (which exist at level zero). Click OK.

Select Check Base Members and use the > arrow to select the products:

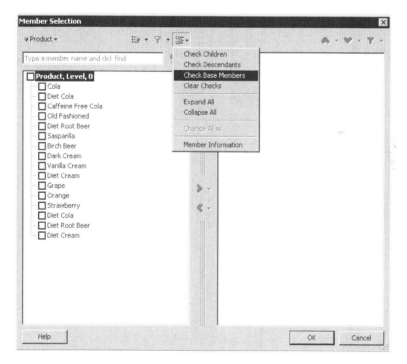

Click OK.

Under Value, you need to identify how the data filter should be applied. Do we want to see the top 5 products based on quarter 1, 2, 3 or 4? The Value setting will use the dimension that is placed in the columns.

Select the ... icon to choose the dimension Year and the member "Qtr1" to be used in the evaluation for the data filter:

Click *OK* to return to the Data Filter dialog box:

Click *OK* when you are done with the data filter definition. The Query Designer is still open and an MDX query that represents your data filtering criteria is inserted into the grid:

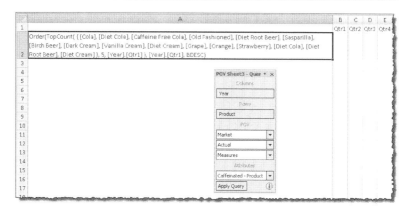

 Note! MDX is a standard query language for Essbase databases (sort of like SQL for relational databases). You can modify the MDX to define more complex selection criteria.

Select *Apply Query* or *Run Report*. The result displays:

	A	B	C	D	E
2		Qtr1	Qtr2	Qtr3	Qtr4
3	Cola	5096	5892	6583	5206
4	Diet Root Beer	2963	3079	3149	2834
5	Diet Root Beer	2963	3079	3149	2834
6	Grape	2838	2998	3201	2807
7	Diet Cream	2695	2723	2855	2820

See any concerns? Notice that "Diet Root Beer" is displayed twice. This is because this member exists twice in the products hierarchy; once under the main rollup and another time under the Diet products. When we selected members to filter, did you see that "Diet Root Beer" and others were listed twice? Let's see how we fix it.

To modify the query and its data filter, click *Query >> Query Designer*. Once the Query Designer is open, select *Query >> Data Filter*. Select the ... icon next to Set. Remove the three duplicate members listed in the selection:

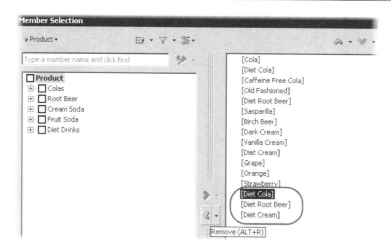

Click *OK* and *OK*. Click *Apply Query* to run the report and the correct data should display with members only listed once:

To summarize, when would you use the Query Designer vs. a regular ad hoc query? The following table illustrates a comparison of the two options:

	Regular Ad hoc Query	Query Designer
You know the query layout at the beginning	Good	Best
Apply Data filters	N	Y

	Regular Ad hoc Query	*Query Designer*
Your list of members changes often and you need to include new members automatically	N	Y
You've drilled into a query and want to get back to the original starting point	Good	Best
Allows free form MDX	N	Y

In addition to Query Designer, if you are on version 11.1.2.2, you have one more tool in your Smart View MacGyver tool belt - Smart Query.

Lumberght has done it again. He's asked for the impossible, thinking he's found a sure fire way to make you work through the weekend. He wants you to find the following information and be able to provide this analysis on a weekly basis:

- Request 1 - The Bottom 5 Markets for Sales of Cola with Diet Cola sales also displayed
- Request 2 - The Top 5 Markets for Sales of Old Fashioned with sales for Diet Root Beer also displayed
- Request 3 – Profit margin for all products for the markets found in Request 1 and 2

Of course this request makes little sense (right along with those TPS reports) but he's Lumberght and you are stuck with this task. Is there a way in Smart View to create reusable queries to select this information in an easy way? Query Designer is a possibility but if you are on 11.1.2.2, Smart Query a better answer.

SMART QUERY

Smart Query is a tool that you can use to create a complex query using multiple sets, filters, unions and joins for Essbase data sources. Once a Smart Query is created, it can be saved, reused and shared for ad hoc analysis. It can also be used in other Smart Queries.

The process to define a Smart Query is:
1. Define the Set(s)
2. Define the Set Filter(s)
3. Build the Smart Query
4. Set Options and Save the Query

Define the Smart Query Set

Let's knock out Lumberght's crazy request so that we can head to Chuy's (if you are on a version prior to 11.1.2.2, you can skip this section and use the Smart View features that you've learned so far or you can just shut down the computer and start thinking about margaritas.

Navigate to the Smart View Panel by selecting the Panel icon. Under the Shared Connections for Essbase, expand the tree to find Sample.Basic. Right click on Sample.Basic and select *New Smart Query Sheet* (or just click *New Smart Query Sheet* at the bottom of the Smart View panel):

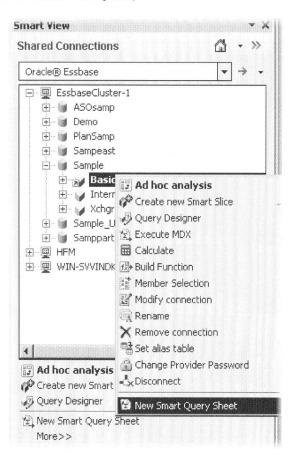

The Smart Query Panel will display with the default dimensions for the Essbase source:

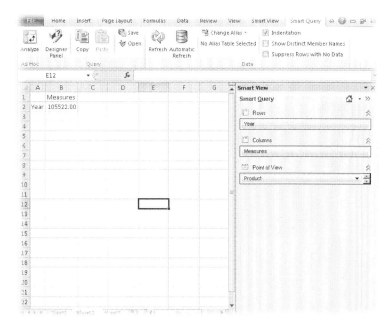

Like you did in the Query Designer, you can drag dimensions to Rows, Columns and Point of View. You can then further select members for the set. In addition to normal member selection methods, you can use MDX expressions to choose members from a dimension.

Drag Product to the Rows:

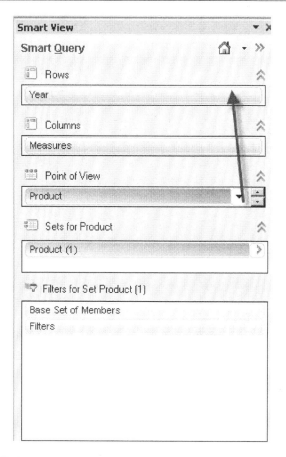

Within the Point of View use the arrow keys to navigate to difererent dimensions in the Rows, Columns or Point of View (or select the ⩔ icon to display all Point of View dimensions):

Drag Markets to the Columns. Drag Measures and Years to the POV. The resulting Smart Query should look as follows:

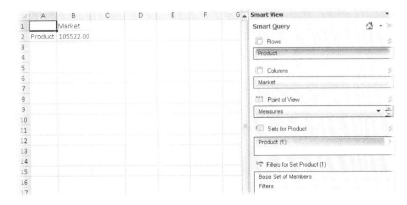

In the Smart Query, select Products under Rows. The Sets for Products becomes active. Select the arrow next to Product (1) under *Sets for Products*:

The following menu will display, providing different alternatives for further defining the member selection for the product dimension:

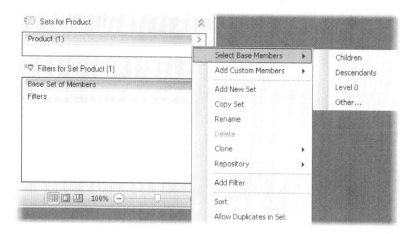

Select *Select Base Members >> Other.* When the Member Selection dialogue displays, choose products 100-10 and 100-20:

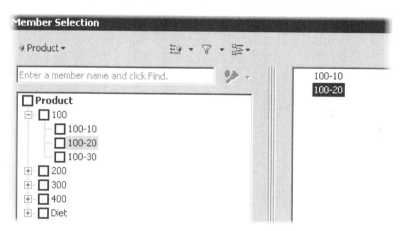

Click OK. Repeat the steps to select "Actual" for Scenario, "Sales" for Measures. "Year" is already defined for the Year dimension so no change is required.

Select Market under columns. Select *Select Base Members>>Level 0:*

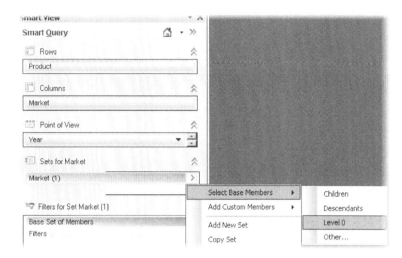

Notice the Smart Query worksheet is updated for the member selections:

Click Save from the Smart Query ribbon:

Name the set Request 1 and optionally add a description:

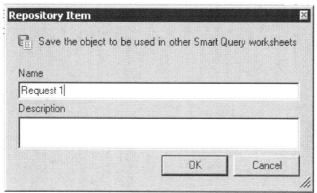

You've just defined your first set!

Define the Smart Query Filter

...But we're not finished. We have a listing of all of the markets for Cola and Diet Cola. But which markets have the worst sales for product 100-10? We'll add a Smart Query Filter to apply to the set.

Select Market dimension. Under the Sets for Market, click the arrow key. Choose *Add Filter:*

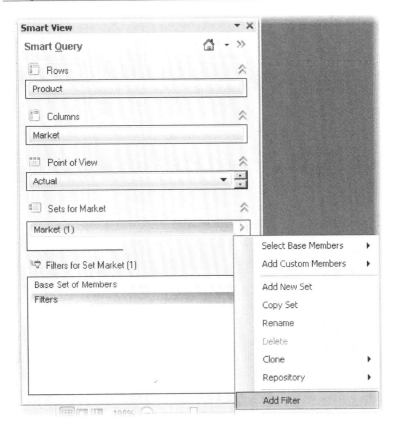

Choose *Top/Bottom:*

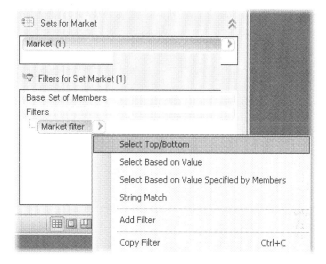

From this dialogue window, you can choose between the *Top* and *Bottom*. You can apply this based on *Count, Percent* or *Sum*. For Lumberght's request, select *Bottom*. Change the setting to *Count* with the number set to "5":

Click *Add*.

Select Measures from the dimension drop down in the upper left hand corner. Select "Sales" and move it over to the Selected panel:

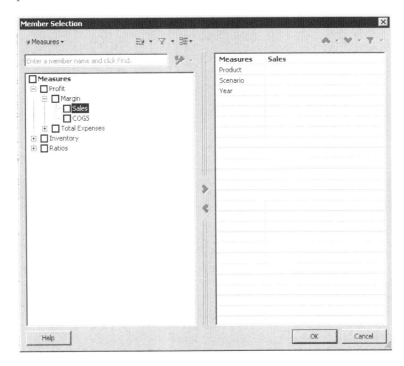

Click *OK* and the resulting filter definition should display:

Click *Add*.

Select Product from the dimension drop down in the upper left hand corner. Select "100-10" and move it over to the Selected panel. Click *OK*:

Click *OK*.

The filter is applied to the Smart Query:

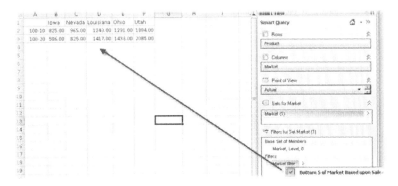

Click *Save* from the Smart Query windo to save Request 1 with the updated filter.

Request 1 is complete. Now we need to create a Smart Query for Request 2. We could start from scratch but the Request 2 is similar to Request 1 so let's modify that Smart Query to create Request 2. We can accomplish this two different ways: You can copy and paste Smart Query across spreadsheets. We could also save the Request 1 Smart Query with a new name. The Save feature also works like a "Save As".

Follow along to learn the possibilities with Copy & Reuse of Smart Query components; we're going to show you the round-a-bout method to hit all of the features.

Select *Copy* from the Smart Query ribbon:

Select a new spreadsheet. Click Paste from the Smart View panel, pasting the Smart Query definition into the active sheet:

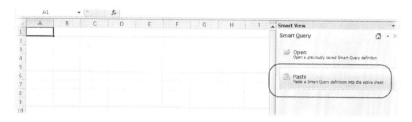

Select Product. Under Sets for Product, select *Select Base Members>>Other*:

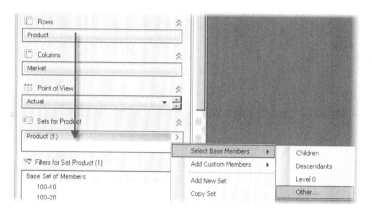

Change the member selection to 200-10 and 200-20:

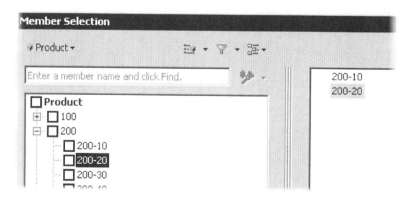

Click *OK*.

Select Market. Under Sets for Market, click the arrow next to Market filter. Select Bottom 5 of Market based upon 100-10...:

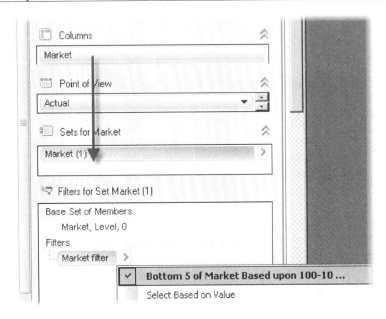

Update the filter to select the top 5 markets based on sales for 200-10:

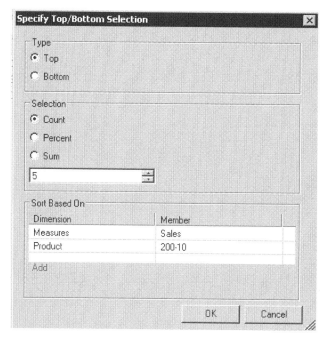

Click *OK*.
The Smart Query results are updated:

	A	B	C	D	E	F
1		Illinois	Ohio	California	Texas	Florida
2	200-10	7151.00	3810.00	3768.00	3183.00	2890.00
3	200-20	5875.00	1418.00	7151.00	2276.00	2393.00

Save Smart Query Filter

Now let's save the filters so we can used them for future queries. Navigate back to the spreadsheet containing Request 1. Right click on the Bottom 5 Market Based upon 100-10... and select *Repository >> Save Filter:*

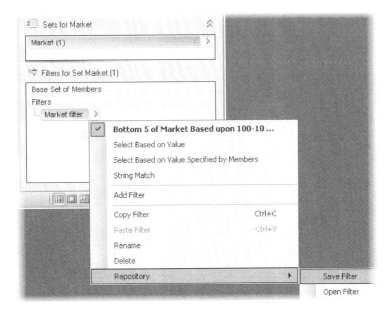

Enter a name and description for the filter:

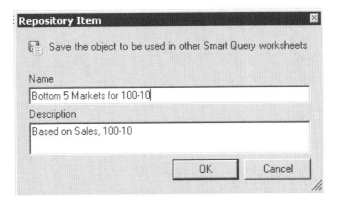

Click *OK*.

   Navigate to the spreadsheet containing Request 2. Right click on the Top 5 Market Based upon 200-10... and select *Repository >> Save Filter*. Enter a name and description for the filter:

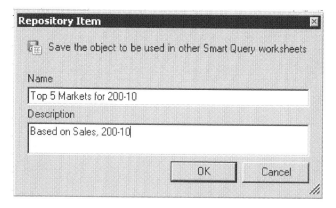

Click *OK*.

Two requests complete! Chuy's here we come!

Navigate to the spreadsheet with Request 1. Select *Copy* from the Smart Query ribbon:

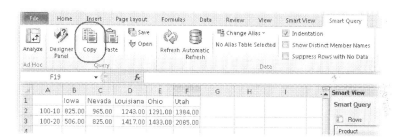

In a blank worksheet, click *Paste* from the Smart Query panel:

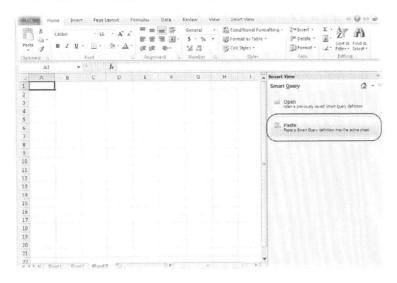

Under Sets for Market, selec the > and choose *Add Filter:*

A new filter is added to the Smart Query definition for Markets. Select > next to Market Filter(2) and choose *Repository* *>>Open Filter:*

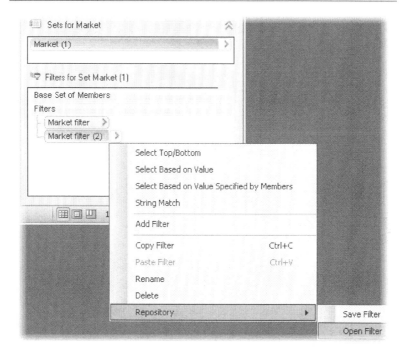

Navigate to and select the "Top 5 Markets for 200-10" filter:

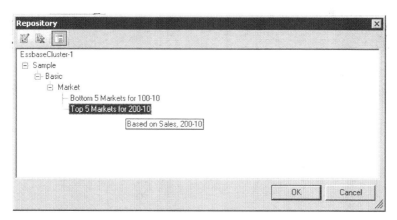

Click *OK*.

The Smart Query definitions and results are updated showing the 5 markets from each filter (note there are 9 because Ohio exists in both filter results):

	A	B	C	D	E	F	G	H	I	J
1		Iowa	Nevada	Louisiana	Ohio	Utah	Illinois	California	Texas	Florida
2	100-10	825.00	965.00	1243.00	1291.00	1384.00	5199.00	8940.00	6210.00	2799.00
3	100-20	506.00	825.00	1417.00	1433.00	2085.00	3651.00	1832.00	1863.00	3068.00

This is called a "Union" of a filter set. Lumberght requested to see Profit for all products so we need to modify the member selections for Products and Measures.

Select Product under Rows. Under Sets for Product, select *Select Base Members >> Level0*:

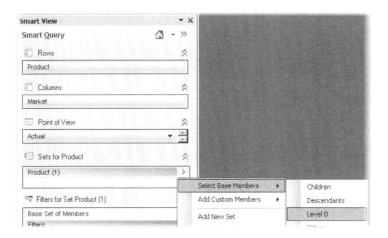

Select Measure under Point of View. Under Sets for Measures, select *Select Base Members >> Other*:

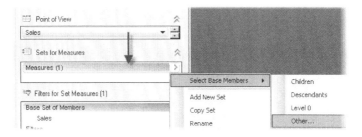

In the Member Selection window, remove "Sales" and select "Profit":

Click _OK_. Lumberght's final request is complete:

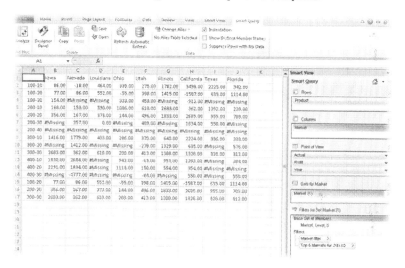

Click _Save_ from the Smart Query ribbon. Enter a name and description for Request 3:

Repository Item

Save the object to be used in other Smart Query worksheets

Name

Request 3 Profit for Select Markets

Description

OK | Cancel

Click *OK*.

More on Sets

We've just skimmed the surface of how you can define Smart Query Sets. Within a set definition, you can choose members based on functions like Children, Descendants or Level Zero. You can choose Other to launch the Member Selection window:

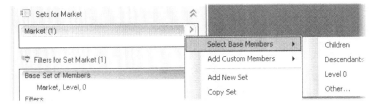

You can also add Custom Members like Totals or Counts:

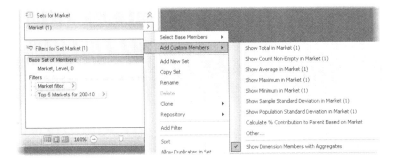

In our example, our Smart Queries just contained one set but you can select many sets in a single Smart Query definition. To add a new set, choose Add New Set from the menu:

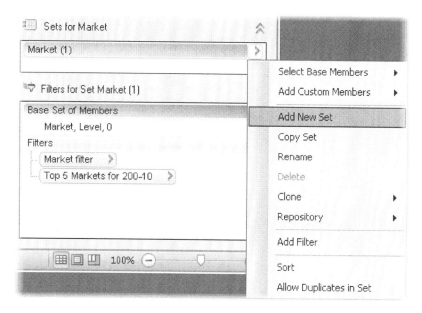

You can save a set definition for use in future Smart Query definitions or you can open a saved set by selecting *Repository>> Save Set* or *Open Set*:

More on Filters

You can define custom filters or used a filter wizard to filter data based on a value or based on a value for specific members:

The *Select Based on Value* menu option launches the following dialogue window:

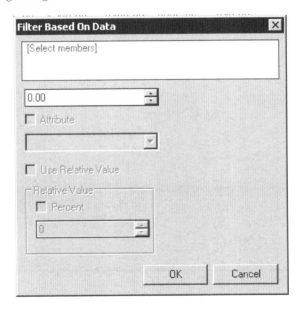

The Member Selection window is displayed when you click on [Select members]:

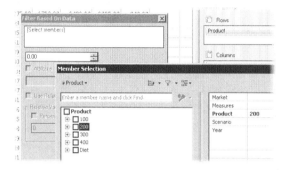

You can then set the criteria (=,<>, <,>) and the amount to be applied in the filter:

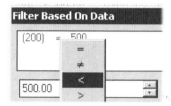

You can also use the wizard to apply filters based on attribute dimensions:

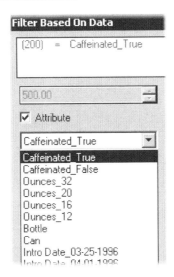

Multiple filters can be added to a Smart Query definition. Lumberght's example showed us a Union of two filters.

You can also create an Interection of filters. Intersections will combine only members that belong to all member sets. For example, Lumberght wants to only see the markets that contain "io" in its name from Request 1 – bottom 5 markets based on Sales for product 100-10. From the first Market filter >, choose *Add Filter*:

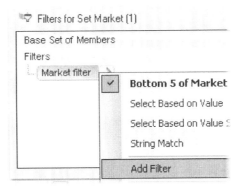

Select *String Match*:

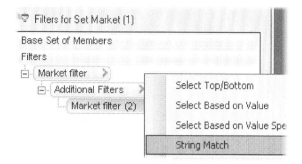

Enter "io". Choose *Contains* and check *Ignore Case*:

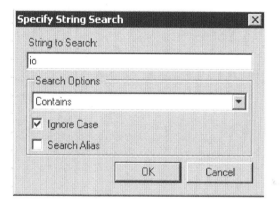

Click *OK* and the intersection is created:

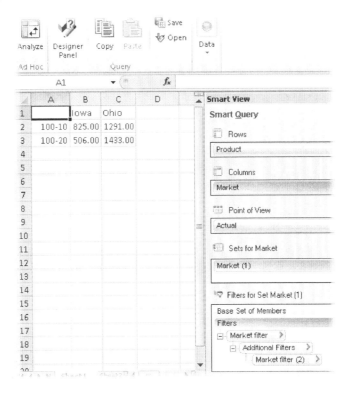

Complements will select members from one set that are not members of the other specified set. Simply choose "Exclude" option when adding the additional features:

And then, of course, you can save and reuse these filter definitions.

Apply Smart Query Options

In the Smart Query ribbon, you can choose options to apply indentation with *Indentation*, *Show Distinct Member Names* and *Suppress Rows with No Data*:

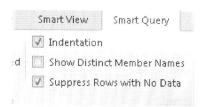

You can also change the alias table used in the result set:

Analyze Data with the Smart Query

At any point within a Smart Query, you can jump into adhoc mode. From the Smart Query ribbon, click *Analyze*:

	A	B	C	D	E	F	G	H	I	J	K
1		Iowa	Nevada	Louisiana	Ohio	Utah	Illinois	California	Texas	Florida	
2	100-10	86.00	-18.00	464.00	335.00	275.00	1782.00	3498.00	2225.00	942.00	
3	100-20	77.00	86.00	552.00	-55.00	398.00	1415.00	-1587.00	639.00	1114.00	
4	100-30	154.00	#Missing	#Missing	333.00		459.00	#Missing	-912.00	#Missing	#Missing
5	200-10	168.00	153.00	590.00	1086.00	610.00	2683.00	362.00	1392.00	239.00	
6	200-20	356.00	167.00	373.00	144.00	496.00	1833.00	2685.00	955.00	709.00	
7	200-30	#Missing	357.00	0.00	#Missing		409.00	#Missing	1834.00	550.00	#Missing
8	200-40	#Missing	#Missing	#Missing	#Missing	#Missing	#Missing	#Missing	#Missing	#Missing	
9	300-10	1416.00	1779.00	403.00	286.00	370.00	640.00	2224.00	336.00	203.00	
10	300-20	#Missing	1412.00	#Missing	#Missing	-278.00	1329.00		635.00	#Missing	576.00
11	300-30	2683.00	362.00	610.00	200.00	413.00	1388.00	1328.00	328.00	312.00	
12	400-10	1830.00	2684.00	#Missing	942.00	-63.00	953.00	1393.00	#Missing	384.00	
13	400-20	2291.00	1834.00	#Missing	1113.00	150.00	554.00	954.00	#Missing	#Missing	
14	400-30	#Missing	-4777.00	#Missing	#Missing		-84.00	#Missing	550.00	#Missing	550.00
15	100-20	77.00	86.00	552.00	-55.00	398.00	1415.00	-1587.00	639.00	1114.00	
16	200-20	356.00	167.00	373.00	144.00	496.00	1833.00	2685.00	955.00	709.00	
17	300-30	2683.00	362.00	610.00	200.00	413.00	1388.00	1328.00	328.00	312.00	
18											

Try that now!

	A	B	C	D	E	F	G	H	I	J
1		Actual	Profit	Year						
2		Iowa	Nevada	Louisiana	Ohio	Utah	Illinois	California	Texas	Florida
3	100-10	86	-18	464	335	275	1782	3498	2225	942
4	100-20	77	86	552	-55	398	1415	-1587	639	1114
5	100-30	154	#Missing	#Missing	333		459	#Missing	-912	#Missing #Missing
6	200-10	168	153	590	1086	610	2683	362	1392	239
7	200-20	356	167	373	144	496	1833	2685	955	709
8	200-30	#Missing	357	0	#Missing		409	#Missing	1834	550 #Missing
9	200-40	#Missing	#Missing	#Missing	#Missing	#Missing	#Missing	#Missing	#Missing	#Missing
10	300-10	1416	1779	403	286	370	640	2224	336	203
11	300-20	#Missing	1412	#Missing	#Missing	-278	1329		635	#Missing 576
12	300-30	2683	362	610	200	413	1388	1328	328	312
13	400-10	1830	2684	#Missing	942	-63	953	1393	#Missing	384
14	400-20	2291	1834	#Missing	1113	150	554		954	#Missing #Missing
15	400-30	#Missing	-4777	#Missing	#Missing		-84	#Missing	550	#Missing 550

You've shut down the computer and head to Lumberght's office with the three printed requests in hand. Two more minutes and you are out the door on your way to Chuy's.

Lumberght looks up surprise to see you and is a bit stunned when you hand him the results. Just as you are about to get in the elevator he catches you and says, "I've entered a few last transactions that could impact this data. I'm going to need you to rerun this." On a day before Smart Query, this would have likely caused you several broken pencils and a bit tongue. But you have Smart Query and this will literally take you a few seconds (booting up the computer will take longer).

Manage Smart Queries

Once the computer is booted up and Excel is Open. Select the Smart View ribbon and choose Panel. From the Home drop down, select *Smart Query:*

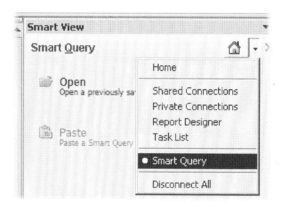

Click *Open* and the local repository of saved Smart Queries display:

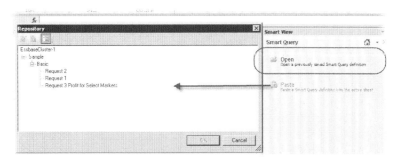

From this window, you can rename and delete Smart Queries.

The Smart Queries are stored locally under your Windows Id. The Smart Queries are not stored on the Essbase server and cannot be opened by other users by using the "Open" feature. You can however share Smart Queries with other users by simply sending them the spreadsheet.

Select Request 1. Enter id and password if prompted and the Smart Query will rerun with Lumberght's new transactions considered. Repeat the steps for Request 2 and 3. This time you decide to just email Lumburght the spreadsheet containing the 3 Smart Queries with instructions on how to run the queries himself (just in case he has any last minute transactions). You smile as you click send and this time take the stairs at the opposite end of the hall from Lumberght's office. As you skip down the stairs, you ponder the adhoc and query options of Smart View:

	Regular Ad hoc Query	*Query Designer*	*Smart Query*
You know the query layout at the beginning	Good	Best	Best
Apply Data filters	N	Y	Y
Your list of members changes often and you need to include new members automatically	N	Y	Y

	Regular Ad hoc Query	*Query Designer*	*Smart Query*
You've drilled into a query and want to get back to the original starting point	Good	Better	Best
Reusable Query	Good	Better	Best
Complex, reusable member sets and filters using unions, complements, and intersections	N	N	Y
Allows free form MDX	N	Y	Y

COPY DATA POINTS

Just as you put the key in the ignition, your cell phone rings. "What's happening? Yeah. I'm gonna need that analysis you did on Margin and Profit by Ounces in Word format. Along with the three Market requests. And I may need an updated version after a few more data transactions are entered. Is that going to be a problem? No? OK. That would be terrific. By the end of the weekend is fine," says Lumberght with a wish-I-could-wipe-that-grin-off-your-face smirk.

Fortunately for you, this request isn't a problem. One of the coolest features in Smart View is the copy and paste data points feature. Available since its infancy days of 9.3x, this feature allows you to copy data points from spreadsheet to spreadsheet, spreadsheet to Word document, PowerPoint to spreadsheet, and more. What's the coolest is that the data points remained linked to the database (yes, we are still geeks!) so if the underlying data changes, you can just refresh the copied data points.

Note!

You may want to toggle of the floating POV so that the point of view members will be pasted into the target (for reference). It is not required but will help you remember the data intersections displayed.

Create the following spreadsheet. To copy and paste data points, select the grid to copy in Excel:

	A	B	C	D	E	F
1		Market	Sales	Actual		
2		Qtr1	Qtr2	Qtr3	Qtr4	
3	Colas	25048	27187	28544	25355	
4	Root Beer	26627	27401	27942	27116	
5	Cream Soda	23997	25736	26650	25022	
6	Fruit Soda	20148	21355	22079	20648	
7	Product	95820	101679	105215	98141	
8						

Select *Copy Data Point* from the Smart View ribbon:

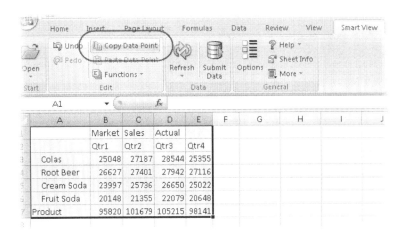

Select a new spreadsheet and select *Paste Data Point:*

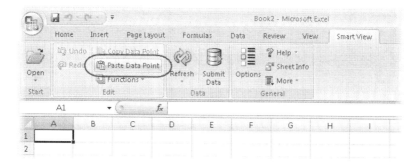

The copied grid will be pasted into the spreadsheet:

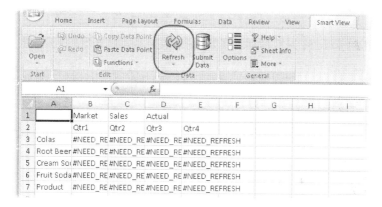

Click *Refresh* to refresh the data points.

	A	B	C	D	E
1		Market	Sales	Actual	
2		Qtr1	Qtr2	Qtr3	Qtr4
3	Colas	25048	27187	28544	25355
4	Root Beer	26627	27401	27942	27116
5	Cream Soc	23997	25736	26650	25022
6	Fruit Soda	20148	21355	22079	20648
7	Product	95820	101679	105215	98141

Each cell that contains a number is a single data point. When you use the Copy / Paste Data Point feature, you are no longer operating with an ad hoc grid (you cannot zoom or pivot data points). Each data point is a self-contained component. Each individual cell (or data point) is linked information about the data point (server, application, cube / database, member intersection for all dimensions and alias table):

Because the data point stores this information, it is fully refreshable. As the underlying data changes, simply click *Refresh* to see the up to date information.

The header information like "Colas" and "Qtr1" is just text. This means you could change this information but it will not change the data point and what is retrieved/refreshed.

Note!   Mouse over a data point to see the connection information.

That's good and all but what about Word or PowerPoint? You have this new request for Lumberght to fill. The real benefit of copying data points is using this feature with Word and PowerPoint. Simply open a Word or PowerPoint document and choose *Paste Data Point* from the Smart View ribbon:

After pasting the data points into Word (or PowerPoint), hit *Refresh* to pull in the current data values.

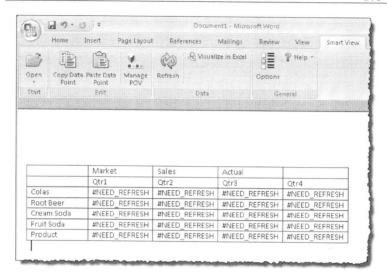

	Market	Sales	Actual	
	Qtr1	Qtr2	Qtr3	Qtr4
Colas	#NEED_REFRESH	#NEED_REFRESH	#NEED_REFRESH	#NEED_REFRESH
Root Beer	#NEED_REFRESH	#NEED_REFRESH	#NEED_REFRESH	#NEED_REFRESH
Cream Soda	#NEED_REFRESH	#NEED_REFRESH	#NEED_REFRESH	#NEED_REFRESH
Fruit Soda	#NEED_REFRESH	#NEED_REFRESH	#NEED_REFRESH	#NEED_REFRESH
Product	#NEED_REFRESH	#NEED_REFRESH	#NEED_REFRESH	#NEED_REFRESH

Wala! Essbase numbers in a Word document (can't nobody hold you down, including Lumberght!).

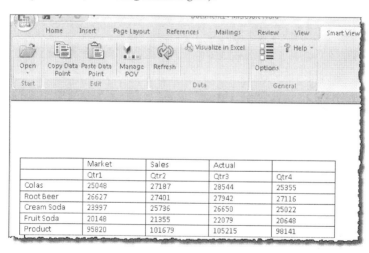

	Market	Sales	Actual	
	Qtr1	Qtr2	Qtr3	Qtr4
Colas	25048	27187	28544	25355
Root Beer	26627	27401	27942	27116
Cream Soda	23997	25736	26650	25022
Fruit Soda	20148	21355	22079	20648
Product	95820	101679	105215	98141

Just like Excel, each one of the numbers is a single self-contained data point. "Colas" and Qtr1" headers are plain ol' text and not tied to Essbase..

For example, in the Word document, change the headers to Quarter One, Quarter Two, Quarter Three, and Quarter Four (these are not valid member names or aliases). What do you think will happen when you click Refresh?

A successful refresh happens. These "headers" are not tied to the data points. We didn't change information related to the data point so it refreshes as normal.

	Market	Sales	Actual	
	Quarter One	Quarter Two	Quarter Three	Quarter Four
Colas	25048	27187	28544	25355
Root Beer	26627	27401	27942	27116
Cream Soda	23997	25736	26650	25022
Fruit Soda	20148	21355	22079	20648
Product	95820	101679	105215	98141

So what if you are looking at Essbase data in Word or PowerPoint and you want to further analyze that data set? Simple. Select the desired data point and click the *Visualize in Excel* button on the Smart View ribbon to pull the grid back into Excel where you can perform further analytics:

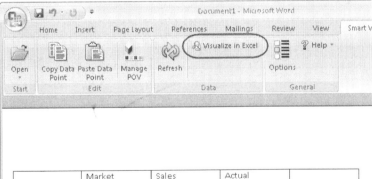

This step brings you to a linked query in Excel:

	A	B	C	D	E	F	G
2		Qtr1	Qtr2	Qtr3	Qtr4		
3	Colas	25048	27187	28544	25355		
4	Root Beer	26627	27401	27942	27116		
5	Cream Soda	23997	25736	26650	25022		
6	Fruit Soda	20148	21355	22079	20648		
7	Product	95820	101679	105215	98141		
8							
9							

POV Linked ∀ ▾ ✕

Market ▾

Sales ▾

Actual ▾

Refresh ⓘ

Copy data points between a spreadsheet and a Word document. Change the underlying data and refresh the Word document.

Try It!

Do you have to copy the full grid? Nope, you can just copy a single data point (the data).

Open	Copy Data Point	Paste Data Point	Manage POV	Refresh		Options
Start		Edit			Data	General

	Market	Sales	Actual	
	Quarter One	Quarter Two	Quarter Three	Quarter Four
Colas	25048	27187	28544	25355
Root Beer	26627	27401	27942	27116
Cream Soda	23997	25736	26650	25022
Fruit Soda	20148	21355	22079	20648
Product	95820	101679	105215	98141

I want to highlight Q3 sales of #NEED_REFRESH.

Click *Refresh* and you have dynamic content in Word (or PowerPoint).

| Open | Copy Data Point | Paste Data Point | Manage POV | Refresh | | Options |
| Start | | Edit | | | Data | General |

	Market	Sales	Actual	
	Quarter One	Quarter Two	Quarter Three	Quarter Four
Colas	25048	27187	28544	25355
Root Beer	26627	27401	27942	27116
Cream Soda	23997	25736	26650	25022
Fruit Soda	20148	21355	22079	20648
Product	95820	101679	105215	98141

I want to highlight Q3 sales of 28544.

You can also copy and paste data points from Smart Queries.

We've now taken you through the advanced analytics portion of the book, analyzing data at the speed of light (well, almost the speed of light, for relativistic reasons). You are finally off to Chuy's, happy to be free of Lumberght for the weekend. We'll next turn our attention to dynamic formatted reporting with Smart View and Essbase.

Chapter 5:
Create Formatted Reports

"Did you see the memo about this? We're going to need detailed formatting on all of the reports before they go out. So if you could go ahead and try to remember to do that from now on, that'd be great. All right!" Before you throw this book at Lumberght's head (again) bright and early Monday morning, let us learn the ins and outs of formatting with Smart View.

Smart View provides two ways to format: Excel formatting and Smart View formatting. In the next chapter, we'll show you more reporting capabilities with Smart Slices and Report Designer, new features in version 11 (although formatting information covered in this chapter also applies to Report Designer). Trust us; formatting won't be a problem any longer.

USE EXCEL FORMATTING

Everything we've done up to this point has been fairly ad hoc and formatting has been kept to a minimum. One of the reasons we're using Excel to display our data is that it's a great place to pretty up boring numbers (or as we used to say back on the farm: "making 'em look fancy"). Essbase will still be used as the source of the data, but Excel will provide all of our formatting. In the recent versions of Smart View Excel formatting provides much faster retrievals:(http://timtows-hyperion-blog.blogspot.com/2012/03/smart-view-11121102-performance-tip.html).

Using what you've learned so far, create the following P&L statement for TBC:

	A	B	C	D
1		Product	Market	Year
2		Actual	Budget	
3	Sales	400855	373140	
4	COGS	179336	158940	
5	Margin	221519	214200	
6	Marketing	66237	49520	
7	Payroll	48747	35240	
8	Misc	1013	-	
9	Total Expenses	115997	84760	
10	Profit	105522	129440	
11				

We now have a P&L, statement but it doesn't look that great. What we really need to do is apply some formatting to this spreadsheet.

Formatting Options

We are in Excel so we can use all the power that is Microsoft for formatting our spreadsheets. Before you start formatting with Excel, select *Options* from the Smart View ribbon. Choose the Formatting section:

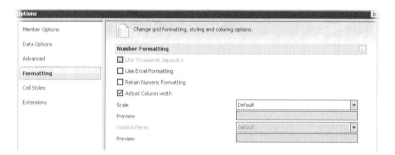

Use Excel Formatting is the key setting to tell Essbase that you want to leverage Excel formatting in your ad hoc grids. Excel formatting will be retained on all operations. However, when you pivot, you may not get what you had planned. The cell itself will maintain the formatting (e.g. in cell C4 you've formatted the data value to be bold with commas but after pivoting C4 holds the member "Jan" which is bold with commas). In version 11.1.2.2, we have a new option available *Move Formatting on Operations*:

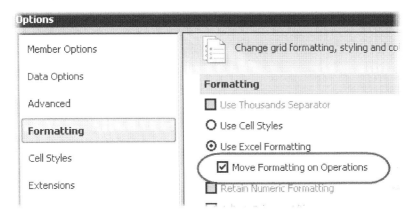

Move Formatting on Operations applies your Excel formatting selections to expanded cells when you zoom in. This formatting also moves with the data when you pivot members.

You can set the Scale if you need to scale Essbase numbers for your report. If you want the column to automatically adjust based on the member length, check *Adjust Column Width*.

Retain Numeric Formatting will maintain the Scale and Decimal settings during drilling actions. You can also set the *Use Thousands* separator.

Add Excel Formatting

Check the box to *Use Excel Formatting*. Click *OK* and you're ready. So what are you waiting for? Get formatting. Format your sheet to look like the following using normal Excel formatting options:

	A	B	C	D
1		Product	Market	Year
2		**Actual**	**Budget**	
3	**Sales**	$ 400,855	$ 373,140	
4	**COGS**	$ 179,336	$ 158,940	
5	***Margin***	*$ 221,519*	*$ 214,200*	
6	**Marketing**	$ 66,237	$ 49,520	
7	**Payroll**	$ 48,747	$ 35,240	
8	**Misc**	$ 1,013	-	
9	***Total Expenses***	*$ 115,997*	*$ 84,760*	
10	**Profit**	$ 105,522	$ 129,440	
11				

Click the *Refresh* button and notice the formatting remains. Save this report. Now drag Year into the rows (or Select cell D1 and click *Pivot*). Oh no! What happened to my formatting?

	A	B	C	D
1			Product	Market
2			**Actual**	Budget
3	**Year**	Sales	$ 400,855	###
4		COGS	$ 179,336	###
5		*Margin*	*$ 221,519*	###
6		Marke	$ 66,237	###
7		Payrol	$ 48,747	###
8		Misc	$ 1,013	-
9		*Total Exp*	*$ 115,997*	###
10		Profit	$ 105,522	###
11				

If you change the grid layout by adding, removing or moving dimensions or if you drill into a report, you can probably count on some formatting issues. So the biggest lesson learned from this chapter: **Always format last!**

Click *Undo* to get back to our pretty report. Let's continue with other formatting capabilities.

At this point you want to finalize the layout. Once we add formulas and formatting, be wary of changes to the layout. While we have improved support for formatting on drills and pivots, there is still the possibility of rework or updates to the formulas and/or formatting. So ask yourself this question: are you sure this is the final layout? Really sure? If so, then you are ready to move on to the next step.

Add Blank Columns or Rows ("Spacing")

Since this is the data layout we want to see on our final report, let's add some spacing to the report by moving our row, column, and page members around. Our data is a bit cramped at the moment, so let's space it out by inserting some blank rows. Highlight the rows (by clicking the row number) and select *Insert >> Rows* from the Excel menu. Make your spreadsheet look like the following:

	A	B	C	D	E
1					
2					
3					
4		Product		Market	Year
5					
6					
7					
8		Actual		Budget	
9	Sales	$ 400,855		$ 373,140	
10	COGS	$ 179,336		$ 158,940	
11	*Margin*	$ 221,519		$ 214,200	
12	Marketing	$ 66,237		$ 49,520	
13	Payroll	$ 48,747		$ 35,240	
14	Misc	$ 1,013		-	
15	*Total Expenses*	$ 115,997		$ 84,760	
16	Profit	$ 105,522		$ 129,440	
17					

Even though we've inserted a bunch of extra lines, this is still a valid Essbase retrieval. Click *Refresh* to just prove it.

Add Titles and Other Text

As Smart View is scanning the sheet, it will often run into names it doesn't recognize. The retrieve will still function even though unknown names are present.

We can use this to our advantage by adding extraneous text to our retrieve knowing that the retrieve will continue to work just fine. Extra text can include header information such as the company or the name of the report. In our case, we're going to add a title and headers for the POV:

- In cell A2, "Profit and Loss Statement:"
- In cell A3, "for:"
- In cell A4, "Product:"
- In cell A5, "Market:"
- In cell A6, "Period":

The top of your retrieve should now look like this:

	A	B	C	D	E
1					
2	**Profit and Loss Statement**				
3	for				
4	*Product:*	Product			
5	*Market:*	Market			
6	*Period:*	Year			
7					
8		**Actual**		**Budget**	
9	**Sales**	$ 400,855		$ 373,140	
10	**COGS**	$ 179,336		$ 158,940	
11	***Margin***	*$ 221,519*		*$ 214,200*	
12	**Marketing**	$ 66,237		$ 49,520	
13	**Payroll**	$ 48,747		$ 35,240	
14	**Misc**	$ 1,013		-	
15	***Total Expenses***	*$ 115,997*		*$ 84,760*	
16	**Profit**	$ 105,522		$ 129,440	

Click *Refresh* and note the text was saved.

Tip!

Smart View will support merged cells. In the example above, we could have each merged and centered the B-D4 Markets, B-D5 Products, and B-D6Year cells.

Tip!

Be careful not to add text that matches a member name or Essbase will try to retrieve it and may give you weird error messages. In the example above, we added a " :" to make the text different from the dimension or member names, Product, Market and Year,

Insert Excel Formulas

At times, you may want to add formulas to your report to calculate things that aren't in Essbase. We are of the belief that, whenever possible, you should try to add these types of calculations to the Essbase database itself. The main reason is that if you add the calculation to Essbase anyone else will be guaranteed to calculate that value the exact same way you do. This prevents the embarrassing situation of two people walking into a meeting with different ideas of what Profit as a percent of Sales was last month. This is likely to get one or both people fired (usually, they'll fire the one who has the lower Profit number). If both people were getting their Profit % from Essbase, then they'd at least have the same number.

The other benefit of performing the calculation in Essbase is that the next time you need the calculation, you don't have to remember how you calculated it last time. There's a member waiting for you to use with the calculation already defined. Sample.Basic, for instance, has members called "Profit %" and "Margin %" in the Measures dimension. Go ahead and type Profit % into cell A18 and *Refresh*. You'll see that Profit as a percent of Sales is about 26% for the year:

	A	B	C	D	E
1					
2	Profit and Loss Statement				
3	for				
4	*Product:*	Product			
5	*Market:*	Market			
6	*Period:*	Year			
7					
8		**Actual**		**Budget**	
9	**Sales**	$ 400,855		$ 373,140	
10	**COGS**	$ 179,336		$ 158,940	
11	*Margin*	*$ 221,519*		*$ 214,200*	
12	**Marketing**	$ 66,237		$ 49,520	
13	**Payroll**	$ 48,747		$ 35,240	
14	**Misc**	$ 1,013		-	
15	*Total Expenses*	*$ 115,997*		*$ 84,760*	
16	**Profit**	$ 105,522		$ 129,440	
17					
18	**Profit %**	26.3		34.7	
19					

While adding all of your calculations to Essbase may be great in theory, there are plenty of times when a calculation will occur to you on the spot and you don't want to bother your Essbase admin asking her to add the calculation to the database. For instance, say we want to add a line to our report that calculates Total Expenses as a percent of Sales. "Expense %" is not a member in the database. Type in the following:

- In cell A20, "Expense %"
- In cell B20, "=B15/B9*100"

Copy the formula in cell B20 to cell D20. Your report should now look like this:

	A	B	C	D	E
			f∗	=B15/B9*100	
		B19			
1					
2		**Profit and Loss Statement**			
3		for			
4	*Product:*	Product			
5	*Market:*	Market			
6	*Period:*	Year			
7					
8		**Actual**		**Budget**	
9	**Sales**	$ 400,855		$ 373,140	
10	**COGS**	$ 179,336		$ 158,940	
11	*Margin*	*$ 221,519*		*$ 214,200*	
12	**Marketing**	$ 66,237		$ 49,520	
13	**Payroll**	$ 48,747		$ 35,240	
14	**Misc**	$ 1,013		-	
15	*Total Expenses*	*$ 115,997*		*$ 84,760*	
16	**Profit**	$ 105,522		$ 129,440	
17					
18	**Profit%**	26.3		34.7	
19	**Expense%**	28.9		22.7	
20					

Formulas can be in the rows or the columns just like a normal Excel spreadsheet. Refresh your data and something really cool will happen: your Expense % formulas remains.

Note!

By default, Smart View will retain formulas (the *Preserve Formulas and Comments in ad hoc operations* option is checked). In the old days of the Excel Add-in, we had to first turn on Formula Preservation.

Your report template is now complete. In cell B5, type in "East". Click *Refresh* and the report refreshes for the East region:

	A	B	C	D	E
1					
2	**Profit and Loss Statement**				
3	for				
4	*Product:*	Product			
5	*Market:*	East			
6	*Period:*	Year			
7					
8		**Actual**		**Budget**	
9	**Sales**	$ 87,398		$ 79,010	
10	**COGS**	$ 37,927		$ 32,250	
11	*Margin*	$ 49,471		$ 46,760	
12	**Marketing**	$ 14,721		$ 11,210	
13	**Payroll**	$ 10,389		$ 7,100	
14	**Misc**	$ 200		-	
15	*Total Expenses*	$ 25,310		$ 18,310	
16	**Profit**	$ 24,161		$ 28,450	
17					
18	**Profit %**	27.6		36.0	
19	**Expense%**	29.0		23.2	

Type "Jan" in cell B6. Click *Refresh*.

	A	B	C	D
1				
2	**Profit and Loss Statement**			
3	for			
4	*Product:*	Product		
5	*Market:*	East		
6	*Period:*	Jan		
7				
8		**Actual**		**Budget**
9	**Sales**	$ 6,780		$ 6,240
10	**COGS**	$ 3,007		$ 2,590
11	*Margin*	*$ 3,773*		*$ 3,650*
12	**Marketing**	$ 1,161		$ 890
13	**Payroll**	$ 865		$ 620
14	**Misc**	$ 15		-
15	*Total Expenses*	*$ 2,041*		*$ 1,510*
16	**Profit**	$ 1,732		$ 2,140
17				
18	**Profit %**	25.5		34.3
19	**Expense%**	30.1		24.2
20				

Add Excel Conditional Formatting

One of our favorite Excel features is the built in conditional formatting available in Excel 2007 and on. You can create a dashboard-like report with traffic lighting indicators to understand how you are performing in relation to other data sets or specific criteria that you determine. This is an Excel feature but let's show you how you can apply it to data from Essbase.

Select the cells for the Profit %:

	A	B	C	D	E
1					
2	**Profit and Loss Statement**				
3	for				
4	*Product:*	Product			
5	*Market:*	East			
6	*Period:*	Jan			
7					
8		**Actual**		**Budget**	
9	**Sales**	$ 6,780		$ 6,240	
10	**COGS**	$ 3,007		$ 2,590	
11	*Margin*	$ 3,773		$ 3,650	
12	**Marketing**	$ 1,161		$ 890	
13	**Payroll**	$ 865		$ 620	
14	**Misc**	$ 15		-	
15	*Total Expenses*	$ 2,041		$ 1,510	
16	**Profit**	$ 1,732		$ 2,140	
17					
18	**Profit %**	25.5		34.3	
19	**Expense%**	30.1		24.2	

Select Conditional Formatting on the Excel Home ribbon. Choose Color Scales >> Green/Yellow option:

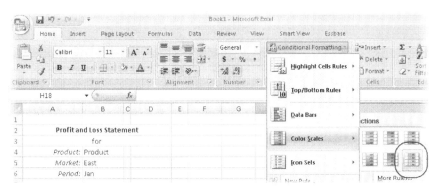

The final report should look as follows:

	A	B	C	D	E
1					
2	**Profit and Loss Statement**				
3	for				
4	*Product:*	Product			
5	*Market:*	East			
6	*Period:*	Year			
7					
8		**Actual**		**Budget**	
9	**Sales**	$ 87,398		$ 79,010	
10	**COGS**	$ 37,927		$ 32,250	
11	*Margin*	$ 49,471		$ 46,760	
12	**Marketing**	$ 14,721		$ 11,210	
13	**Payroll**	$ 10,389		$ 7,100	
14	**Misc**	$ 200		-	
15	*Total Expenses*	$ 25,310		$ 18,310	
16	Profit	$ 24,161		$ 28,450	
17					
18	**Profit %**	27.6		36.0	
19	**Expense%**	29.0		23.2	
20					

You can apply color scales, data bars, icons and more in Excel conditional formatting.

Note! If you use Smart View for Planning, FM or Enterprise you may see an option *Preserve Formula on POV Change.* Unfortunately, this option is not available for Essbase connections. But never fear - By default formula will be maintained with floating POV change.

Save

Before you save the workbook, blank out all your numbers (keep your formulas, though). This makes the file size that much smaller thereby making the file that much faster to open next time.

The next time you want to use this report, open it up, connect to the database, use Member Select to select your Market, Product, and Scenario members (or just type them in), and finally choose *Refresh*.

Save your spreadsheet where you'll be able to find it later. We'll be using it in future exercises.

Try It!

Create and save the following Product Analysis report for Lumberght:

Try It!

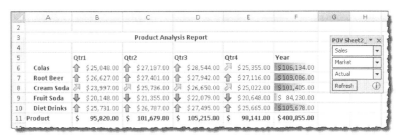

Note!

In the example above, zooming in on Colas should also expand the formatting (if you have *Use Excel Formatting* on).

PRINT POV IN HEADERS AND FOOTERS

Because POV members are hidden in row 1, you can include them in standard headers and footers for the report.

Another way to print the POV in Excel headers and footers is to use the POV{} function. In Excel, navigate to Page Setup. Under Headers/Footers, choose *Custom Header* or *Custom Footer*. Type in the statement POV:{} to pull in the current POV selections:

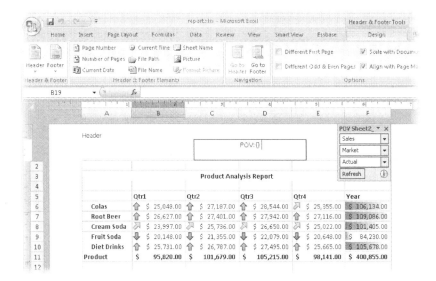

Click *OK* and *OK* to confirm changes and the POV should display in the header or footer when you print the spreadsheet.

MULTI-GRID / MULTI-SOURCE REPORTS

There are certain times when you'll want to have two sets of Essbase data on one sheet. Say we wanted to create a report that had Actual on the top half of the page and Budget on the bottom half:

	Qtr1	Market Qtr2	Product Qtr3	Actual Qtr4	Year
Sales	95,820	101,679	105,215	98,141	400,855
COGS	42,877	45,362	47,343	43,754	179,336
Margin	52,943	56,317	57,872	54,387	**221,519**
Marketing	15,839	16,716	17,522	16,160	**66,237**
Payroll	12,168	12,243	12,168	12,168	**48,747**
Misc	233	251	270	259	**1,013**
Total Expenses	28,240	29,210	29,960	28,587	**115,997**
Profit	**24,703**	**27,107**	**27,912**	**25,800**	**105,522**

	Qtr1	Market Qtr2	Product Qtr3	Budget Qtr4	Year
Sales	89,680	95,240	98,690	89,470	**373,080**
COGS	38,140	40,460	42,280	38,060	**158,940**
Margin	51,540	54,780	56,410	51,410	**214,140**
Marketing	11,900	12,700	13,370	11,550	**49,520**
Payroll	9,060	9,210	9,060	7,910	**35,240**
Misc	-	-	-	-	**-**
Total Expenses	20,960	21,910	22,430	19,460	**84,760**
Profit	**30,580**	**32,870**	**33,980**	**31,950**	**129,380**

In the old Excel Add-in, if you created this spreadsheet and chose *Essbase >> Retrieve*, you'd receive the following error:

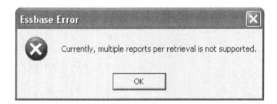

This was actually our favorite Essbase Add-In error, because it almost comes across as a poorly worded marketing message. The presence of the word "Currently" gives you hope that if you just wait until the next release, Essbase will support multiple reports per retrieval! Not to dash your hopes, but this error message has been there for over ten years and they still haven't added it. Give up and stop waiting, because there is a workaround (check out our *Look Smarter Than You Are with Essbase System 9: An End User's Guide* for those steps).

So is it possible in Smart View? Beginning in 11.1.2.1.102, multiple grids in a single worksheet are possible for Essbase connections. The grids may be connected to the same or different Essbase data sources.

A few limitations exist with multi – grid reports:

- You may only submit data for one grid at a time
- You cannot set a cell style for dirty cells
- Comments are not supported
- Undo, Redo, Pivot to POV and POV buttons are disabled on the Smart View and Essbase ribbons

Open a blank worksheet. Open the Smart View panel (click *Open* on the Smart View ribbon). Select the Essbase server. Click the + sign on the Essbase server and navigate to Sample.Basic. Right click on Basic and click *Connect*.

Next select a range of cells (it must be a range of cells and not a single cell). Right click on Basic and select *Ad Hoc Analysis:*

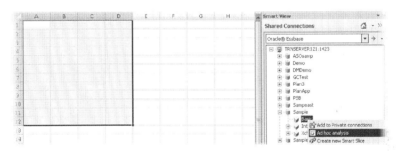

Be careful with how many cells you select in the starting range. Any empty rows are still considered part of the grid and might give you unwanted whitespace.

Tip!

When prompted, click *Yes* to change the sheet to support multiple grids:

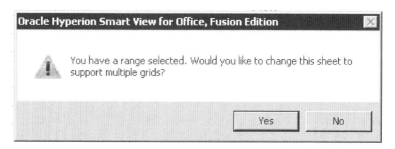

In the spreadsheet, use member selection and/or zooming to create the following grid:

	A	B	C	D
1		Jan	Market	
2		Actual	Budget	Variance
3		Sales	Sales	Sales
4	Colas	8314	9040	-726
5	Root Beer	8716	8500	216
6	Cream Soda	7874	6650	1224
7	Fruit Soda	6634	5350	1284
8	Diet Drinks	8454	8260	194
9	Product	31538	29540	1998

Next select a range of cells below the first ad hoc grid. Right click on Basic and select *Ad Hoc Analysis:*

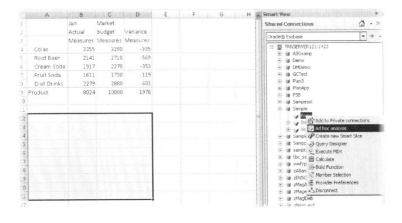

Use member selection and/or zooming to create the second grid. Update both grids to use the "Sales" member in the Measures dimension:

	A	B	C	D
1		Jan	Market	
2		Actual	Budget	Variance
3		Sales	Sales	Sales
4	Colas	8314	9040	-726
5	Root Beer	8716	8500	216
6	Cream Soda	7874	6650	1224
7	Fruit Soda	6634	5350	1284
8	Diet Drinks	8454	8260	194
9	Product	31538	29540	1998
10				
11				
12		Feb	Market	
13		Actual	Budget	Variance
14		Sales	Sales	Sales
15	Colas	8327	9040	-713
16	Root Beer	8960	8730	230
17	Cream Soda	8046	6800	1246
18	Fruit Soda	6736	5430	1306
19	Diet Drinks	8610	8410	200
20	Product	32069	30000	2069
21				

Once you've finalized the layout, you can apply formatting just as we learned earlier in this chapter.

Create the following multi grid report that retrieves data from Sample.Basic and Sample.Intntl:

Try It!

	A	B	C	D	E	F
1						
2		Sales	Product	Actual	From Sample.Basic	
3		Qtr1	Qtr2	Qtr3	Qtr4	Year
4	East	$ 20,621	$ 22,449	$ 22,976	$ 21,352	$ 87,398
5	West	$ 31,674	$ 33,572	$ 35,130	$ 32,555	$ 132,931
6	South	$ 12,113	$ 12,602	$ 13,355	$ 12,776	$ 50,846
7	Central	$ 31,412	$ 33,056	$ 33,754	$ 31,458	$ 129,680
8	Market	$ 95,820	$ 101,679	$ 105,215	$ 98,141	$ 400,855
9						
10		Sales	Product	Actual	From Sample.Intntl	
11		Qtr1	Qtr2	Qtr3	Qtr4	Year
12	US	$ 24,703	$ 27,107	$ 27,912	$ 25,800	$ 105,522
13	Canada	$ 3,851	$ 3,856	$ 3,983	$ 3,840	$ 15,530
14	Europe	$ 1,521	$ 3,245	$ 3,726	$ 3,044	$ 11,536
15	Market	$ 30,075	$ 34,208	$ 35,620	$ 32,684	$ 132,588
16						

Apply some creative formatting to the multi-grid / multi-source report (make sure *Use Excel Formatting* is turned on). Click *Refresh* when finished and formatting should remain.

Try It!

	A	B	C	D	E	F
1						
2						
3						
4			Sales Report			
5						
6		Qtr1	Qtr2	Qtr3	Qtr4	Year
7	East	$ 20,621	$ 22,449	$ 22,976	$ 21,352	$ 87,398
8	West	$ 31,674	$ 33,572	$ 35,130	$ 32,555	$ 132,931
9	South	$ 12,113	$ 12,602	$ 13,355	$ 12,776	$ 50,846
10	Central	$ 31,412	$ 33,056	$ 33,754	$ 31,458	$ 129,680
15	US	$ 95,820	$101,679	$105,215	$ 98,141	$ 400,855
16	Canada	$ 16,461	$ 16,506	$ 16,781	$ 16,351	$ 66,099
17	Europe	$ 21,336	$ 26,255	$ 28,680	$ 24,926	$ 101,197
18	Market	$ 133,617	$144,440	$150,677	$139,418	$ 568,151

Tip!

Excel Formatting Hints for Multiple Grids:
- Make sure *Use Excel Formatting* is turned on for the worksheet
- Apply no borders to the cells
- Change background to white
- Change text to "white" to hide headers and rows (do *not* delete grid headers or POV members because that could impact your ability to refresh)
- Apply lines, bolding, etc.
- Adjust row size to help with white space

BUTTERFLY REPORT

Using the multi-grid features of Smart View, you can create a "butterfly" report, a report that has data points before member names. Follow along.

In a new spreadsheet, select a range of cells. Right click on Sample.Basic and select *Ad hoc Analysis*. When prompted, click *Yes* to enable the sheet for multiple grids if you will need to have multiple grids (this isn't mandatory for creating a butterfly report). Next, using zooming, member selection, or direct typing, create the following grid:

	A	B	C
1		Year	Market
2		Actual	Budget
3		Sales	Sales
4	Colas	106134	114370
5	Root Beer	109086	106740
6	Cream Soda	101405	85230
7	Fruit Soda	84230	66800
8	Diet Drinks	105678	103300
9	Product	400855	373140

At this point you have a standard grid. Insert a column between Actual and Budget. Using Excel functionality, copy and paste the product names from column A to the new blank column, column C. Click *Refresh* and you have a butterfly report! Apply some Excel formatting and then save this report.

	A	B	C	D	E
1		Sales		Year	Market
2		**Actual**		**Budget**	
3		$106,134.00	Colas	$114,370.00	
4		$109,086.00	Root Beer	$106,740.00	
5		$101,405.00	Cream Soda	$85,230.00	
6		$84,230.00	Fruit Soda	$66,800.00	
7		$105,678.00	Diet Drinks	$103,300.00	
8		**$400,855.00**	Product	**$373,140.00**	

MULTI-SOURCE REPORT WITH DATA POINTS

You can also create a multi-source report using data points, the pre-11.1.2.1.102 method. While multi-grid spreadsheets are the recommended method, we'll review this alternative so you'll have the full bag of Smart View tricks.

Create the following grid in a separate worksheet, sourced from Sample.Basic:

	A	B	C	D	E	F
1		Actual	Product			
2		Qtr1	Qtr2	Qtr3	Qtr4	Year
3		Sales	Sales	Sales	Sales	Sales
4	East	20621	22449	22976	21352	87398
5	West	31674	33572	35130	32555	132931
6	South	12113	12602	13355	12776	50846
7	Central	31412	33056	33754	31458	129680
8	Market	95820	101679	105215	98141	400855
9						

Create the following grid in a separate worksheet, sourced from Sample.Interntl:

	A	B	C	D	E	F
1		Product	Actual			
2		Qtr1	Qtr2	Qtr3	Qtr4	Year
3		Sales	Sales	Sales	Sales	Sales
4	US	95820	101679	105215	98141	400855
5	Canada	16461.27	16505.64	16781.04	16351.11	66099.06
6	Europe	21335.923	26254.93	28680.47	24925.64	101196.963
7	Market	133617.193	144439.57	150676.51	139417.75	568151.023
8						

Next, select the first grid from the worksheet and select *Copy Data Point* from the Smart View ribbon:

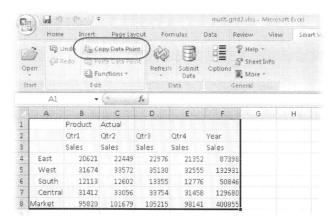

Select a blank worksheet and select *Paste Data,* pasting the data points into a blank worksheet:

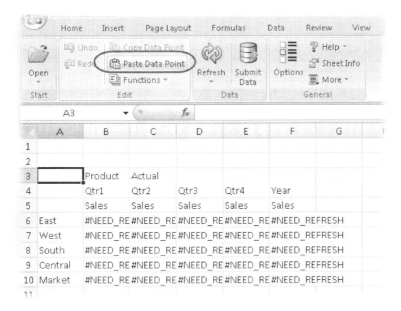

"Behind the scenes", the Paste Data Points feature is creating a report with each cell using the HSGetValue function.

Repeat the same steps for the second grid, copying and pasting the data points below the first grid. Notice each data cell is an individual data point that is tied to a specific intersection of dimension members, database and server:

	A	B	C	D	E	F	G
1							
2							
3		Product	Actual				
4		Qtr1	Qtr2	Qtr3	Qtr4	Year	
5		Sales	Sales	Sales	Sales	Sales	
6	East	#NEED_RE	#NEED_RE	#NEED_RE	#NEED_RE	#NEED_REFRESH	
7	West	#NEED_RE	#NEED_RE	#NEED_RE	#NEED_RE	#NEED_REFRESH	
8	South	#NEED_RE	#NEED_RE	#NEED_RE	#NEED_RE	#NEED_REFRESH	
9	Central	#NEED_RE	#NEED_RE	#NEED_RE	#NEED_RE	#NEED_REFRESH	
10	Market	#NEED_RE	#NEED_RE	#NEED_RE	#NEED_RE	#NEED_REFRESH	
11							
12		Qtr1	Qtr2	Qtr3	Qtr4	Year	
13	US	#NEED_RE	#NEED_RE	#NEED_RE	#NEED_RE	#NEED_REFRESH	
14	Canada	#NEED_RE	#NEED_RE	#NEED_RE	#NEED_RE	#NEED_REFRESH	
15	Europe	#NEED_RE	#NEED_RE	#NEED_RE	#NEED_RE	#NEED_REFRESH	
16	Market	#NEED_RE	#NEED_RE	#NEED_RE	#NEED_RE	#NEED_REFRESH	

Click *Refresh* to refresh the data for each data point. From this point you can follow the same formatting steps for the spreadsheet.

Try It!

Apply some creative formatting to the data points / multi-source report (*Use Excel Formatting* is only applicable for grids so it can be turned on or off with no impact to formatting on data points). Click *Refresh* when finished and formatting should remain.

	A	B	C	D	E	F
1						
2			Market Report for Sales			
3						
4		Qtr1	Qtr2	Qtr3	Qtr4	Year
5	East	$ 20,621	$ 22,449	$ 22,976	$ 21,352	$ 87,398
6	West	$ 31,674	$ 33,572	$ 35,130	$ 32,555	$ 132,931
7	South	$ 12,113	$ 12,602	$ 13,355	$ 12,776	$ 50,846
8	Central	$ 31,412	$ 33,056	$ 33,754	$ 31,458	$ 129,680
10	US	$ 95,820	$ 101,679	$ 105,215	$ 98,141	$ 400,855
11	Canada	$ 16,461	$ 16,506	$ 16,781	$ 16,351	$ 66,099
12	Europe	$ 21,336	$ 26,255	$ 28,680	$ 24,926	$ 101,197
13	Market	$ 20,621	$ 22,449	$ 22,976	$ 21,352	$ 87,398

Tip!

Excel Formatting Hints for Reports using Data Points:
- Apply no borders to the cells
- Change background to white
- Change text to "white" to hide headers and rows (do *not* delete grid headers or POV members because that could impact your ability to refresh)
- Apply lines, bolding, etc
- Adjust row size to help with white space

You can then refresh the report daily, monthly or as necessary and the current data stored in Essbase will display.

Change POV for Data Points with POV Manager

Notice that if you select the data point a tool tip will display showing you the attributes about the data point. Notice also all of our data points reference Product. What if we wanted to run this report for product category for "Colas"? How do I change each cell and, more importantly, is there a way to change it once for all data points?

We'll show you how you can do this once for each data source. Select a data point in our multi-source report and choose *Functions >> Manage POV* on the Smart View ribbon:

		Qtr1		Qtr2		Qtr3		Qtr4		Year
5	East	$	20,621	$	22,449	$	22,976	$	21,352	$	87,398
6	West	$	31,674	$	33,572	$	35,130	$	32,555	$	132,931
7	South	$	12,113	$	12,602	$	13,355	$	12,776	$	50,846
8	Central	$	31,412	$	33,056	$	33,754	$	31,458	$	129,680
10	US	$	95,820	$	101,679	$	105,215	$	98,141	$	400,855
11	Canada	$	16,461	$	16,506	$	16,781	$	16,351	$	66,099
12	Europe	$	21,336	$	26,255	$	28,680	$	24,926	$	101,197
13	**Market**	$	**20,621**	$	**22,449**	$	**22,976**	$	**21,352**	$	**87,398**

The POV Manager will display showing the two Smart View queries used for the data points (two in this case because we have one for Sample.Basic and one for Sample.Interntl):

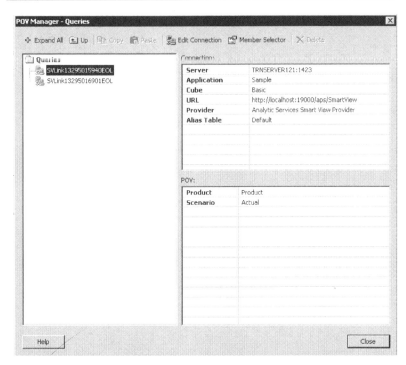

For each SVLinkxxx (one for Sample.Basic and one for Sample.Interntl), change the Product dimension selection from Product to "Colas" by highlighting "Product" in the POV section and using the Member selection window:

Repeat the member selection steps so that both SVLinks are updated to point to "Colas":

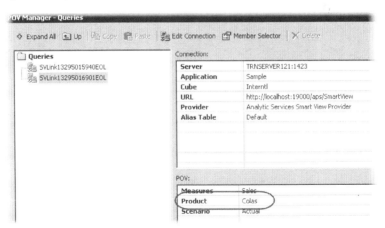

Click *Close.* Choose *Refresh* and note all of the data points are updated for the product category "Colas":

	A	B	C	D	E	
1						
2			Market Report for Sales			
3						
4		Qtr1	Qtr2	Qtr3	Qtr4	
5	East	$ 6,292	$ 7,230	$ 7,770	$ 6,448	$
6	West	$ 6,950	$ 7,178	$ 7,423	$ 6,755	$
7	South	$ 3,732	$ 4,078	$ 4,457	$ 4,013	$
8	Central	$ 8,074	$ 8,701	$ 8,894	$ 8,139	$
10	US	$ 25,048	$ 27,187	$ 28,544	$ 25,355	$

Note, as you copy and paste new data points into a target, more queries are added. It will become difficult to tell which SVLinkxxx belongs to which data points, so keep this in mind as you use data points and the POV Manager.

Another alternative is to use HsGetValue formulas and have the formulas reference a cell with the desired data/point of view.

CREATE A REPORT IN WORD OR POWERPOINT

As we mentioned earlier Smart View works with Excel as well as Word and PowerPoint. Integration with all of the Office products is bread and butter for Smart View. The easiest way to get data into Word or PowerPoint is to copy and paste data points just as we did in the Power User chapter. You can copy and paste data points from:

- Excel to Word and PowerPoint
- Word to Word and PowerPoint
- PowerPoint to Word and PowerPoint

These live data points are tied to a specific server, database and dimension member intersection (just like the data points in Excel). This means you can refresh them at any time and get the most current data.

When creating reports in Word or PowerPoint, make sure to apply Excel formatting first before you copy and paste data points to Word and PowerPoint. The numeric formatting is preserved as you copy and paste the data points. Member formatting, however, is not saved. You'll need to apply the desired formatting in Word or PowerPoint.

Let's now create a report in Word. Pull up our saved butterfly report. Select the grid and choose *Copy Data Point* from the Smart View ribbon:

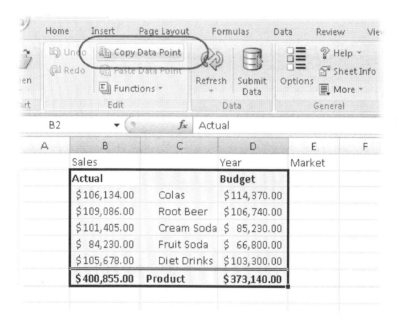

Next open a blank Word document. Add a title and text to the word document (just to give you a feel for what is possible):

Find the desired location for the copied grid and choose *Paste Data Point* from the Smart View ribbon. Click *Refresh* and the result should look as follows:

Actual		Budget
$ 106,134.00	Colas	$ 114,370.00
$ 109,086.00	Root Beer	$ 106,740.00
$ 101,405.00	Cream Soda	$ 85,230.00
$ 84,230.00	Fruit Soda	$ 66,800.00
$ 105,678.00	Diet Drinks	$ 103,300.00
$ 400,855.00	Product	$ 373,140.00

As the underlying data changes, you can simply click *Refresh* to pull in the current data set. In this basic example, we've shown you how to pull in data from a single source but you can create multi-source reports in Word and PowerPoint as well.

You can change the POV for the data points just as we did in Excel. Choose a data point and select *Manage POV* from the Smart View ribbon. Change the Market member selection to "West":

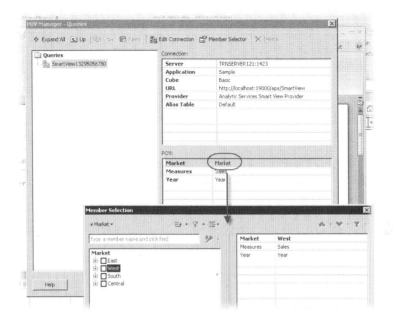

Click *Close* to close the POV Manager and click *Refresh*. The data points in the report should be updated to reflect the new member selections. Make sure to add "West" to the title of the report (so consumers will understand the data set they are viewing):

Product Variance Report for West

Overall product sales beat budget estimates due to reasons xyz.

Actual		Budget
$ 28,306.00	Colas	$ 34,830.00
$ 34,200.00	Root Beer	$ 31,810.00
$ 35,391.00	Cream Soda	$ 30,480.00
$ 35,034.00	Fruit Soda	$ 22,730.00
$ 36,423.00	Diet Drinks	$ 35,690.00
$ 132,931.00	Product	$ 119,850.00

Follow these same steps to create a presentation in PowerPoint. When data points are inserted into PowerPoint, they appear as floating text boxes:

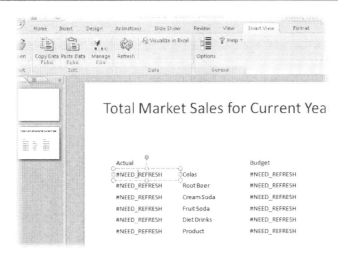

You can move each text box to its desired placement. Click *Refresh* to pull in the data. Add formatting to the text boxes as necessary to create a nicely formatted presentation:

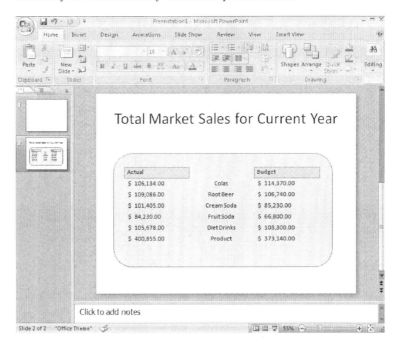

Don't forget the ability to *Visualize in Excel* (amaze your boss with immediate answers during presentation reviews).

Tip!

To Visualize in Excel, you must select a specific data point (not the table).

Create the following PowerPoint presentation:

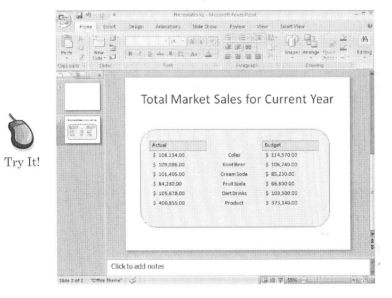

Try It!

Now that Lumberght is happy with your nicely formatted reports in Excel, Word and PowerPoint, he's asked you to create the same version of the P&L report for each different product (and you have over 1000 products). Before you start thinking "I'm just not gonna go" again, let us introduce you to our friend, the magician known as Cascade (you click a button and reports magically appear).

CASCADE

Once you start building reports, the time will come when you want to run the same report for multiple selections. On the report you just built, you might want to run it for every region. While you could use Member Select to pick each region (East,

Central...) and choose *Refresh* after each one, a feature called Cascade will do this in a much faster manner.

For our example, we've been asked to create a P&L by product. Open our saved P&L report and connect to Sample.Basic:

	A	B	C	D	E
1					
2	**Profit and Loss Statement**				
3	for				
4	*Product:*	Product			
5	*Market:*	East			
6	*Period:*	Year			
7					
8		**Actual**		**Budget**	
9	**Sales**	$ 87,398		$ 79,010	
10	**COGS**	$ 37,927		$ 32,250	
11	*Margin*	*$ 49,471*		*$ 46,760*	
12	**Marketing**	$ 14,721		$ 11,210	
13	**Payroll**	$ 10,389		$ 7,100	
14	**Misc**	$ 200		-	
15	*Total Expenses*	*$ 25,310*		*$ 18,310*	
16	**Profit**	$ 24,161		$ 28,450	
17					
18	**Profit %**	27.6		36.0	
19	**Expense%**	29.0		23.2	

You can choose whether you want to cascade the results to a new workbook or the same workbook. In 11.1.2.2 you can also cascade the results with each member to its own workbook:

Click the *Cascade >> New Workbook* option on the Essbase ribbon:

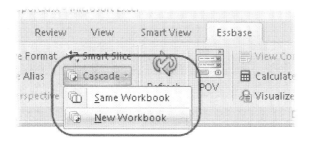

If you are using our example, you received the following error message:

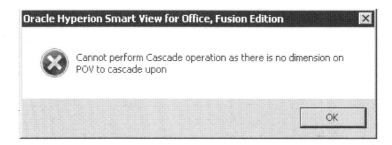

The dimension for which you are cascading (or bursting) must be in the POV. So we need to move Product into the POV. There is little chance that we can do this without impacting the formatting. Valid ways to get Product into the POV are:

- Delete "Product" from the cell and click *Refresh*
- Delete the row containing "Product" and click *Refresh*
- Select "Product' and choose *Pivot >> Pivot to POV*
- Just start over

Go ahead and pick one of the options above or other that you choose. Correct any formatting so that the result is as follows, with "Product" in the floating POV:

	A	B	C	D	E	F
2						
3						
4	Profit and Loss Report					
5					POV Sheet4_ ▼ ×	
6		Actual		Budget	Product ▼	
7	Sales	$ 400,855	$	373,140	Market ▼	
8	COGS	$ 179,336	$	158,940	Year ▼	
9	Margin	$ 221,519	$	214,200		
10	Marketing	$ 66,237	$	49,520	Refresh ⓘ	
11	Payroll	$ 48,747	$	35,240		
12	Misc	$ 1,013	-			
13	Total Expenses	$ 115,997	$	84,760		
14	Profit	$ 105,522	$	129,440		
15						

You now appreciate the importance of finalizing the layout before applying formatting, right? Now click the *Cascade >> New Workbook* button on the Essbase ribbon. Using the Member Selection, filter the Product for the Children of Product (a.k.a Product Category):

Click the option to Check Base Members and move them into the selection panel:

Click *OK* and a new workbook will be created with a worksheet for each product category:

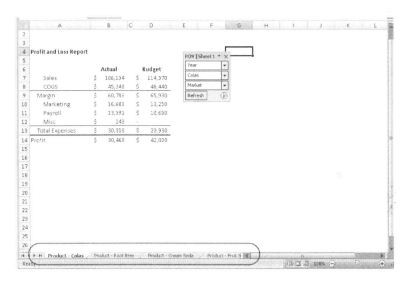

You may be directed back to the original spreadsheet but never fear, the new workbook is there. Was it really that easy to generate reports for all of my product categories? Yes, it was: imagine the possibilities. We now have a number of reports created in a just a few seconds. Imagine running this for hundreds of stores. Go have a venti latte with the time we've just saved you.

Note!
The tabs in the cascaded workbook are renamed to either the member name or alias depending on what you have selected for the current connection. (Remember in the old days when the Excel Add-in just numbered the spreadsheets. Yes, my old friend the Excel Add-in, we think

it is about time you retired.)

SMART VIEW FORMATTING

Now that we've covered Excel formatting options along with some other import report creation "how to's", we'll turn our attention to Smart View formatting options.

You can use either Excel formatting or Smart View formatting but not both. We've already reviewed the most common and, in our opinion, best formatting option for formatting reports, which is Excel. We still must, however, cover two other options available to you. Smart View formatting can be helpful when you are operating in ad hoc analysis mode (though with the new *Move Formatting on operations* feature in 11.1.2.2, the use case for Smart View formatting is reduced). Let's look at basic Smart View formatting features.

First you have to turn off Excel formatting. Go to *Options* on the Smart View ribbon. Under the Formatting section, uncheck "Use Excel Formatting."

Let's do that now for our Profit and Loss report:

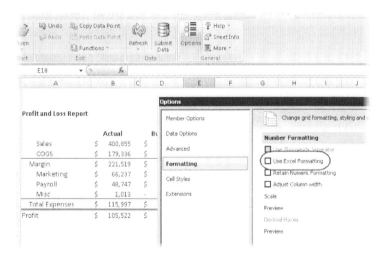

Click *Refresh* and the Excel formatting disappears:

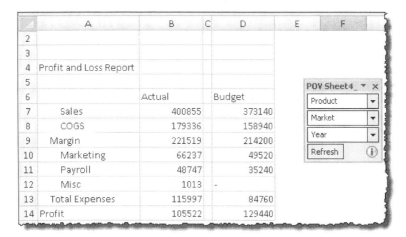

Go back to the options tab and check the *Retain Numeric Formatting:*

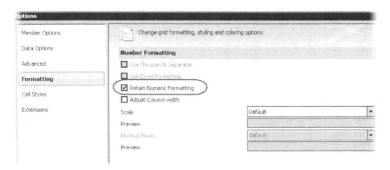

Apply numeric formatting to the grid:

	A	B	C	D
1				
2	Profit and Loss Statement			
3	for			
5		East		
6		Year		
7				
8		Actual		Budget
9	Sales	$ 87,398		$ 79,010
10	COGS	$ 37,927		$ 32,250
11	Margin	$ 49,471		$ 46,760
12	Marketing	$ 14,721		$ 11,210
13	Payroll	$ 10,389		$ 7,100
14	Misc	$ 200		-
15	Total Expenses	$ 25,310		$ 18,310
16	Profit	$ 24,161		$ 28,450
17				
18	Profit %	27.6447974		36.0081002

Click *Refresh*. The numeric formatting is retained. Your excitement will be short lived; zoom out on East (double right click or select *Zoom Out* from the Essbase ribbon). Zoom in on Market. Continue to zoom in and out and pivot on the dimensions. The numeric formatting might be retained for a few zooms but you will end up with an unformatted grid eventually.

Numeric formatting when applying a scale however will be retained. Under *Options >> Formatting*, change the Scale to 1 (to scale to the thousands):

Click *Refresh*. Zoom in and out and notice that the scaling remains:

	A	B	C	D
1				
2	Profit and Loss Statement			
3	for			
4			East	Product
5			Year	
6				
7		Actual	Budget	Variance
8	Sales	8739.8	7901	838.8
9	COGS	3792.7	3225	-567.7
10	Margin	4947.1	4676	271.1
11	Marketing	1472.1	1121	-351.1
12	Payroll	1038.9	710	-328.9
13	Misc	20	-	-20
14	Total Expenses	2531	1831	-700
15	Profit	2416.1	2845	-428.9
16				

Note! Scale is supported in both Excel formatting and Smart View formatting.

PRESERVE FORMATTING

Another formatting feature available in Smart View, Preserve Formatting, is the ability to save the formatting selected for data cells. Any Excel formatting will be saved for the highlighted cells. The formatting remains for those cells through zooming operations but it will not apply to new data cells that are returned to the spreadsheet. This feature is again more helpful as you perform ad hoc analysis as opposed to creating formatted reports.

Open a blank worksheet and retrieve data for Sample.Basic (see our query below to follow along). Zoom in on Year. Set the formatting for the data cells to $. Make sure *Use Excel Formatting* under *Options>>Formatting* is still unchecked.

Next, select the data cells with the formatting defined (just the data cells). Select *Preserve Formatting* from the Essbase ribbon:

	A	B	C	D
1				
2			East	Product
3			Year	
4				
5		Actual	Budget	Variance
6	Sales	$ 8,740	$ 7,901	$ 839
7	COGS	$ 3,793	$ 3,225	$ (568)
8	Margin	$ 4,947	$ 4,676	$ 271
9	Marketing	$ 1,472	$ 1,121	$ (351)
10	Payroll	$ 1,039	$ 710	$ (329)
11	Misc	$ 20	-	$ (20)
12	Total Expenses	$ 2,531	$ 1,831	$ (700)
13	Profit	$ 2,416	$ 2,845	$ (429)
14				

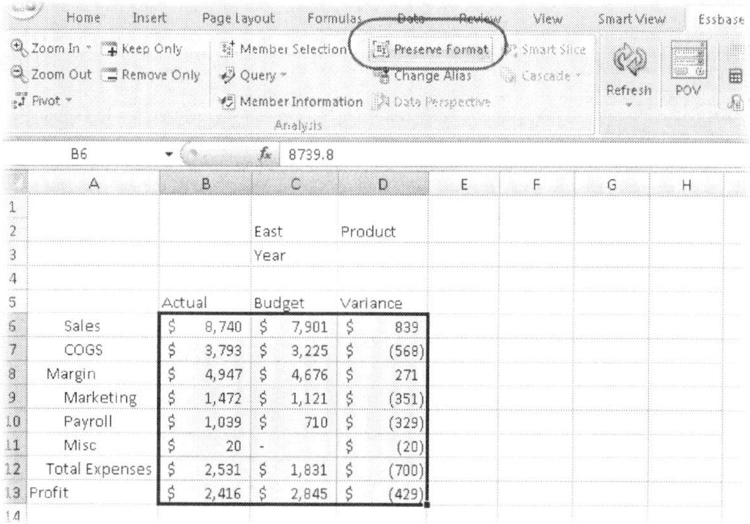

Now when you perform a refresh or basic drilling, the cell formatting will remain for the selected cells. Zoom out on "Sales". Zoom out on "Profit". Zoom back down the Measures dimension. The formatting is retained.

Zoom into Year and you should see the formatting retained as quarters are displayed across the columns:

	A	B	C	D	E	F	G	H	I	J
1										
2			East	Product						
3			Qtr1			Qtr2			Qtr3	
4										
5		Actual	Budget	Variance	Actual	Budget	Variance	Actual	Budget	Variance
6	Sales	$ 2,062	$ 1,895	$ 167	$ 2,245	$ 2,059	$ 186	$ 2,298	$ 2,110	$ 188
7	COGS	$ 908	$ 784	$ (124)	$ 959	$ 826	$ (133)	$ 1,006	$ 864	$ (142)
8	Margin	$ 1,154	$ 1,111	$ 43	$ 1,286	$ 1,233	$ 53	$ 1,291	$ 1,246	$ 45
9	Marketing	$ 352	$ 269	$ (83)	$ 371	$ 289	$ (82)	$ 392	$ 305	$ (87)
10	Payroll	$ 260	$ 186	$ (74)	$ 260	$ 189	$ (71)	$ 260	$ 186	$ (74)
11	Misc	$ 5	-	$ (5)	$ 5	-	$ (5)	$ 5	-	$ (5)
12	Total Expenses	$ 616	$ 455	$ (161)	$ 637	$ 478	$ (159)	$ 657	$ 491	$ (166)
13	Profit	$ 538	$ 656	$ (118)	$ 650	$ 755	$ (105)	$ 635	$ 755	$ (120)
14										

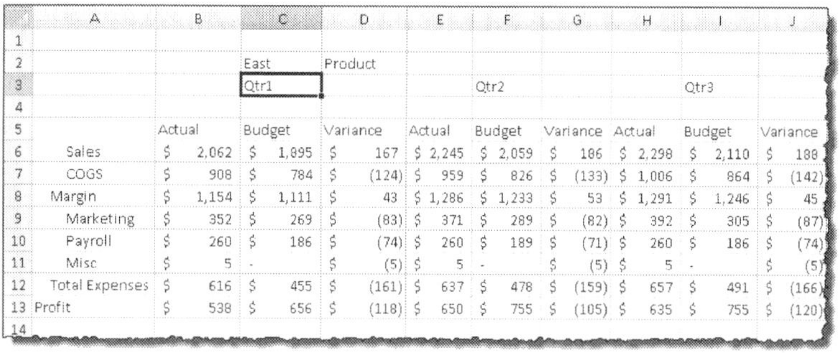

Formatting is retained. However, if we were to zoom in on a dimension that was listed down the row, the formatting would only remain on the data cells that were originally highlighted. Keep Only on "Qtr1" and "Sales". Zoom in on Product:

	A	B	C	D	E
1					
2			Qtr1	East	
3					
4			Actual	Budget	Variance
5	Colas	Sales	629.2	593	36.2
6	Root Beer	Sales	572.6	546	26.6
7	Cream Soda	Sales	486.8	368	118.8
8	Fruit Soda	Sales	373.5	388	-14.5
9	Diet Drinks	Sales	188.4	170	18.4
10	Product	Sales	$ 2,062	$ 1,895	$ 167

The preserved format is only "preserved" for the original data cells.

Note! Preserve formatting is tied to specific member combinations. If you drill down, next levels will not have the applied formatting.

The following chart provides a quick comparison of the formatting features:

	Preserve Formatting	*Use Excel Formatting*
Use When	Ad hoc Analysis	Report Templates
Applies to Data Cells	Y	Y
Applies to Members	N	Y
Retains formatting on drill	Y (for selected cells)	N
Retains formatting on POV change	Y	Y
Retains formatting on pivot	Y (for selected cells)	N

	Preserve Formatting	Use Excel Formatting
Provides the fastest retrievals	N	Y

CELL STYLE OPTIONS

Cell Styles will apply specific formatting (fonts, borders, and backgrounds) to member and data cells. Formatting can be assigned by different characteristics of members and data cells. You may also want to highlight a specific member or data points for a particular reason. For example, we recommend using cell styles for members or data points that may have drill through reports associated with them. If you are inputting data, you may want to apply a special format to highlight intersections with write access (e.g. for budget input templates).

Lumberght wants us to create a budget input template for quarter 1 sales. Create the following query to follow along as we learn how to use Styles:

	A	B	C	D	E	F	G	H	I	J	K	L	M
1			Sales										
2			New York										
3			Jan			Feb			Mar			Qtr1	
4													
5			Actual	Budget	Varianc	Actual	Budget	Varianc	Actual	Budget	Varianc	Actual	Budget	Variance
6	Cola	678	700	-22	645	610	35	675	640	35	1998	1950	48
7	Diet Cola	-	-	-	-	-	-	-	-	-	-	-	-
8	Caffeine Free Col	-	-	-	-	-	-	-	-	-	-	-	-
9	Colas	678	700	-22	645	610	35	675	640	35	1998	1950	48
10	Old Fashioned	61	50	11	61	50	11	63	60	3	185	160	25
11	Diet Root Beer	-	-	-	-	-	-	-	-	-	-	-	-
12	Sasparilla	-	-	-	-	-	-	-	-	-	-	-	-
13	Birch Beer	490	480	10	580	560	20	523	510	13	1593	1550	43
14	Root Beer	551	530	21	641	610	31	586	570	16	1778	1710	68

Select the *Options* button from the Smart View ribbon. First check that *Use Excel Formatting* is unchecked on the Formatting section. (Also make sure scaling is set to zero or you'll go crazy wondering why your numbers are off.)

To use Cell Styles, choose the Cell Styles section:

Expand the *Analytic Services* option. Expand *Member cells* to set member properties or expand *Data cells* to set data cell properties:

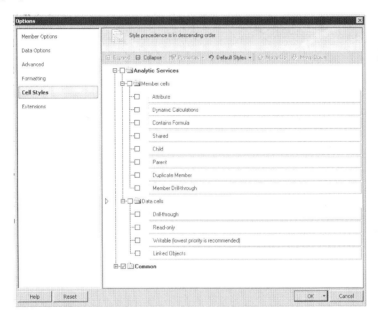

Note!

What's Analytic Services? Back in the old days just as System 9 was introduced and when Hyperion still owned Hyperion, Essbase was renamed to Analytic Services. Thank goodness for Oracle as they have now brought home our beloved Essbase name back to us. Still you may see references to "Analytic Services" throughout the Oracle EPM products. Just think "Essbase" when you see this.

Let's change the cell style for parents. Check the box next to *Parent* to enable a properties box:

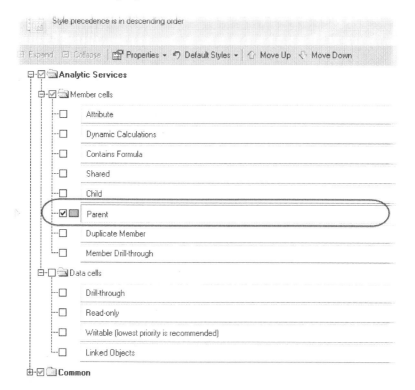

You can set the properties for *Font*, *Background*, and *Border*. From the Properties drop down, choose *Font*:

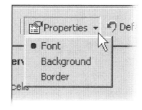

Change the font to bold and some nice earth tone (navy is the new black):

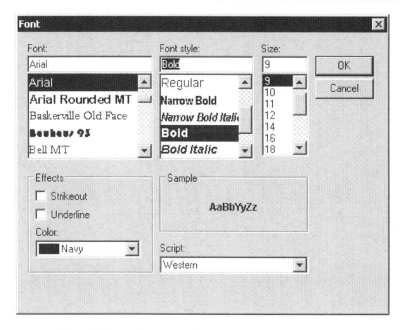

Click *OK* and then click *OK* again to save the settings and close the Options window. Refresh data.

Here is the result:

	A	B	C	D	E	F	G	H	I	J	K	L	M
1			Sales										
2			New York										
3			Jan		Feb			Mar			Qtr1		
4													
5		Actual	Budget	Varianc	Actual	Budget	Varianc	Actual	Budget	Varianc	Actual	Budget	Variance
6	Cola	678	700	-22	645	610	35	675	640	35	1998	1950	48
7	Diet Cola	-	-	-	-	-	-	-	-	-	-	-	-
8	Caffeine Free Col	-	-	-	-	-	-	-	-	-	-	-	-
9	Colas	678	700	-22	645	610	35	675	640	35	1998	1950	48
10	Old Fashioned	61	50	11	61	50	11	63	60	3	185	160	25
11	Diet Root Beer	-	-	-	-	-	-	-	-	-	-	-	-
12	Sasparilla	-	-	-	-	-	-	-	-	-	-	-	-
13	Birch Beer	490	480	10	580	560	20	523	510	13	1593	1550	43
14	Root Beer	551	530	21	641	610	31	586	570	16	1778	1710	68
15													

Notice for any member that is a parent, the font is now bold and a nice earthy "navy" tone. Any member that is a child only (level-zero) is set to the default formatting. If you wanted all members to have the same formatting, go back to the *Options >> Cell Styles* tab and set the same font properties for the Child section. In our example, let's change the font color to *Navy* but leave the font *Regular*:

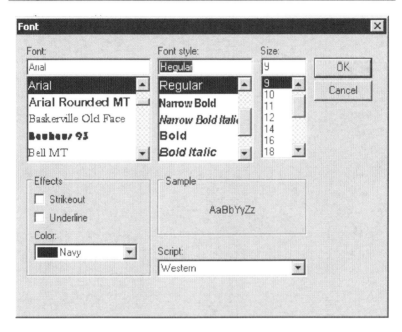

A member can meet more than one criterion. Qtr1 is both a parent and a child. Yo Mamma is both a parent (yours) and a child (of yo Grandmamma). Use the *Move Up* or *Move Down* buttons to define the order of precedence for how cell styles should be applied (we want Parent to have the first priority):

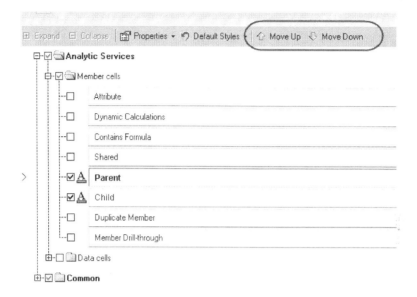

The cells at the top of the list have higher precedence while cells at the bottom of the list have lower precedence.

On Data cells, you can set a background color for writable cells (along with font or border settings). Setting a background color is beneficial when developing budgeting input sheets for end user submissions. In the example below, read-only cells are set to gray and writable cells are set to yellow:

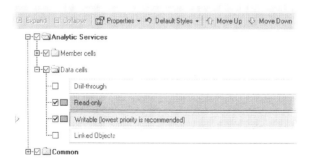

Here is an example of a budget entry spreadsheet with Cell Styles applied for a user who has been assigned write access to the budget scenario for level zero products:

	A	B	C	D	E	F	G	H	I	J	K	L	M
1		Sales											
2		New York											
3		Jan			Feb			Mar			Qtr1		
4													
5		Actual	Budget	Variance	Actual	Budget	Variance	Actual	Budget	Variance	Actual	Budget	Variance
6	Cola	$ 678	$ 700	$ (22)	$ 645	$ 610	$ 35	$ 675	$ 640	$ 35	#####	#####	$ 48
7	Diet Cola	-	-	-	-	-	-	-	-	-	-	-	-
8	Caffeine Free Cola	-	-	-	-	-	-	-	-	-	-	-	-
9	Colas	$ 678	$ 700	$ (22)	$ 645	$ 610	$ 35	$ 675	$ 640	$ 35	#####	#####	$ 48
10	Old Fashioned	$ 61	$ 50	$ 11	$ 61	$ 50	$ 11	$ 63	$ 60	$ 3	$ 185	$ 160	$ 25
11	Diet Root Beer	-	-	-	-	-	-	-	-	-	-	-	-
12	Sasparilla	-	-	-	-	-	-	-	-	-	-	-	-
13	Birch Beer	$ 490	$ 480	$ 10	$ 580	$ 560	$ 20	$ 523	$ 510	$ 13	#####	#####	$ 43
14	Root Beer	$ 551	$ 530	$ 21	$ 641	$ 610	$ 31	$ 586	$ 570	$ 16	#####	#####	$ 68
15													

Tip! You may want to also set dynamically calc'd cells to grey so that you know you can't load data to that member (remember our earlier discussion on dynamically calculated members?).

Tip! *Retain Numeric Formatting* works with cell styles!

Try It! Create your own budget entry spreadsheet for Sample.Basic. You might even impress Lumberght with your "styling" work.

Note! Make sure you uncheck *Use Excel Formatting* on the *Display* tab. If this option is selected, Cell Styles are ignored.

Once you're finished playing with Styles (and before burning matching holes in your retinas due to horrendous color schemes), go to the *Styles* section on your Options and uncheck all the boxes on the Analytic Services *Style* section.

Note! Turning off Styles does not set your spreadsheet back to its "pre-Essbase" formatting. You may have to click *Refresh* or set Excel formatting to return to the desired state.

Smart View provides common styles that are used across connections. By default, "dirty" cells are cells where data has been changed by the user but not submitted to the database. The background for any dirty cells will change to a light yellow. Note you can also set a different font or background for cells containing comments (applicable to Planning and HFM connections).

Now you can see the formatting and reporting options are practically endless with Smart View and our handy Office products. But we're not done yet! Hold on as we jump into two big new features introduced in Smart View 11.1.1, Smart Slices and Report Designer.

END OF THE CHAPTER QUICK REFERENCE – DON'T MISS SMART VIEW LINKS

Blog	Link
Oracle EPM System Documentation for 11.1.2.2	http://docs.oracle.com/cd/E17236_01/index
Smart View Discussion Board	https://forums.oracle.com/forums/forum.jspa?forumID=766
Essbase Discussion Board	https://forums.oracle.com/forums/forum.jspa?forumID=405
Oracle Support	https://support.oracle.com/
Network 54 (great EPM discussion board)	www.network54.com/Forum/58296/
interRel's EPM & Smart View Training & Free Webcasts	http://www.interrel.com/Education

Chapter 6:
Smart Slices & Report Designer

By now you may be asking yourself "What more could I need with Essbase and my trusty Smart View add-in?" We just covered how to create reports and report templates with our Essbase database and that was pretty easy. Can it get any better? See for yourself as we review Smart Slices and Report Designer. Read closely as the topics we cover here could prove beneficial for your upcoming presentation with Lumberght, the consultants and executive management.

SMART SLICES

Introduction to Smart Slices

Smart Slices, introduced in version 11.1.1, allow an administrator to create a filtered data view for a selected cube. For the DBAs reading this book, smart slices are like a view against an Essbase database. For example, say you have a Sales Analysis database for all markets across the United States. However, the Sales Managers only care about analyzing data for their specific region (okay, you're right, they probably want to sneak a peek at their performance in comparison to the other markets, but let's roll with this example anyway). You can create a smart slice for each market, filtering the dimensions and data and setting up a starting point query for the end users. This saves the user time in navigating through the hierarchy to find their "market". They are immediately ready to start analyzing. Users can further filter the smart slice using a sub-query (more on this in a bit). Defining and using smart slices is also another way of distributing and sharing a default point of view for a data source. Once the smart slice is defined, the users can perform analysis and create reports just as they do with a regular Essbase connection (e.g. zoom in, pivot, member select).

Smart slices are only available in Smart View (not visible to the Workspace...today; this functionality will be coming in future versions). So for what products can you create smart slices? Essbase, HFM, and Planning sources. We are of course focusing on Essbase in this book but the steps for defining and using smart slices are similar across the above-mentioned sources.

Create a Smart Slice

The best way to understand smart slices is to create and actually use one so let's get started.

Note!

Only administrators can create smart slices. If you don't see the *Add* option in your right click menu, give your administrator a call and make your case for why you need to create smart slices or ask her to create the sample Smart Slice below for you. In the meantime, jump down to the *Use a Smart Slice* section and follow along in your mind.

Smart Slices can be created with either Shared Connections or Private connections.

In a blank sheet, connect to Sample.Basic. Right click on the Sample.Basic database and click *Create new Smart Slice*:

You will be prompted to select an alias table. Choose *Default* and click *OK*:

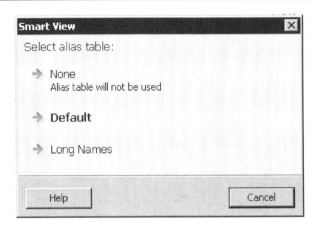

The default Smart Slice definition dialog will display (looks an awful lot like Query Designer, right?). Note the default is descendants of every dimension (the entire cube):

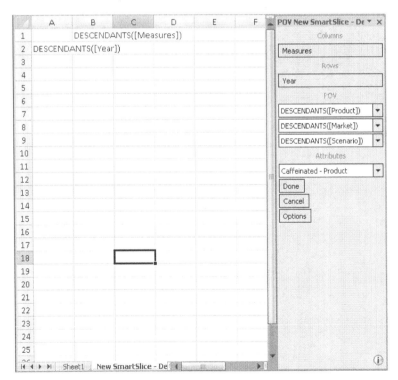

Using member selection and drag/dropping capabilities, we'll define the boundaries of the Smart Slice. Similar to the Query Designer, update the Smart Slice definition to select the descendants of West and Sales.

Double click on Measures in the POV New SmartSlice Definition window. Change the member filter (if necessary) to *Descendants*. Note that if the filter is set to *Children*, you only see the children of Measures. Select "Sales" and use the right arrow button to move Sales into the Selection section.

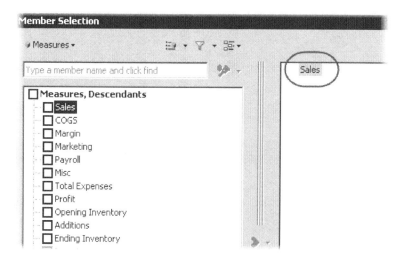

From the drop down box on the POV Smart Slice Definition window, select the ellipsis (...) for Market:

Remove the selection for the descendants of Market by clicking the double left arrow icon. Select "West" and use the arrow icon to move "West" into the Selection section. Click the *Filter* icon in the mid-level right hand portion of the Member Selection window and choose *Descendants*:

(Or you could have selected Descendants from the > arrow drop down):

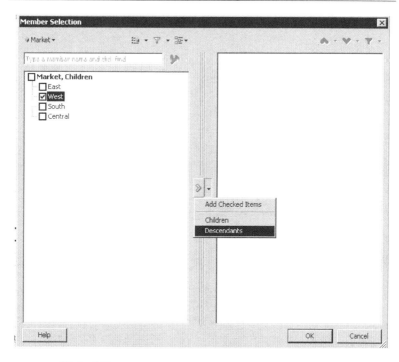

Click *OK* and your smart slice definition and spreadsheet should now look like this:

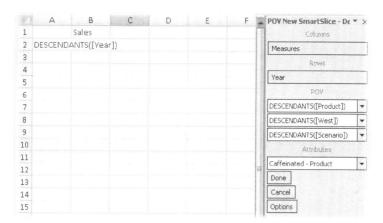

Next, drag Descendants(West) to the Rows. Drag Year to the Column. Move Measures to the POV (you could have also moved these dimensions at the start of the process):

You can define options for smart slices like indentions or display for missing data. Click *Options* on the POV New SmartSlice Definition window to define the preferences for the Smart Slice. In this example, let us set the following options:

- Replace #Missing label with a -.
- Set Thousands separator to *Yes*.
- Confirm the Alias table is set to *Default*.

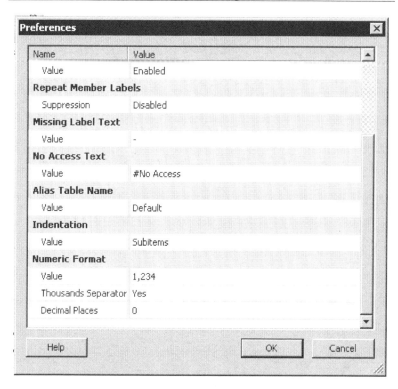

Click *OK* when the options are set.

Click the *Done* button when the Smart Slice Definition is complete.

At this point (in our example), we will be prompted to specify members for the POV (Product, Sales and Year).

The default values are the top members for Product and Year and our only option for Measures – Sales. We can leave the defaults or use Member Selection to change the selections, further filtering the smart slice:

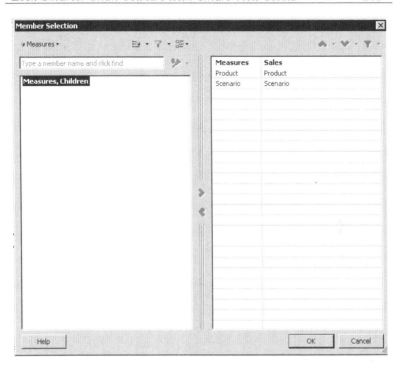

For now leave the selected members and click *OK*. Enter a new name for the Smart Slice – *WestSales*:

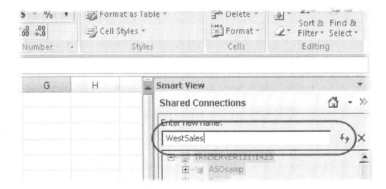

Click the revolving green arrows to accept the new name.

The new slice is added to the Sample.Basic database, indicated by the red cube under the blue Basic cube.

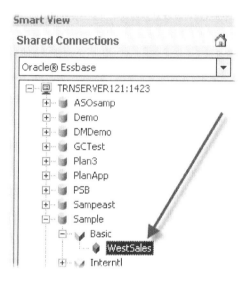

Note that you can have multiple smart slices for a single Essbase database. Beware, though, and don't create so many smart slices that it becomes difficult to use and manage. As of version 11.1.2.1.102 there is not a way to assign or security these smart slices by user or group. Everyone sees every smart slice. There isn't a way to organize the smart slices either, so you may want to think through the naming conventions for the smart slices ahead of time (smart slices are sorted alphabetically).

Note!

Even though Smart Slices are not secured by user, Essbase assigned member and data security still apply.

Use a Smart Slice

To analyze data with smart slices, simply right click on the WestSales Smart Slice and click *Ad-hoc Analysis*:

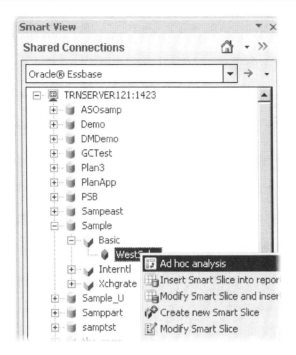

You may be prompted with this message depending on whether you are in a blank spreadsheet or a spreadsheet with data. We've seen this before, but as a reminder, if you need to save the data in the current spreadsheet click *No*. To replace the data in the current spreadsheet with the default view for the Smart Slice click *Yes*.

The following result should display:

	A	B	C	D
1		Year	POV [Book1] ▾ ✕	
2	West	132931	Sales ▾	
3			Product ▾	
4			Scenario ▾	
5				
6			Refresh ⓘ	
7				

You are immediately brought into the default layout and definition of the smart slice, with "West" in the rows, "Year" in the column and a focus on "Sales" in the POV.

Zoom into West. Zoom back up and notice that you can't go any higher than West. When using the smart slice you are limited to the selections or boundaries for the smart slice. Pivot Product to the rows and drill down on product, noting you have full analytical functionality within the smart slice.

Hmm... maybe we should have designed the smart slice to automatically display Actual, Budget and Variance. Can I modify my smart slice? Of course.

Modify a Smart Slice

To modify a smart slice, simply right click and select *Modify Smart Slice.*

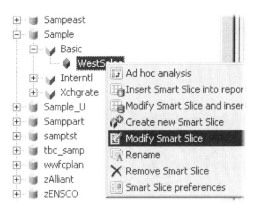

Let's do that now for our WestSales smart slice. When the smart slice definition window displays, double click on Scenario. In the Member Selection window, update the selection to specifically select Actual, Budget, Variance, and Var %.

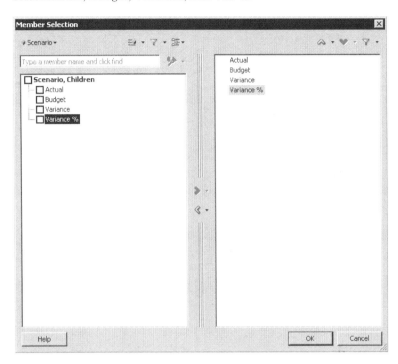

Move the Scenario dimension to the columns. Click *OK* and your smart slice definition should now look like the following:

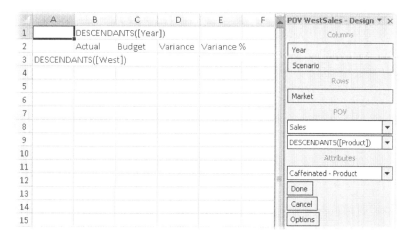

Click *Done* to save your changes and click *OK* at the member selection screen to accept the default members selected. Wait a minute! It didn't refresh automatically. To apply the updated smart slice to the spreadsheet, right click on WestSales and select *Ad hoc Analysis*.

Choose *Clear sheet contents and POV* (we want to clear out anything currently in the spreadsheet):

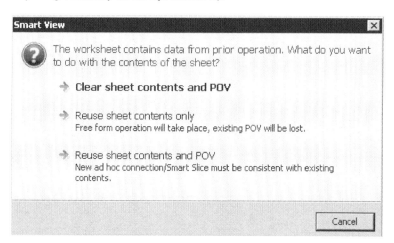

The following result should display:

	A	B	C	D	E	F
1		Year	Year	Year	Year	
2		Actual	Budget	Variance	Variance %	
3	West	132931	119850	13081	10.91448	
4						
5						
6						
7						
8						
9						

POV [Book1] ▼ ✕

Sales ▼

Product ▼

Refresh ⓘ

Create another smart slice similar to your West Sales smart slice but this time for East Sales.

Try It!

Smart Slices - Rename, Remove and Update Preferences

You can easily rename or remove a smart slice by right clicking on the desired smart slice and choosing *Rename* or *Remove:*

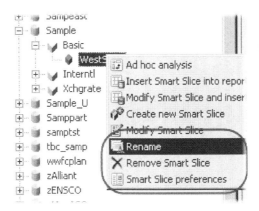

You can also change the options or preferences that you applied by select *Smart Slice preferences.*

Now that we know how to create and use smart slices, let's learn about Report Designer.

REPORT DESIGNER

Introduction to Report Designer

In addition to Smart Slices, version 11.1.1 introduced (drum roll, please) a new user interface that uses existing Smart Slices to create formatted and structured reports. But we've already created nice, formatted reports, you say? Think what've we've done so far, but on steroids. That's the Report Designer. The Report Designer leverages Office – Excel, Word or PowerPoint – for report design. You can combine multiple grids into a document and link controls for those grids. Those sources that leverage the Shared Connections can take advantage of the Report Designer.

Note!

Quiz: What sources in version 11.1.1 use the common provider Services? Essbase, Planning, and OBI Server. A+ for you! HFM was supported beginning in version 11.1.2.0.

Without further ado, let's create a report in Report Designer so that you can fully understand the power of this new tool (imagine the evil laugh of Diego DaSilva as Dr. Dementor ... ah ha ha ha).

Note!

Any Smart View user can use smart slices and create reports with Report Designer (not limited to administrators).

Create a Report with Report Designer

In a blank worksheet, create the following report title and heading:

	A	B	C	D
1	**Product Sales Report**			
2				
3	East Region			
4				
5				

Next add the Smart Slice to the Report Designer by clicking on the East Sales smart slice and selecting *Insert Smart Slice into report*:

The Smart Slice should be added to the Report Designer (this is called a query). The Report Designer is the section under the server and applications listing within the Smart View Panel:

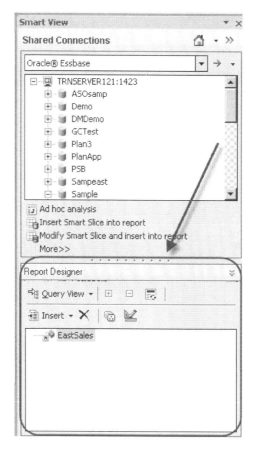

Right click on the smart slice and note the available options:

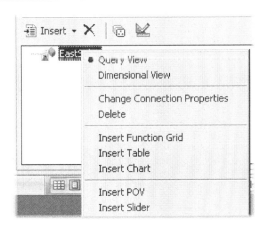

Skipping the first options like Query View / Dimensional View options (we'll cover those in just a moment), we'll focus on the three types of data objects - Function Grid, Table, and Chart - and two control objects - Slider and POV.

Object	*Description*
Function Grid	Displays the query in a dynamic grid format; data points are inserted into individual cells in Excel, individual data points in a Word table, and individual data points in PowerPoint text boxes.
Table	Displays results in a grid format that floats on the document and can be moved and resized. Scroll bars within the table allow you to view larger sets of data in smaller spaces.
Chart	Displays results in a chart format that floats on the document and can be moved and resized.
Slider Control	Control based on one dimension and the defined set of members. Users "slide" the selection to choose different members.
POV Control	Control based on multiple dimensions (those not used in the query in the rows or columns). Users select members from the POV using Member Selection.

Place your cursor in cell A5. Select *Insert Function Grid*. The EastSales Smart Slice should be inserted into the spreadsheet, creating data points for smart slice definition:

	A	B	C	D	E	F	G	H	
1	**Product Sales Report**								
2									
3	East Region								
4									
5		Year	Year	Year	Year	Qtr1	Qtr1	Qtr1	Qt
6		Actual	Budget	Variance	Variance %	Actual	Budget	Variance	V:
7	**East**	#NEED_RE	#NEED_RE	#NEED_RE	#NEED_RE	#NEED_RE	#NEED_RE	#NEED_RE	#N
8	**New York**	#NEED_RE	#NEED_RE	#NEED_RE	#NEED_RE	#NEED_RE	#NEED_RE	#NEED_RE	#N
9	**Massachu**	#NEED_RE	#NEED_RE	#NEED_RE	#NEED_RE	#NEED_RE	#NEED_RE	#NEED_RE	#N
10	**Florida**	#NEED_RE	#NEED_RE	#NEED_RE	#NEED_RE	#NEED_RE	#NEED_RE	#NEED_RE	#N
11	**Connectic**	#NEED_RE	#NEED_RE	#NEED_RE	#NEED_RE	#NEED_RE	#NEED_RE	#NEED_RE	#N
12	**New Ham**	#NEED_RE	#NEED_RE	#NEED_RE	#NEED_RE	#NEED_RE	#NEED_RE	#NEED_RE	#N
13									

Click *Refresh* and the data will display. When you refresh a function grid, the data cells are refreshed and members are not. This would be a problem if, let's say, you created a report with a list of products in the rows. If a new product is added to the database, the report will not dynamically refresh, adding in the new product. If you need to refresh both the data and members (as in our product listing example), you must re-insert the function grid. You could also consider using a table instead (more on tables in just a moment).

Tip!

To apply formatting to function grids, simply use Excel formatting. Formatting defined in the Smart Slice options will not flow through and display in Report Designer objects.

Tip!

Another cool feature is that you can use Excel formulas with function grids. You must leave one empty row between the grid and the cell containing the formula and include the empty row in the range of cells selected for the formula definition.

Next select cell A14 and right click on EastSales smart slice in the Report Designer and select *Insert Chart*:

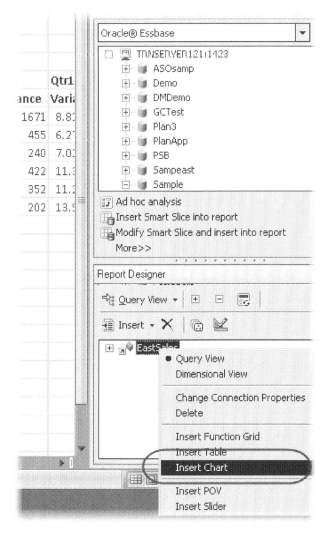

The chart will be inserted into the spreadsheet. Resize and move the chart as desired:

Select *Refresh* and the report is populated with the Essbase data:

	Year Actual	Year Budget	Year Variance	Year Variance %	Qtr1 Actual	Qtr1 Budget	Qtr1 Variance	Qtr1 Variance %	Jan Actual	Jan Budget	Jan Variance
East	87398	79010	8388	10.61638	20621	18950	1671	8.817942	6790	6240	54
New York	34698	31850	2848	8.941915	7705	7250	455	6.275862	2479	2360	11
Massachu	14657	13500	1157	8.57037	3660	3420	240	7.017544	1251	1170	8
Florida	18341	16300	2041	12.52147	4132	3710	422	11.37466	1321	1170	15
Connectic	12411	10920	1491	13.65385	3472	3120	352	11.28205	1197	1080	11
New Ham	7291	6440	851	13.21429	1652	1450	202	13.93103	532	460	7

Well that looks a bit interesting. Because our Smart Slice has the descendants of period selected in the smart slice columns along with actual, budget and variance, this is a wide report and chart. How can we narrow the columns selection? Hold tight; we have a method to our madness and will show you how in just a few short pages.

Select cell A40. Right click on East Sales query and select *Insert >> Table*. It is almost as if we have a spreadsheet within a spreadsheet:

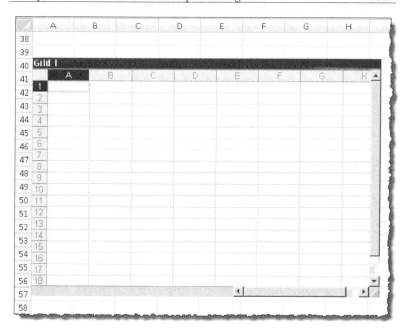

Resize the table accordingly and then select *Refresh* on the Smart View ribbon:

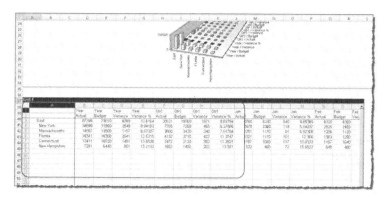

Tip!

After the initial positioning, you must be in Excel Developer mode to resize or move the charts or tables.

To enable the Excel Developer mode, select the Office icon in the upper left corner of the screen. Choose the *Excel Options* button. Check the *Show Developer tab in the Ribbon* option:

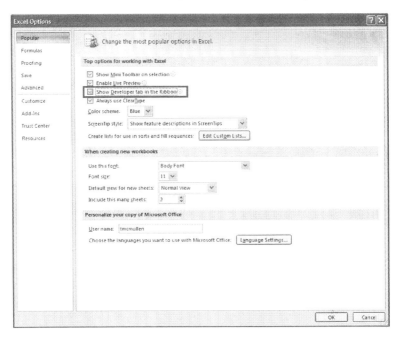

The Developer tab should display. Select *Design Mode* and resize the objects accordingly:

The other quick way to change to Excel Design Mode is to select the  icon in the Report Designer:

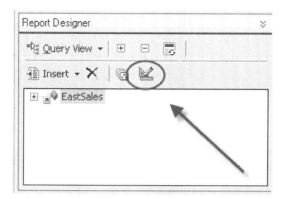

As we mentioned earlier, the table is a floating grid object that contains linked members and data. If you perform a refresh, both members and data will be re-queried and displayed to the user (whereas function grids only refresh the data points).

Within tables you have basic zoom in and out capabilities using right click and double right click actions. (Other analytic ad hoc features are not available against tables.) Try it now. Using your right double click and double click, zoom out on "Jan" and "Qtr1" until just "Year" is listed. Zoom out and in on members in the Market dimension. Notice the chart member selections are updated to be consistent with the table members:

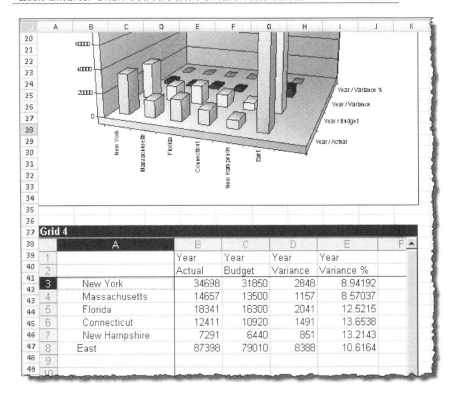

Let's review the use cases for function grids versus tables.

Why Function Grids?
- Function grids are most useful for reports in which members remain reasonably static
- Member formulas / formula preservation
- Data point inserted into a cell
- More control over formatting
- Available in Excel, Word, PowerPoint

Why Tables?
- For reports whose members that change often (tables will refresh both the members and the data)
- Basic zooming
- Show large amount of data in smaller display areas
- Available in Excel, PowerPoint

Now that we've inserted the content of the report, let's use some controls to select the members for the remaining dimensions. We'll start with the slider control. The slider displays a selected set of dimension members from a query. When you drag the slider marker to a member, its data is displayed in all reports associated with the query on the sheet.

Go back to the top of the report and insert several rows just below the report title:

	A	B	C	D	E	F
1	**Product Sales Report**					
2						
3						
4						
5						
6	East Region					
7						
8		**Actual**	**Budget**	**Variance**	**Variance %**	
9	**East**	87398	78950	8448	10.70044	
10	**New York**	34698	31790	2908	9.147531	
11	**Massachu**	14657	13500	1157	8.57037	

Select cell A3. Right click on East Sales query and select *Insert >> Slider*:

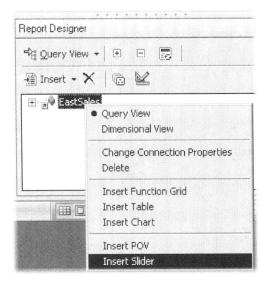

The Member Selection window will display. Choose the Product dimension (note the filter is set to *None* by default and all descendants of Product are displayed). Set the filter to Children. Select the children of Product:

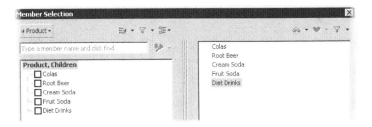

Click *OK*. The slider will insert into the spreadsheet:

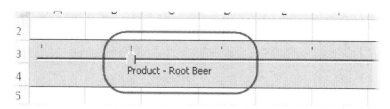

	A	B	C	D	E	F	G	H
2								
3								
4				Product - Colas				
5								
6	East Region							
7								
8		Year	Year	Year	Year	Qtr1	Qtr1	Qtr1
9		Actual	Budget	Variance	Variance %	Actual	Budget	Varia
10	East	27740	25560	2180	8.52895	6292	5930	
11	NewYork	8940	8360	580	6.9378	1998	1950	
12	Massachu	6518	6030	488	8.09287	1456	1360	
13	Florida	5867	5360	507	9.45896	1240	1150	
14	Connectic	3378	3100	278	8.96774	944	880	
15	NewHam	3037	2710	327	12.0664	654	590	
16								
17								
18								

Move the slider to choose different products and note how the data is refreshed for the selected grids throughout the spreadsheet:

2						
3						
4			Product - Root Beer			
5						

A new control called the POV control was added in the 11.1.1.1 release. We've changed our mind on the slider control and decided to use the new POV control instead.

Note!

You can either use sliders or POV controls in a single query but not both.

To delete the slider control, expand the EastSales query by clicking the + sign. Click the + icon next to controls to view all the controls for the current query. Right click on *Slider 1* and select *Delete* (you could also click the delete icon ✕).

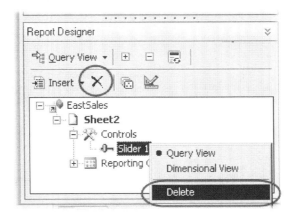

 You can also delete reporting objects from a query like
Note!   tables (a.k.a. Grids), function grids and charts.

Right click on the EastSales query and choose *Insert POV*:

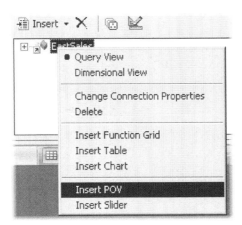

A POV control is inserted into the report. Change the member selections in the POV and your data will be refreshed to reflect the selection in all report objects:

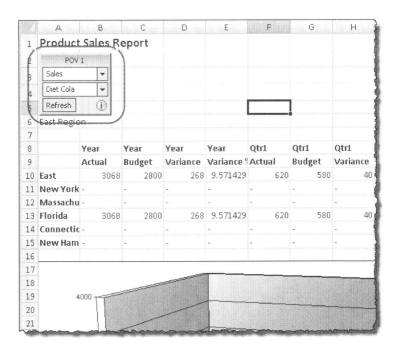

To move the POV control, you must be in Excel Design Mode.

Congratulations, you've created your first report with the Report Designer. See what we mean about report creation on steroids? Save this as the Product Sales Report.xls and let's explore some additional features to help us fine-tune our reporting capabilities.

FINE TUNE REPORT DESIGNER REPORTS

Remember our earlier question "how can we narrow the columns selection from the smart slice definition"? In our first report example, the report was too wide and displayed too much information for our tastes because our East Sales smart slice has the descendants of period selected in the smart slice columns. We were able to address this concern somewhat by zooming in and out within the table, which fixed the table and the chart. But the function grid / data points didn't change. So now to the part where we answer "how can you narrow the member selections from a smart slice definition?"

Instead of selecting *Insert Smart Slice into report*, choose *Modify Smart Slice and insert into report*. The modified smart slice will only exist within the report / workbook where it is created (the smart slice is not available for other reports or users in the Smart View panel).

In a blank spreadsheet, right click on the East Sales Smart slice. Select *Modify Smart Slice and insert into report*:

The Smart Slice definition window displays:

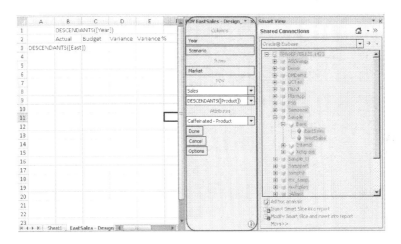

Click the Year dimension to launch the Member Selection. Choose the four quarters.

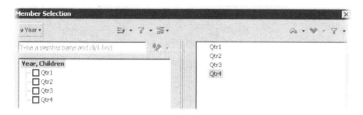

For the Scenario dimension, select Actual.

Click *Done*. Click *OK*.

When modifying the smart slice, you can change member selections but you can't change the dimension layout (whether a dimension is in the POV, rows or columns).

Type in the new name for the modified smart slice – *EastSales-Quarterly*:

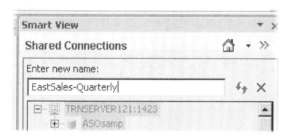

Click the green revolving arrows icon to save. Notice the subquery is inserted into the report designer but not saved as a smart slice.

Try It!

Follow the same steps to create a modified smart slice from East Sales for the twelve months for Actual called EastSales – Monthly.

We are now ready to put the modified smart slice into action. Select A6. Right click on East-Sales-Quarterly and select *Insert Function Grid*:

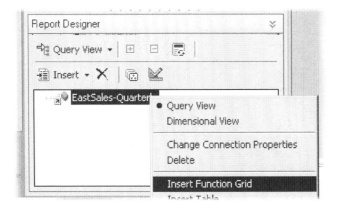

Repeat the steps to insert a table and a chart. Click *Refresh*. This report should look a little cleaner than our first pass at a report designer report:

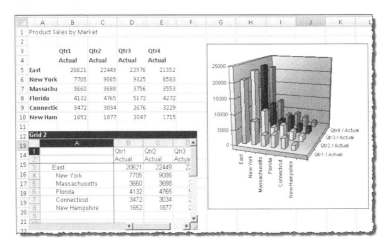

Remember for the function grid / data points, you can add Excel formatting.

Dimensional View

Before we learn our next Report Designer feature, let's remove the table and the chart from the current report. In Report Designer, expand EastSales-Monthly. Expand Sheet1 and Reporting objects. Right click on ChartX and select *Delete*:

Right click on Gridx (Grid = table) and select *Delete*.

Below the Quarterly function grid, insert the EastSales-Monthly grid:

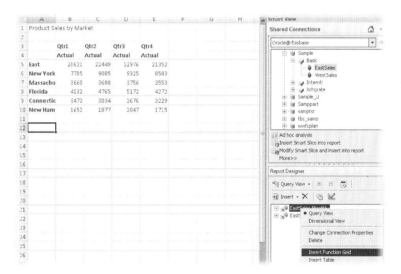

Now we want to insert a slider control to allow us to choose between products. Within Report Designer, you can insert a control that can control multiple smart slices as long as a common dimension exists. You can even have smart slices from different Essbase databases. As long as they share a common dimension, a single control can be used to control both sources.

In the Report Designer, change the view from *Query View* to *Dimensional View*:

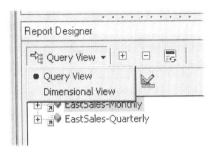

Note!   Query View shows Report Designer objects grouped by query. Dimensional View shows Report Designer objects by dimension. Dimensional view is important when you want to use the same dimension in a control for two different queries.

Select cell A22. Select Product in the Dimensional View window in the Report Designer. Right click on Year and select *Insert Slider*:

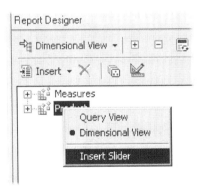

Using the member selection window, choose the product categories to display for the slider:

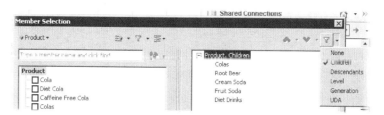

Click *OK* and notice the slider refreshes data for both function grids:

	A	B	C	D	E	F
1	Product Sales by Market					
2						
3		Qtr1	Qtr2	Qtr3	Qtr4	
4		Actual	Actual	Actual	Actual	
5	East	$ 4,868	$ 5,327	$ 5,142	$ 4,904	
6	New York	$ 2,033	$ 2,543	$ 2,421	$ 2,308	
7	Massachu	$ 391	$ 354	$ 326	$ 347	
8	Florida	$ 1,149	$ 1,211	$ 1,279	$ 1,065	
9	Connectic	$ 1,070	$ 977	$ 857	$ 945	
10	New Ham	$ 225	$ 242	$ 259	$ 239	
11						
12		Jan	Feb	Mar	Apr	May
13		Actual	Actual	Actual	Actual	Actual
14	East	$ 1,609	$ 1,621	$ 1,638	$ 1,753	$ 1,779
15	New York	$ 663	$ 675	$ 695	$ 827	$ 849
16	Massachu	$ 130	$ 132	$ 129	$ 121	$ 118
17	Florida	$ 380	$ 382	$ 387	$ 381	$ 410
18	Connectic	$ 360	$ 358	$ 352	$ 345	$ 321
19	New Ham	$ 76	$ 74	$ 75	$ 79	$ 81
20						
21						
22						
23						
24			Product - Cream Soda			

In order for a slider to work against multiple grids, the following rules must be met:

- Same dimension

- Same dimension definition (both grids must say "children of Year"; one cannot say children of Year and the other say descendants of Year)

Note!

Note – the POV control is only available for a single grid.

Try It!

Create the report below using Smart Slices and Report Designer.

Hints:

- Insert two modified Smart Slices, one selecting Colas and one selecting Root Beer
- Add an Excel formula to calculate the total for Root Beer and Colas for all East regions
- Apply formatting to the headers and data values

	A	B	C	D	E
1	East Sales - Colas & Root Beer Report				
2					
3	East Sales Colas				
4		Year	Year	Year	Year
5		Actual	Budget	Variance	Variance %
6	New York	$ 8,940	$ 8,360	$ 580	6.94
7	Massachusetts	$ 6,518	$ 6,030	$ 488	8.09
8	Florida	$ 5,867	$ 5,360	$ 507	9.46
9	Connecticut	$ 3,378	$ 3,100	$ 278	8.97
10	New Hampshire	$ 3,037	$ 2,710	$ 327	12.07
11					
12	East Sales Root Beer				
13					
14					
15	New York	$ 7,939	$ 7,630	$ 309	4.05
16	Massachusetts	$ 5,180	$ 4,930	$ 250	5.07
17	Florida	$ 5,283	$ 5,030	$ 253	5.03
18	Connecticut	$ 3,090	$ 2,900	$ 190	6.55
19	New Hampshire	$ 2,180	$ 2,000	$ 180	9.00
20					
21	Colas - Root Beer Total	$ 51,412	$ 48,050	$ 3,362	
22					

Now change the slider and note the formula and formatting are preserved. You're in love with Smart View now, aren't you? Us too. Save this report as EastSales-Detail.xls.

CASCADE WITH REPORT DESIGNER

Remember the totally awesome cool magician-like feature called Cascade (we realize we sound a bit silly with all the adjectives but we truly feel cascading is deserving of such a description). Cascade was the one that generated a number of reports based on a list of members. Guess what? You can use Cascade on reports created with the Report Designer.

Open the Product Sales spreadsheet:

	A	B	C	D	E	F	G	
1	Product Sales by Market							
2								
3		Qtr1	Qtr2	Qtr3	Qtr4			
4		Actual	Actual	Actual	Actual			
5	East	$ 5,726	$ 5,902	$ 5,863	$ 6,181			
6	New York	$ 1,778	$ 1,989	$ 1,879	$ 2,293			
7	Massachu	$ 1,385	$ 1,263	$ 1,206	$ 1,326			
8	Florida	$ 1,185	$ 1,323	$ 1,494	$ 1,281			
9	Connectic	$ 869	$ 772	$ 678	$ 771			
10	New Ham	$ 509	$ 555	$ 606	$ 510			
11								
12		Jan	Feb	Mar	Apr	May	Jun	Jul
13		Actual	Actual	Actual	Actual	Actual	Actual	Act
14	East	$ 1,853	$ 1,966	$ 1,907	$ 1,935	$ 1,896	$ 2,071	$
15	New York	$ 551	$ 641	$ 586	$ 630	$ 612	$ 747	$
16	Massachu	$ 467	$ 468	$ 450	$ 442	$ 412	$ 409	$
17	Florida	$ 370	$ 400	$ 415	$ 422	$ 425	$ 476	$
18	Connectic	$ 310	$ 285	$ 274	$ 269	$ 267	$ 236	$
19	New Ham	$ 155	$ 172	$ 182	$ 172	$ 180	$ 203	$
20								
21								
22								
23								
24			Product - Root Beer					
25								

Delete the Product slider control.

Click on the *Cascade Report Across the Workbook* icon in the Report Designer:

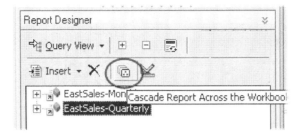

Tip!

Don't click the Cascade for Ad hoc Analysis.

Tip!

You must be in Query View to cascade a Report Designer report.

The Member Selection window will display. Choose the Product dimension and select the children of Product (we want a different report for each product category). Click *OK*.

The different reports will generate (be amazed):

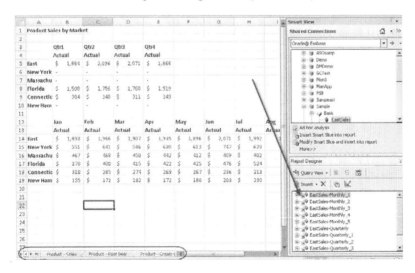

Note!

You may have to refresh the report by selecting *Refresh*.

New modified smart slices are added in the Report Designer and each tab is named the member name or alias depending on your selection for the alias table.

Tip!

Don't forget to format before cascading.

To make reporting a little easier going forward, modify the EastSales and WestSales smart slices:

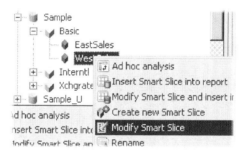

Move the Year dimension into the POV:

CREATE A REPORT WITH REPORT DESIGNER IN WORD

As with all things Smart View, Smart Slices and Report Designer are available in Word and PowerPoint. Let's create a report with Report Designer in Word. Open a new Word document and in the Smart View panel connect to Sample.Basic. Click the + sign to expand Sample.Basic:

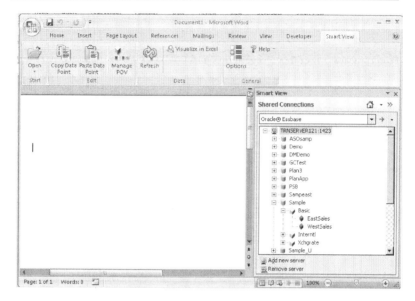

Insert EastSales and WestSales smart slices into the Report Designer:

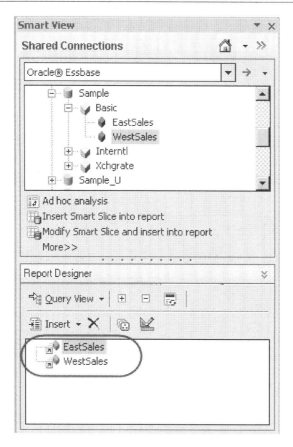

Select EastSales and select *Insert Function Grid* to place the grid in the Word document. Select *Refresh:*

	Actual	Budget	Variance	Variance %
East	87398	78950	8448	10.700443
New York	34698	31790	2908	9.147531
Massachusetts	14657	13500	1157	8.570370
Florida	18341	16300	2041	12.521472
Connecticut	12411	10920	1491	13.653846
New Hampshire	7291	6440	851	13.214286

Individual data points are inserted into a table in Word. You can now add table formatting and other font formatting as necessary. Although note that in the example above we're missing commas, dollar signs, etc. in the function grid.

Note! Remember that Smart Slice formatting options will not be applied in Report Designer.

If you manually add commas or $ to the function grid, they will be deleted upon refresh. There is really no good way to format numbers in a function grid in Word, unfortunately. An alternative would be to copy and paste data points that have been formatted with Excel formatting. But this option doesn't use our handy Report Designer. What's the best answer (as of 11.1.1.)? If you really want to use the Report Designer and function grids, use Excel with Excel formatting to create the report and not Word.

Note! The POV Manager does not work with Report Designer objects.

We've just inserted a function grid into a Word document. How about tables and charts? Sorry, no luck. These two objects are unavailable in Word documents. Cascade isn't supported in Word either. But do these features work in PowerPoint? Let's turn our attention to using Report Designer in PowerPoint and find out.

CASCADE A REPORT IN POWERPOINT

You should be a pro now at using the Report Designer. In a new PowerPoint document, connect to our old friend Sample.Basic. Insert the EastSales Smart Slice into the Report Designer (right click on the Smart Slice and select *Insert Smart slice into Report*). Select EastSales query and select *Insert Function Grid*:

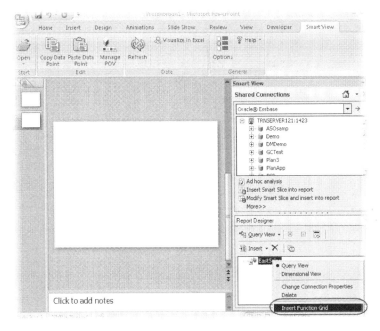

The function grid is inserted as text boxes in PowerPoint:

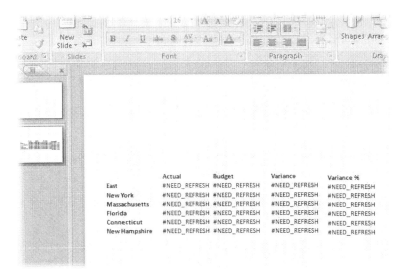

Tip!

Your grid may be sized a bit differently than above. Function grids are inserted as text boxes into PowerPoint where you can move, resize and align as needed (more on this in just a moment).

Click *Refresh* to retrieve the data. Now let's assume we are putting together a PowerPoint presentation with a slide on each product (level zero products). Do I have to go into each slide and insert the grid for each product? Of course not. Cascade to the rescue!

Click on the *Cascade* icon:

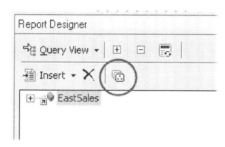

Choose the Product dimension and level zero products.

Click *OK* once the products have been selected. Wait a few seconds – note processing time will increase as the bursting member list increases. The report should display, one slide for each level zero product:

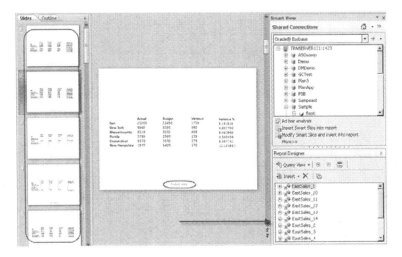

Wow. You just said that out loud, didn't you? Notice "footers" are automatically created identifying the cascaded member. And don't forget these are full refreshable data points. As the underlying data changes, you simply click *Refresh* or *Refresh All* to pull in the current data.

Does anyone see an issue with what we've done so far? We just cascaded an unformatted report. Now we have to go and reformat all of the slides individually. Lesson learned? Always finalize the formatting before you cascade (you don't want to have to recreate those TPS reports or worse, have Lumberght remind you several times about the memo on formatting).

The same rules for formatting in Word apply in PowerPoint. You can't format the data points themselves. Any numeric formatting applied will be removed after refreshing the data. You can manually add in text boxes with the "$":

East Sal

	Actual	Budget
East	$	1378 $
New York	$	521 $
Massachusetts	$	189 $
Florida	$	317 $
Connecticut	$	222 $

As you can see in our example, inserting the Function Grid actually inserts the data points as floating text boxes in the PowerPoint slide. You can format the text box background, border and font:

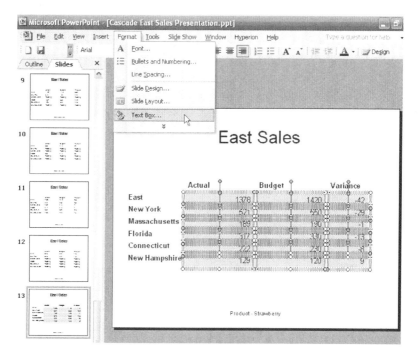

You can resize and reposition as necessary using PowerPoint features like alignment and distribution:

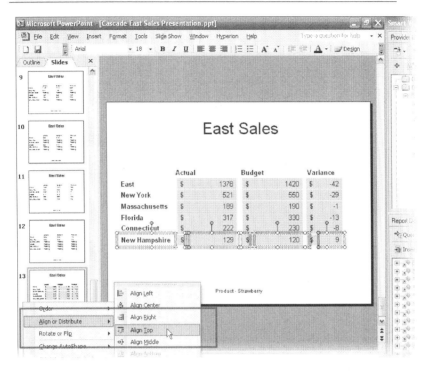

Try It!

Apply formatting to the data points in our PowerPoint presentation. For example, format the color of the data point text boxes. Add in text boxes containing $.

Try It!

Insert a table and chart from the Report Designer into your PowerPoint presentation. Tables and charts are available!

Tip!

To fully view tables and charts in PowerPoint, you will need to switch to slideshow / presentation mode.

Create a slide similar to the following, inserting the same Smart Slice (EastSales) as a table:

Notice the difference between the function grids (floating text boxes for each individual data point) vs. tables (single object with scroll bars). Now for the really cool part!

Change to Slide Show view in PowerPoint. Zoom in and out on the Market dimension. The same basic zoom features are supported in the Slide Show view of PowerPoint.

Now what if we wanted to be able to change the POV? Instead of cascading this slide for all of the different products, let's add a POV control for selecting products dynamically for our upcoming meeting.

Right click on the East Sales smart slice in the Report Designer and select *Insert POV*.

The POV Control is inserted into the slide as a grey box:

	A	B	C	D	E
		Actual	Budget	Variance	Variance %
2	New York	34698	31850	2848	8.94192
3	Massachusetts	14657	13500	1157	8.57037
4	Florida	18341	16300	2041	12.5215
5	Connecticut	12411	10920	1491	13.6538
6	New Hampshire	7291	6440	851	13.2143
7	East	87398	79010	8388	10.6164

Don't panic (like we did the first time we tried this) – in Normal PowerPoint mode, you won't be able to use the control. Change your mode to Slide Show / Presentation and you can use the POV to select new POV members for the slide:

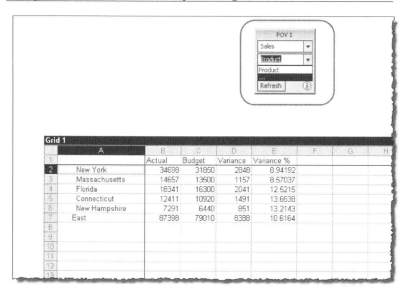

Note!

The same grey box will appear after inserting slide controls as well. Never fear – switch to slide show / presentation mode and the slider becomes available for use.

Note!

You can only use one control per query, either a slide or POV control. You cannot reuse the control on other slides for that query.

In summary, check out the following table to review what objects are available across multiple Office Products:

	Excel	*Word*	*PowerPoint*
Function Grid	Y	Y	Y
Table	Y	N	Y
Chart	Y	N	Y
Slider Control	Y	N	Y
POV Control	Y	N	Y

Congratulations! You did it. The interactive presentations, documents and spreadsheets that you created with Smart Slices and

Report Designer knocked the socks off the consultants and executive management and left Lumberght speechless. The dynamic session with live data resulted in the compliment for you "just a straight shooter with upper management written all over" from the consultants. And apparently Lumberght had been laid off five years ago and was still getting a paycheck. Thank you to Essbase for helping to find this glitch. Now you are ready to conquer the world with value added reporting and analysis for your organization.

COMPARING THE REPORTING OPTIONS

At this point you might be so overwhelmed with all of the reporting options, you're wondering which is best. There is no right answer and how you proceed will depend partly on requirements and partly on your preference. Here are a few considerations when creating reports with Smart View.

You can easily create reports that come from multiple databases or different data sets within the same database.

	Ad hoc Grids	*Plain Ol' Data Points*	*Report Designer*
Creation	Member Selection, Query Designer, Zooming	Starting point from an ad hoc query	Requires a Smart Slice with specific smart slice layout
Maintenance	Refresh / Refresh All	Refresh / Refresh All	Refresh / Refresh All
Update report if hierarchy changes (e.g. Products are in rows; a new product is added to the outline). Is the report updated?	Must Zoom Out and then Zoom In or type in the new product and Refresh	No	No for Function Grid; Yes for Table
Performance	Faster for large amounts of data	OK for small to medium amounts of data	OK for small to medium amounts of data

	Ad hoc Grids	*Plain Ol' Data Points*	*Report Designer*
Formatting Options	Use Excel Formatting or Smart View Formatting	Use Excel Formatting	Use Excel Formatting
Change POV	Yes – Update spreadsheet or toggle on the POV	Yes with POV Manager	Yes with POV control
Use of Floating POV	Yes	No	Yes – POV control
Supports Multi-Source Reports	Yes – Must enable sheet for multi-source	Yes	Yes
Use of Floating POV with Multi-Source Report	No	No	Yes – you can create a POV control to multiple smart slices as long as there is a common dimension
Supported in Excel	Yes	Yes	Yes
Supported in Word	No	Yes	Yes
Supported in PowerPoint	No	Yes	Yes

You're almost to the end of the road, but before we conclude the book let's review some last tips and tricks to solidify your Smart View skills.

Chapter 7:
Smart View Tips and Tricks

Now that you've mastered the majority of the Smart View Add-In menu items, we'll take your skills to the next level of mastery in a short but important chapter.

SPEEDY RETRIEVES

It is not enough to simply understand how to retrieve and report data. Grasshopper, you must understand *why* data retrieves the way it does. One of the questions you must have been asking yourself at this point is "why do some retrieves take longer than others?"

Essbase retrieves are normally measured in seconds or sub-seconds. If your retrieves ever take more than thirty seconds, there are some things to check:

- Hardware performance
- Retrieval size
- Use of attribute dimensions
- Use of dynamically calculated members
- Use of dynamic time series
- Dense vs. sparse retrievals
- Essbase database settings

Let's begin by assuming that your desktop, network, and Essbase server aren't older than dirt. If your hardware is more than a few years old, replace it, because doing so will definitely make things faster. Computers are easier to upgrade than people.

If your hardware is fairly recent, begin by looking at how much data you're retrieving. While 500 rows by 20 columns doesn't seem like much, that's over 10,000 cells of data you're asking Essbase to return. While you can't exactly eliminate every other row on your report to save space ("Sorry about the missing numbers, boss, but Edward Roske told me that deleting even numbered rows on my reports would cut my retrieval time in half!"), you'll at least be aware of why your report is taking a long time.

The next thing to review is your use of members from attribute dimensions, dynamically calculated members, and dynamic time series members. As mentioned earlier, none of these members are pre-calculated. A retrieve that is accessing stored members will almost always run more quickly than one that accesses dynamic members.

One of the most common mistakes people make is putting the top member from an attribute dimension on their report. Notice the "Caffeinated" member on this retrieve:

	A	B	C	D	E	F
1			Market	Product	Actual	Caffeinated
2		Qtr1	Qtr2	Qtr3	Qtr4	Year
3	Sales	95,820	101,679	105,215	98,141	400,855
4	COGS	42,877	45,362	47,343	43,754	179,336
5	Margin	52,943	56,317	57,872	54,387	221,519
6						
7	Marketing	15,839	16,716	17,522	16,160	66,237
8	Payroll	12,168	12,243	12,168	12,168	48,747
9	Misc	233	251	270	259	1,013
10	Total Expenses	28,240	29,210	29,960	28,587	115,997
11						
12	Profit	24,703	27,107	27,912	25,800	105,522
13						

The presence of this member usually doesn't change the totals at all (we still have 105,522 in the bottom-right corner) but it takes a retrieve that would be against stored information and makes it entirely dynamic. Why? Because we are telling Essbase to go grab all the products that are Caffeinated_True and add them together, and then grab all the products that are Caffeinated_False and add them together, and finally, add Caffeinated_False to Caffeinated_True to get total Caffeinated. Well, this is the same value as if we'd never asked for Caffeinated at all!

The solution is obvious: delete the Caffeinated member and our retrieve will speed up by more than an order of magnitude. The more cynical among you might ask why Essbase isn't smart enough to notice that it's dynamically adding up every product when it could just take the stored Product total and be done with it. We don't have a good answer for that, so we'll pretend that we can't hear your question.

Dense vs. Sparse Retrievals for BSO

Density vs. Sparsity for Essbase Block Storage Cubes is a tricky subject, because it really gets in to how Essbase stores data behind the scenes and that's normally only of interest to an Essbase administrator, a developer, or a highly paid (but deservedly so) consultant. We're going to touch on the subject just enough so that you understand how it affects your retrieval times.

Our base dimensions (i.e., not the attribute dimensions) fall into one of two types: dense and sparse. Dense dimensions are dimensions for which most combinations are loaded with data. Sparse dimensions are often missing values.

In Sample.Basic, the dense dimensions are Year, Measures, and Scenario. This is because when there's a value for one month (say, Sales) there tends to be a value for every month. If there's a value for Sales, there tends to be a value for COGS, Marketing, and so on. If there's a number for Actual, there tends to be a value for Budget. As such, Year, Measures, and Scenario are said to be dense dimensions.

The sparse dimensions for Sample.Basic are Product and Market. This is because not every product tends to be sold in every state. As we saw earlier, out of seven possible caffeinated drinks, Massachusetts only sold three of them. As such, Product and Market are said to be sparse dimensions.

Why does this matter to you? Well, a retrieve consisting of dense dimensions (and only dense dimensions) in the rows and columns will tend to be much, much faster than a report with a sparse dimension in the rows or the columns.

When a report only has dense dimensions in the rows and columns, we refer to this as a dense retrieval. Here is an example of a dense retrieval against Sample.Basic:

	A	B	C	D	E	
1		Product	Market	Scenario		
2		Jan	Feb	Mar	Apr	Ma
3	Sales	31,538	32,069	32,213	32,917	33
4	COGS	14,160	14,307	14,410	14,675	15
5	Margin	17,378	17,762	17,803	18,242	18
6	Marketing	5,223	5,289	5,327	5,421	5
7	Payroll	4,056	4,056	4,056	4,081	4
8	Misc	75	71	87	96	
9	Total Expenses	9,354	9,416	9,470	9,598	6
10	Profit	8,024	8,346	8,333	8,644	

It's a dense retrieval because Measures is in the rows, Year is in the columns, and both are dense dimensions. Notice that all the intersections tend to have values loaded to them. This is an example of a sparse retrieval against Sample.Basic:

	A	B	C	D	E	F
1		Jan	Sales	Actual		
2		New York	Massachusetts	Florida	Connecticut	New Hampshire
3	Cola	678	494	210	310	120
4	Diet Cola			200		
5	Caffeine Free Cola					93
6	Old Fashioned	61	126	190	180	90
7	Diet Root Beer			180	130	
8	Sasparilla					
9	Birch Beer	490	341			65
10	Dark Cream	483	130	120	190	76
11	Vanilla Cream	180		150	170	
12	Diet Cream			110		
13	Grape	234	80	80	123	45
14	Orange	219				
15	Strawberry	134	80	81	94	43

This is a sparse retrieval because Product is in the rows, Market is in the columns, and both are sparse dimensions. Notice that a number of the values are missing. Though it doesn't have many more cells to retrieve, this retrieval will take many times longer than the one above because of how Essbase retrieves data from sparse dimensions. Simply put, for sparse retrievals, Essbase retrieves a lot of data into memory on the server side that you'll never see or use.

While we can't change which dimensions are dense or sparse (that's a setting controlled for each database by the Essbase Administrator), we can be aware that sparse retrievals will take much longer than dense retrievals.

If you've tried all of the tips above and your retrieval is still taking a long time, it might be an issue with some of the database settings on the Essbase server. There are a number of settings such as density/sparsity (mentioned above), data caches, index caches, and so forth that someone qualified in Essbase can tune to improve retrieval performance. The bad news is that you can't tweak these yourself, but the good news is that they can be tweaked by someone else.

COPY SPREADSHEET

You will inevitably create a spreadsheet that you want to copy to another spreadsheet without having to start over. You know the feature – right click on the Excel spreadsheet and click *Move or Copy*:

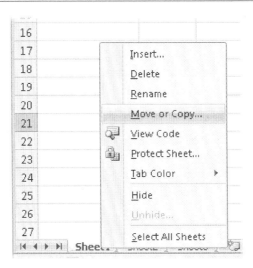

Once you've completed the copy, the new spreadsheet isn't connected to the Essbase database (no Essbase ribbon). To connect the new spreadsheet, right click on the desired Essbase database and click Ad Hoc analysis:

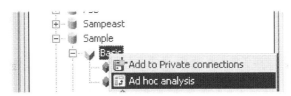

The data is refreshed and will include any POV member selections if you are using the floating POV.

If you are using Private Connections (more on this in the next chapter), you can also just apply the Active Connection to the spreadsheet.

EXCEL FORMULA RETENTION

We skipped one member option in the first chapter of the book. Let's revisit this helpful feature now – formula retention when zooming. You can build Excel formulas into your analyses and retain those formulas as you zoom in and out (with a few constraints). Set up the following worksheet:

	A	B	C	D
1		Sales	East	Actual
2		Qtr1	Qtr2	
3	Product	20621	22449	

We want to add a subtotal for Qtr1 and Qtr2 to see how we are fared for the first half of the year. This subtotal does not exist in Essbase so we need to add it in Excel. In E3 add an Excel formula to perform this subtotal:

	A	B	C	D	E	F	G
1		Sales	East	Actual			
2		Qtr1	Qtr2				
3	Product	20621	22449		=SUM(B3:D3)		
4					SUM(**number1**, [number2], ...)		

Click *Refresh*. The formula is retained. Now before you start zooming, select *Options* from the Smart View ribbon. Under *Member Options*, check the box to *Preserve Formulas and Comments on Ad hoc operation* and *Formula/Format Fill*:

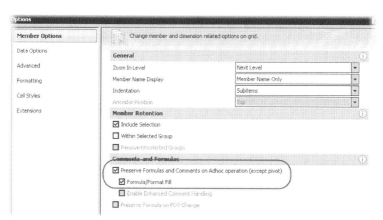

Click *OK*.

Zoom on Product and notice the formula "fills" as you zoom:

	A	B	C	D	E
1		Sales	East	Actual	
2		Qtr1	Qtr2		
3	Colas	$ 6,292	$ 7,230		$ 13,522
4	Root Beer	$ 5,726	$ 5,902		$ 11,628
5	Cream Soda	$ 4,868	$ 5,327		$ 10,195
6	Fruit Soda	$ 3,735	$ 3,990		$ 7,725
7	Diet Drinks	$ 1,884	$ 2,096		$ 3,980
8	Product	$ 20,621	$ 22,449		$ 43,070
9					

This works great up until you decide to pivot. Select "East" and click *Pivot* from the Essbase ribbon. You should be prompted with the following window:

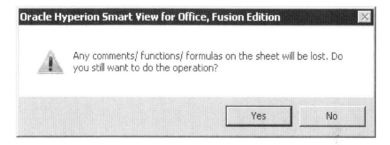

Click *Yes* and note the formula is removed.

#NUMERICZERO VS. ZERO

We want to highlight one additional selection under Data Options that is important if you are writing data back to Essbase. Select *Options* from the Smart View ribbon. Under the Data Options section, select the drop down for Replacement options #NoData/Missing label:

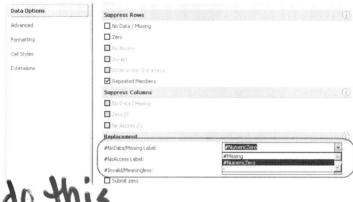

When you retrieve data from Essbase, you choose how you want missing data to be displayed. It can be any text value you choose (e.g. "-") or the default value #Missing but this may cause issues for the Excel formulas. To address this issue, some users may even choose "0" (in version 11x, you can't use just "0"; you have to use '0 or (0)). This works fine for reporting but if you need to submit data back to Essbase and you've used "0" as the replacement option, you will be writing a lot of zeroes back to the Essbase database, increasing the database size unnecessarily. A better alternative is to choose the #NumericZero which will display a "0" so Excel formulas work but "zero data" will not be submitted back to the database. The only way to submit zeros back to Essbase is to explicitly check *Submit Zero* (though in most cases, leave this unchecked):

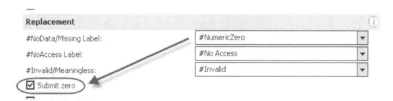

MEMBER INFORMATION

At any point in time you can find out more information about a member. What is the member name or alias? Is this member dynamically calculated or stored? What is the consolidation tag? To find out all there is to know about a member (and then some), select the member in the spreadsheet. Click *Member Information* from the Essbase ribbon:

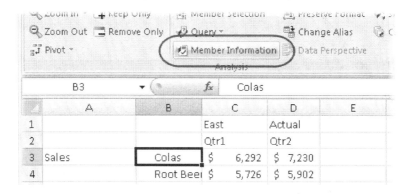

The Member Information window will display:

Click *Save* if you would like to save this information into a separate Excel spreadsheet:

	A	B
1	Information	
2		
3	Property	Value
4	Member Name	100
5	Dimension Name	Product
6	Level Number	1
7	Generation Number	2
8	Parent Member Name	Product
9	Child Member Name	100-10
10	Next Member Name	200
11	Consolidation	Addition
12	Two Pass Calculation	False
13	Expense	False
14	Share	Store Data
15	Storage	Sparse
16	Category	None
17	Storage Category	Other
18	Child Count	3
19	Attributed	False
20	Relational Descendants	False
21	HA Enabled	False
22	Default Alias	Colas
23	Hierarchy Type	Not a Hierarchy Member
24	Dimension Solve Order	0
25	Solve Order	0

MDX QUERIES

For the more technically inclined users who want to the option to write an MDX query directly to Essbase, you can! Simply click *Query >> Execute MDX*:

Enter in valid MDX syntax and click *Execute*:

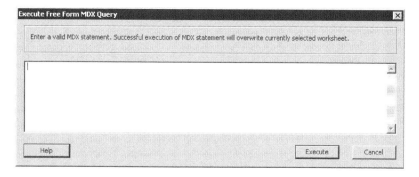

For more information on MDX, check out Look Smarter Than You Are with Essbase: An Administrator Guide.

IMPORT A FINANCIAL REPORTING REPORT

The last tip that we want to share includes an additional EPM software component, Financial Reporting. Financial Reporting is a reporting tool within the Oracle EPM System that is used to create nicely formatted reports against Essbase, Planning and HFM applications. Financial Reporting reports and books are accessible over the web via the EPM workspace and can also be distributed via PDFs in emails, shared network drive, or static websites. This is a great tool for your standard reports that are generated on a consistent basis like your monthly financials. Why do we mention Financial Reporting here in the Smart View book? Because you can import a Financial Reporting document into Excel, Word and PowerPoint using Smart View.

The steps to import a Financial Reporting document into Excel, Word and PowerPoint are the same. We'll show you Note! the basic steps in Excel.

In the Smart View panel, click the drop down next to the Home icon and select *Shared Connections:*

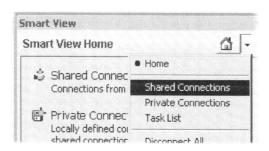

Choose *Reporting and Analysis Framework* (this is the connection to the EPM Workspace directory):

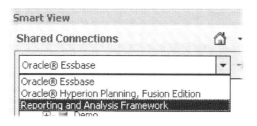

Click the + sign to expand and navigate through the EPM Workspace directory structure. Double click to select the desired report (or right click and select *Open*):

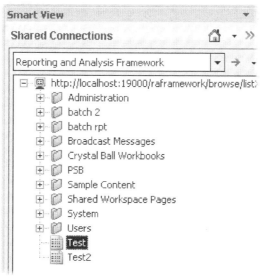

The Import Workspace Document window will display. First make any desired changes to the POV. Select the member and the member selection window will display:

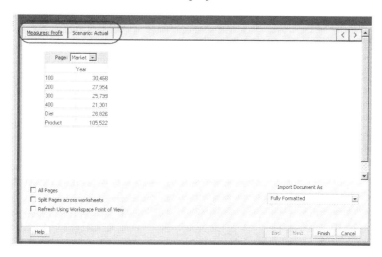

You can also choose to refresh the report using your POV that is defined in the Workspace (whichever POV selection you last used in the web will be used for this import):

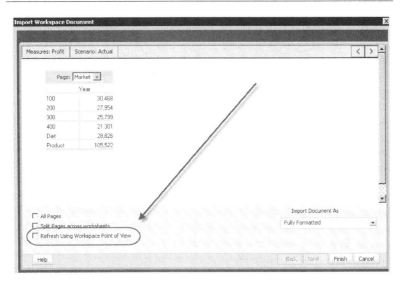

Next choose how the "Pages" section should be handled. In our example, the Market dimension is defined as the pages section of the Financial Reporting document:

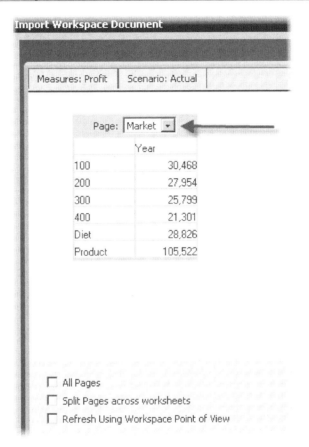

Choose the desired Page options:
* Bring in *All Pages* (which could take a while depending on how many members are defined in the Page definition)
* *Split Pages across worksheets* (so if you have "Market", "East", and "West" in the page definition, three worksheets will be created)

The last step is to define how the report will be imported - *Fully Formatted* or *Query-Ready*:

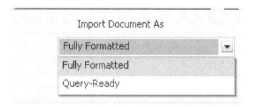

In our example we will select Fully Formatted, which will bring in the Financial Reporting report with all of the formatting applied in Excel:

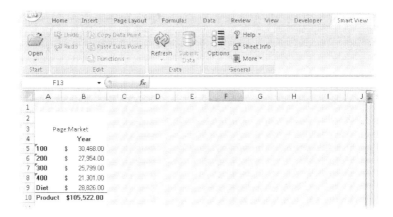

You can refresh the report at any time, bringing in any report changes along with refreshed data. Simply click *Refresh*.

Query ready imported documents have no formatting but allow you to switch to a Smart View Essbase connection and begin zooming and pivoting. Just right click on the applicable Essbase database and select *Ad hoc Analysis.*

Tip!

You can import Financial Reporting documents into Excel as a fully formatted grid or query ready grid.

Tip!

You can import Financial Reporting documents into Word or PowerPoint as an image.

Chapter 8:
SMART VIEW ADMINISTRATION

By now you think you are a Smart View expert, and rightly so; you've mastered almost every Smart View feature. You've used a number of the administration features so far, including Smart View Panel. We want to make sure you understand a few other more administrative options before we conclude this captivating book on Smart View.

MANAGE CONNECTIONS

You've now connected to the Sample.Basic database several times. Pretty straight-forward, right? Yes, in the Essbase world, life is gloriously simple; but is there more (should we settle or embrace change)? Before we digress into life lessons, let's focus and say yes, there are some additional connection features that can help you in your Essbase reporting and analysis process. In the previous chapter we saw that we can also connect to the EPM Workspace and import Financial Reporting documents (and Web Analysis documents). Also many of you may be using Smart View for Planning, Financial Management or other BI / EPM tools so let us expand on our connecting capabilities.

Two types of connections exist in the Oracle EPM and BI environment - Shared Connections and Private Connections:

Shared Connections are stored in a central location and are available for multiple users. End users cannot change Shared Connections.

Private connections are created by end users by saving a shared connection to the local computer or entering a URL. When you create a private connection, it becomes the active connection.

You've worked with a Shared Connection through this book. Let's now take a quick look at Private Connections.

CREATE A PRIVATE CONNECTION

Private connections (used for backward compatibility and for HsGetValue and other functions) are created one of two ways: saving a shared connection as private or manually entering in a provider URL.

In the Smart View panel, select the drop down box next to the home icon and choose *Private Connections:*

If you haven't created a private connection, the list should be blank:

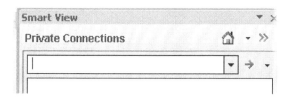

Toggle back to Shared Connections. Select the Essbase server if necessary. Expand down to Sample.Basic. Right click and select *Add to Private Connection:*

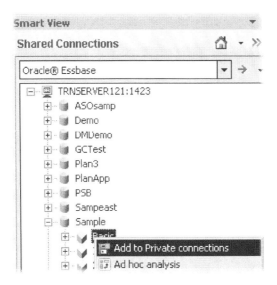

Give the connection a name. You can leave the default name or create your own (in our example we want to easily see that this is the connection to a development database vs. a production database, so we name it accordingly).

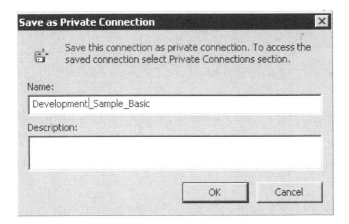

Click *OK*. The new name displays in the Smart View panel.

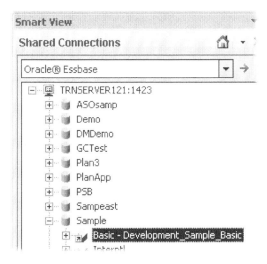

Now that Sample.Basic is a private connection, you can use the *Activate* option on the Smart View ribbon. In a new worksheet, select *Open >> Active Connections>>Development_Sample_Basic*:

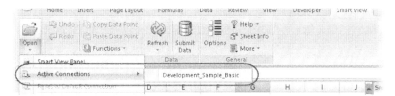

The worksheet is connected and the Essbase ribbon displays. You are ready to analyze!

Toggle back to Private Connections in the Smart View panel. You should now see the Essbase server in the drop down box. Select it:

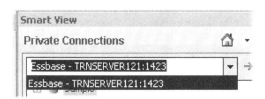

Notice that you just see the Sample.Basic database and not the full list of applications:

This may be preferable if you have access to a long list of Essbase databases but only use a few of them. Private connections are your way of saving connections as "favorites".

To manually create a Private connection, choose the drop down next to the connection window. Select *Create new connection:*

Enter the URL:

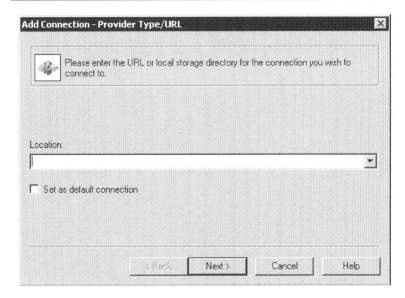

Valid URLs for 11.1.2 (your Hyperion administrator can provide the server and port):

Financial Management	http(s)://*servername*:*port*/hfmofficeprovider/hfmofficeprovider
Hyperion Enterprise	http://*servername*:*port*/heofficeprovider/heofficeprovider
Planning	http(s)://*servername*:*port*/HyperionPlanning/SmartView
Essbase	http(s)://*servername*:*port*/aps/SmartView
Reporting and Analysis	http(s)://*servername*:*port*/raframework/browse/listxml
Financial Close Management	http://*servername*:*port*/fcc/servlets/smartview/fcmsvservlet

Click *Next* and the connection is added. Now you know how to add connections, but what if you want to change the connection for an existing grid?

CHANGE CONNECTION FOR AD HOC GRID

You can easily change the connection for an ad hoc grid. With the ad hoc grid open, right click on the desired database and select *Ad hoc analysis*. You might be prompted to clear or keep POV and sheet options:

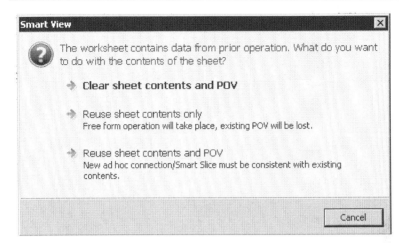

If additional dimensions exist in the new database, those will be added to the point of view.

CHANGE THE CONNECTION FOR MULTI-GRID REPORT

Select the range of cells for which you want to change the connection. Using the Excel Name Manager, delete the associated name range:

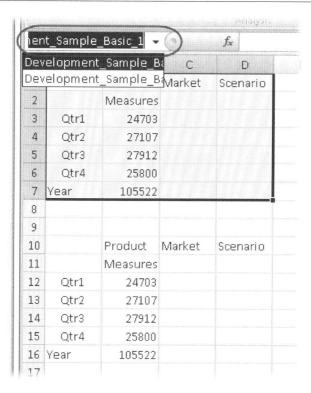

In the Smart View panel, right click on the desired source and select *Ad hoc Analysis*.

Now that you are fully fluent in managing Smart View connections, let's review the remaining Options in Smart View.

OPTIONS – ADVANCED

The Advanced section under Smart View Options contains a number of administrative settings for Smart View. The Advanced Options are global operations that apply to the entire workbook and any worksheets and workbooks going forward.

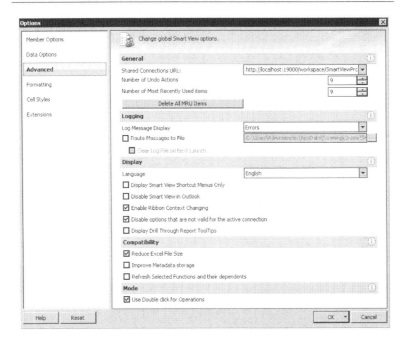

You've likely already set the first setting, the Shared Connections URL. You set the *Number of Undo* (and Redo) actions permitted from 0 to 100. You set the number of *Most Recently Used Items* from 0-15. This number of your most recently used connections will display in the Smart View home panel. If you'd like to clear your Most Recently Used connections list, click *Delete All MRU Items.*

You can define the level of logging for Smart View actions to display and record. Log levels for version 11.1.2.1.102 include Information, Warnings, Errors, None. Information level will track all messages including errors and warnings. Because a large amount of information is tracked, performance could be negatively impacted and this setting is usually set for troubleshooting. Warnings will track warnings and error messages. Errors level will track error messages only and this is the setting that is typically recommended for Smart View logging.

Two new logging levels were introduced in version 11.1.2.2 to help with troubleshooting and debugging efforts: Extended Info and Profile. Extended Info provides information level messages plus all of the server responses. Profile level provides extended information log entries plus most function calls. XML files are created for each Office application with an active Smart View instance. Both options will negatively impact performance and should only be set for debugging purposes for a small period of time.

To route log messages to a file, check the *Route message to files* and specify the log file location. *Clear Log File on Next Launch* will clear the log file when Excel is closed.

Under the Display section of Advanced options, you can choose the language that is used throughout Smart View (sort of like when Buzz Lightyear is switched to Spanish mode with the simple flip of a switch in Toy Story 3). Select *Spanish* as the language for Smart View display:

When prompted, click *OK*. In order for the language setting to take place, you must restart Excel:

Close and reopen Excel. Be amazed at your new Spanish speaking Smart View ribbon:

Open a recently used query from Sample.Basic. Note that the Essbase members and data still displays according to the Essbase outline.

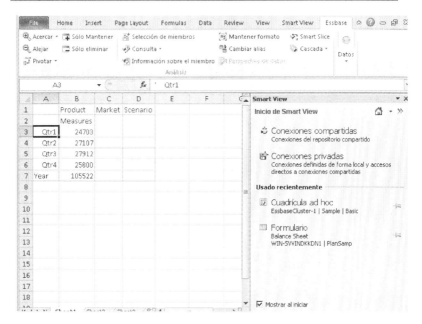

To view the members in Spanish or another language, the Essbase administrator should build an alternate alias to house the additional descriptions. Then you simply select the *Change Alias* option to choose that Alias table.

Click on *Opciones* (Options). Select *Advanzado (*Advanced) and change the language back to *Ingles* (English):

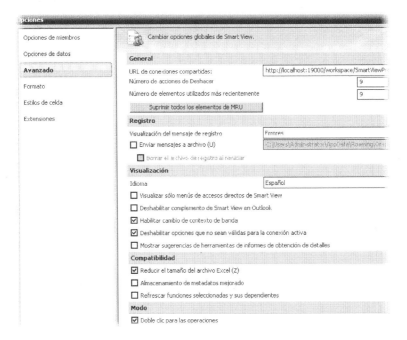

Click *Apply* and then *OK*. Close and reopen Excel and you are back to plain ol' English.

The default setting in Smart View is to see both Excel and Smart View options in your right click short cut menus (which results in a pretty long menu selection):

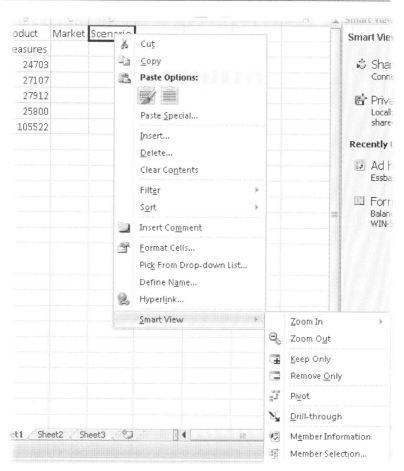

To just view Smart View short cut menus, check *Display Smart View Short Cut Menus Only*:

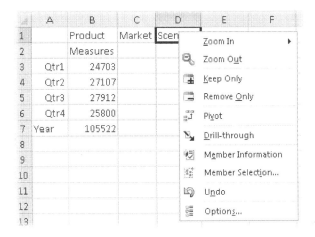

 Did you know that Smart View right click menus are context sensitive?

Note!

Right click on a Member and view the available actions:

	A	B	C	D	E	F
1		Product	Market	Scen	Zoom In ▶	
2		Measures			Zoom Out	
3	Qtr1	24703			Keep Only	
4	Qtr2	27107			Remove Only	
5	Qtr3	27912			Pivot	
6	Qtr4	25800			Drill-through	
7	Year	105522			Member Information	
8					Member Selection...	
9						
10					Undo	
11					Options...	
12						
13						

Right click on a data point and view the available actions:

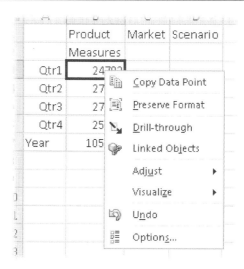

Disable Smart View in Outlook is an option that is used with Hyperion Planning and Hyperion Financial Management task lists.

If *Enable Ribbon Context Changing* is checked, the active data provider ribbon (e.g. Essbase) will display for the new connection. If this setting is unchecked, the Essbase ribbon opens but the view remains on the Smart View ribbon.

Disable options that are not valid for the active connection will keep you sane. Keep this option checked so that you aren't banging your head against the wall trying to figure out why a button isn't working the way you want. Some features in Smart View are data source specific.

If you are using Essbase Studio Drill Through reports, check the *Display Drill Through Report Tooltips*. This option must be checked to see tool tips for Studio drill through reports:

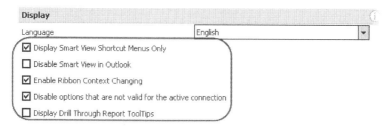

The last settings under the Compatibility section *Reduce Excel File Size* and *Improve Metadata Storage* should always be checked unless you are sending the workbook to a user on Smart View 9.3.1.6:

Compatibility

☑ Reduce Excel File Size

☑ Improve Metadata storage

☐ Refresh Selected Functions and their dependents

Refresh Selected Functions and their dependents is a setting you will consider if you have worksheets using functions like HsGetValue.

The last setting under the Mode section will turn off double-clicking for Zoom actions if unchecked:

Mode

☑ Use Double click for Operations

OPTIONS – EXTENSIONS

The Extensions section under options lists the extensions that are installed to use Smart View for other Oracle products. Currently supported products are Financial Reporting and Hyperion Disclosure Management (so if you don't use these products, you won't see anything). These settings also support power packs, add-ins designed to do special tasks like Grid Formatter, Member Search, Substitution Variable manager, MDXScript Library, and more. For more information, check out the following link:

http://www.oracle.com/technetwork/middleware/smart-view-for-office/downloads/index-088403.html.

In this section, you choose how to handle the extensions. Do you want to enable or disable a particular extension? Do you want to check for an update? Do you want to enable logging for extension installation?

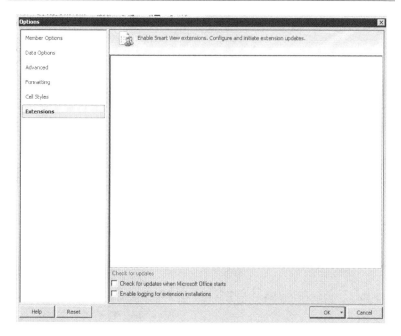

Extension options are global (they will apply to all worksheets).

OPTIONS - PROVIDER PREFERENCES

Provider preferences under Smart View Options are set by the administrator. She can define the following preferences for Essbase connections:

- Force Client to Upgrade
- Warn Client to Upgrade
- Session Timeout
- Number of Rows (maximum number of rows returned in an ad hoc grid)
- Number of Columns (maximum number of columns returned in an ad hoc grid

You are almost to the end of your journey with Smart View. We'll leave you with one last chapter, a visionary chapter, to help you understand what is possible with Essbase data sources and reporting and analysis with Smart View. The consultants will love you after you show them all of the possible reports. Why did they ever hire Lumberght in the first place?

Chapter 9:
DIFFERENT APPLICATIONS

Everything we've done up to this point has been using the Sample.Basic database that comes with Essbase. While it's workable for exercises in this book, it's not terribly representative of databases in the real world. The goal for this chapter is to describe a few common types of databases in case you should ever run into them. For each application type, we'll review how the application is generally used and what the dimensions tend to be for that type of application. The most important take-away from this chapter: while Essbase is very good at financial analysis, it can support many, many different types of applications.

Note!

While an application can house one or more databases, most applications contain just one database. With that said, this chapter uses the terms "application" and "database" in the broader Information Technology sense.

COMMON DIMENSIONS

While every application will be different, most applications draw from a common set of dimension templates. The details within each dimension may change and the names of the dimensions may differ, but the same dimensions will keep appearing throughout many Essbase applications at your company. While we'll review later the differences for each specific application, it seems like a good idea to start with what we all have in common.

Time

All of us experience the constant effects of time and likewise (with very few exceptions) every Essbase database has one *or more* time dimensions. This is the dimension that contains the time periods for your database. Sample.Basic calls this dimension "Year":

In addition to Year, other common names for this dimension include Periods, All Periods, Time (my personal favorite), Time Periods, Full Year, Year Total, and History. As you can tell from the plus signs above next to each member, this dimension generally aggregates from the bottom-up.

A Time dimension will usually have one or more of the following generations:

- Years
    - Seasons
        - Halves
            - Quarters
                - Months
                    - Weeks
                        - Days

While it is not unheard of to have an application that looks at hours or portions of hours, this is normally split off into its own dimension and called something like "Hours" or "Time of Day." Call center analysis applications and some retail sales applications analyze data by portions of a day.

It is quite common for an Essbase application to have two time dimensions. One dimension will house the quarters, months, days, and so forth. A separate dimension, generally called "Years" or "FY" (for Fiscal Year), will contain the calendar year. Here's an example of a Years dimension:

```
⊟ Years (Alias: Current Year)
   ├─ FY03 (~) (Alias: 2003)
   ├─ FY04 (~) (Alias: 2004)
   ├─ FY05 (~) (Alias: 2005)
   ├─ FY06 (+) (Alias: 2006)
   ├─ FY07 (~) (Alias: 2007)
   ├─ FY08 (~) (Alias: 2008)
   ├─ FY09 (~) (Alias: 2009)
   └─ FY10 (~) (Alias: 2010)
```

Unlike the Time dimensions that usually contain quarters and months, Years dimensions typically do not aggregate. Most often, the top member of a Years dimension is set to equal the data in the current year. In the above image, the tilde (~) signs (also called "no consolidate" tags) denote which years are not to be added into the total. As you can see, only FY06 has a plus next it, and therefore is the only one to roll into Years. As such, Years equals FY06.

Some applications will combine a Time and Years dimension into one. This is often done when the Time dimension goes all the way down to the day-level and a company wants to do analysis by day of the week:

```
⊟ Time {Day of Week}
   ⊞ 2005 (+)
   ⊞ 2006 (+)
   ⊟ 2007 (+)
      ⊞ Jan, 2007 (+)
      ⊞ Feb, 2007 (+)
      ⊞ Mar, 2007 (+)
      ⊞ Apr, 2007 (+)
      ⊞ May, 2007 (+)
      ⊟ Jun, 2007 (+)
         ├─ Jun 1, 2007 (+) {Day of Week: Friday}
         ├─ Jun 2, 2007 (+) {Day of Week: Saturday}
         ├─ Jun 3, 2007 (+) {Day of Week: Sunday}
         ├─ Jun 4, 2007 (+) {Day of Week: Monday}
         ├─ Jun 5, 2007 (+) {Day of Week: Tuesday}
         ├─ Jun 6, 2007 (+) {Day of Week: Wednesday}
         ├─ Jun 7, 2007 (+) {Day of Week: Thursday}
         ├─ Jun 8, 2007 (+) {Day of Week: Friday}
         ├─ Jun 9, 2007 (+) {Day of Week: Saturday}
         ├─ Jun 10, 2007 (+) {Day of Week: Sunday}
         ├─ Jun 11, 2007 (+) {Day of Week: Monday}
         ├─ Jun 12, 2007 (+) {Day of Week: Tuesday}
         └─ Jun 13, 2007 (+) {Day of Week: Wednesday}
```

Each date in the dimension has a "Day of Week" user-defined attribute (UDA) assigned to it. "Jun 1, 2007," for instance, has a "Day of Week" attribute of Friday. If we had the years in a separate dimension, we would have to declare every June 1ˢᵗ to be a Friday. While the people born on June 1ˢᵗ would absolutely love this, the calendar makers would not. As such, we have to put the year in to specify a specific date as being a specific day of the week. Here is the "Day of Week" attribute dimension that is used in conjunction with the dimension above:

```
⊟ Day of Week [Type: Text]
  ─ Sunday
  ─ Monday
  ─ Tuesday
  ─ Wednesday
  ─ Thursday
  ─ Friday
  ─ Saturday
```

While most Time dimensions use Essbase Dynamic Time Series functionality to calculate year-to-date and quarter-to-date members, it's not uncommon to come across an older Essbase outline that has actual YTD and QTD members. Usually, there will be a member called YTD (and/or QTD) in the Time dimension that will have a child for each month. For January, the member would be called either "Jan YTD" or "YTD Jan." Here's an example of a Time dimension with stored YTD members:

```
⊟ All Periods
  ⊟ MTD (+) (Alias: Full Year)
    ⊟ Qtr1 (+)
      ─ Jan (+)
      ─ Feb (+)
      ─ Mar (+)
    ⊞ Qtr2 (+)
    ⊞ Qtr3 (+)
    ⊞ Qtr4 (+)
  ⊟ YTD (~)
    ─ Jan YTD (~)
    ─ Feb YTD (~)
    ─ Mar YTD (~)
    ─ Apr YTD (~)
    ─ May YTD (~)
    ─ Jun YTD (~)
    ─ Jul YTD (~)
    ─ Aug YTD (~)
    ─ Sep YTD (~)
    ─ Oct YTD (~)
    ─ Nov YTD (~)
    ─ Dec YTD (~)
```

Measures

Like Time, almost every Essbase application has a dimension that lists the metrics for the database. While common practice is to call this dimension Measures (as Sample.Basic does), other frequently used names include Accounts and Metrics.

In Sample.Basic, the Measures dimension contains some profit and loss accounts, inventory metrics, and three calculated ratios:

You'll notice that under "Profit," there are two members for "Margin" and "Total Expenses." Each one of these members has members below it. It's quite common for a Measures dimension to have many levels of hierarchy. A financial reporting application, for instance, might have hierarchy all the way down to a sub-account level.

While most every application will have a Measures dimension, what constitutes the Measures dimension will differ wildly:

- A financial reporting application will have accounts for income statement, balance sheet, and sometimes cash flow.
- An inventory analysis application will have measures for beginning inventory, ending inventory, additions, returns, adjustments, and so forth.
- A sales analysis application will have measures for sales dollars, units sold, and average sales price.

- A human capital analysis application will have metrics for payroll, FICA, FUTA, sick days, vacation days, years of employment, and so on.

The Measures dimension is the most important dimension in any application since it lets you define what metrics you're going to analyze, but you can safely expect every Measures dimension to be unique for every application.

It's worth pointing out that the Measures dimension in Sample.Basic is very odd. It's not normal to see inventory statistics along with profit and loss accounts in the same database. From what we can tell, this was only done to show in a sample database that Essbase can handle things beyond just financial metrics.

Scenario

This dimension is common to applications that in addition to actual data also have budget, forecast, or planning information. The "Scenario" dimension usually houses members such as Actual, Budget, Forecast, What-If, and several variances (differences between one scenario and another). While the most popular name for this dimension is Scenario (or Scenarios), other common names include Category, Ledger, Cases, and Versions.

As a general rule, we try to avoid calling my Scenario dimension "Versions," because Hyperion Planning also has a dimension called "Versions" in addition to a "Scenario" dimension. In Planning, the Versions dimension is used to differentiate between different drafts of budget and plan data. Members in a Versions dimension could be Initial, Draft 1, Draft 2, Draft 3, and Final. To avoid confusion in case you run across any lost Planning users at your company, don't name your Scenario dimension "Versions" when there are so many other good names from which to choose.

Here is Sample.Basic's Scenario dimension:

Most Scenario dimensions are non-aggregating (since it doesn't make a lot of sense to add Actual and Budget together). In Sample.Basic, the only child of Scenario to roll-up is Actual, in effect setting Scenario equal to Actual.

⊟⋯**Scenario**
⋮⋯**Actual** (+)
⋮⋯**Budget** (~)
⋮⋯**Variance** (~)
⋮⋯**Variance %** (~)

Other Dimensions

Many applications have a dimension that differentiates between different organizational entities. Commonly, this dimension is called Entities (the name Hyperion Planning prefers), Organization (the name we prefer), Departments, Cost Centers, Companies, Locations, and other industry specific names (like

Stores or Branches). The closest Sample.Basic has to an Organization dimension is the Market dimension.

Another common dimension that you might run across is Product, which houses the relationships between products and their categories and families. This is one of the few dimensions where just about everyone calls it the same thing although the alias differs at the top of the dimension, containing something like "All Products" or "Total Products." The greatest difference in this dimension is the depth to which different applications go. Some Product dimensions stop at different classes of products while others will go all the way down to individual parts, items, or SKUs (Stock Keeping Units).

Other dimensions tend to be specific to different types of applications. For instance, a Customer dimension will tend to show up in Sales Analysis and Accounts Receivable applications. We'll cover some of the major applications you'll tend to see. This is by no means thorough, because every day a company comes up with some new way to use Essbase that no one has ever tried before.

Please don't think that Essbase can only be used for financial applications. We once built an Essbase cube to track projects that families signed up for at our church Advent workshop. Okay, that's really geeky, but it goes to show you what you can do if you get out of the finance realm.

FINANCIAL REPORTING

Financial reporting (often called General Ledger, or GL analysis) databases are by far the most common type of Essbase application (not to be confused with the Oracle product called Hyperion Financial Reporting which is a reporting tool that sits on top of Essbase, HFM and Planning). This goes back to the early days of Essbase when the Arbor Software sales team used to sell pretty much exclusively into finance and accounting departments. Even today, the first Essbase database most companies build is to facilitate general ledger analysis.

In all fairness, Essbase is very good at doing GL analysis. Essbase has hundreds of built-in financial functions that make it a good fit for GL reporting. The Essbase outline provides a user friendly view of how accounts, departments, and other entities roll up within hierarchies and dimensions. It is also very easy for finance-minded personnel to manage those hierarchies. The most attractive thing about Essbase to accountants, though, is that accountants love Excel and as you just saw from the earlier chapters, Excel loves Essbase (or is that the other way around?).

Financial Reporting applications generally receive data from one or more GL Systems (including those that are part of a larger

ERP solution). Generally, this data is loaded monthly right after a financial close, but it is sometimes loaded more frequently during the close process.

Typical Financial Reporting dimensions include those common dimensions just discussed: Time, Measures, Scenario, Organization and Years. Measures will contain your account hierarchies for income statement, balance sheet, metrics, and cash flow. You can have alternate hierarchies to support different reporting requirements (more on that later).

In addition to the common dimensions, you will have those dimensions for which you'd like to perform analysis – by Geography, Product, Channel, or any other imaginable dimension that makes sense for your company. That's the beauty of Essbase: dimensionality is flexible and 100% customizable.

SALES ANALYSIS

Sales Analysis applications are a natural fit for Essbase, because they require fast retrievals at detailed levels. We once built a Sales Analysis application (sometimes called Flash Sales) that had data by store (for over 5,000 stores) by SKU (for over 100,000 products) by day for three years. It was an obscene amount of detail, but Essbase handled it flawlessly with retrievals measured in seconds.

Typical dimensions for this class of application include Product, Location, and Geography. You can also view sales data by demographics (like age and income level of buyer), by store information (like store manager, square footage, store type, or location), or by product information (like promotion or introduction date):

```
⊟ Income Level
   ┝ Under 20,000 ( + )
   ┝ 20,000-29,999 ( + )     ⊟ Payment Type
   ┝ 30,000-49,999 ( + )        ┝ Cash ( + )
   ┝ 50,000-69,999 ( + )        ┝ ATM ( + )
   ┝ 70,000-99,999 ( + )        ┝ Check ( + )
   ┕ 100,000 & Over ( + )       ┕ Credit Card ( + )
```

Age
  Teens (+)
    1 to 13 Years (+)
    14 to 19 Years (+)
  Adults (+)
    20 to 25 Years (+)
    26 to 30 Years (+)
    31 to 35 Years (+)
    36 to 45 Years (+)
    46 to 54 Years (+)
  Senior (+)

Time dimensions will often go to the day level (and be tracked across multiple years) and have attributes for day of week. Measures or accounts will often include units sold, cost of goods sold, price, revenue, and much more. Some sales applications have inventory data as well and include weeks of supply calculations.

With the introduction of Aggregate Storage Option (known in System 9 as "Enterprise Analytics"), the level of detail that can be loaded into Sales Analysis applications has grown exponentially. The advent of 64-bit Essbase has expanded the size of some of these databases even further since 64-bit Essbase allows far more RAM to be allocated to individual Essbase applications.

Unlike financial reporting applications which are generally fed from GLs or ERPs, Sales Analysis applications are generally fed from data warehouses, operational data stores, and legacy systems. It is not uncommon for Sales Analysis databases to be loaded every night with the prior day's sales data.

HUMAN CAPITAL ANALYSIS

Human Capital Analysis applications allow companies to analyze one of their most important assets: their people. (How important are certain people in your organization? Discuss.) Sometimes these applications are called Human Resources analysis, Employee analysis, or Salary analysis. We'll go with "Human Capital" analysis because it's trendy. "Human Resources" is *so* five minutes ago.

In addition to the ubiquitous Measures and Time, common dimensions for Human Capital applications include employee, employee status, job grade, and function. Detailed applications could also include title, start dates, and other employee-level information. It's also not uncommon to have Equal Employment Opportunity Commission attributes such as race, gender, age, and veteran status.

The Measures dimension will have accounts that tend to map to the General Ledger (particularly, the payroll or compensation section of the income statement).

- 501000 (+) (Alias: Total Compensation)
  - 501100 (+) (Alias: Salaries and Wages)
    - 501110 (+) (Alias: Total Salary)
    - 501120 (+) (Alias: Overtime)
    - 501130 (+) (Alias: Bonus Expense)
    - 501150 (+) (Alias: Auto Allowance)
  - 501200 (+) (Alias: Taxes and Benefits)

You can also use different drivers to budget and plan employee costs. Headcount, Start Month, Vacation Days, Sick Days, and many more can be used in calculations to complete accurate planning numbers.

These drivers can also provide invaluable insight into historical employee trends. We once knew a company that analyzed employee sick time patterns to find out which employees tended to be "sick" on Mondays more than any other day of the week. Apparently, the Monday morning flu was a big problem at their company.

CAPITAL EXPENDITURE ANALYSIS

Capital Expenditure applications (often abbreviated to "Cap Ex" and sometimes called Capital Equipment or Fixed Asset) are another frequent type of Essbase cube. Whether it's determining the rate of return on an investment or tracking capital equipment requests from your organization, you can implement a CapEx application to suit your company's needs. Dimensions include capital equipment item, equipment type, asset category, and asset life.

Here are some examples of capital equipment dimensions:

```
⊟ Category
    ─ Capacity (+)
    ─ Capability (+)
    ─ Cost Reduction (+)
    ─ Maintenance (+)
    ─ Market Opportunity (+)
    ─ Quality (+)
    ─ No Category (+)
⊟ Projects
  ⊟ All Projects (+)
      ─ Laser Weld (+)
      ─ Plasma R&D (+)
      ─ Networking (+)
      ─ BPM Implementation (+)
    ─ No Project (+)

⊟ Equip Type
  ⊟ All Equip Types (+)
      ─ Building (+)
      ─ Leasehold Improv (+)
      ─ Mfg Machinery (+)
      ─ Office Furniture (+)
      ─ Computer Equip (+)
      ─ New Software (+)
      ─ Auto (+)
    ─ No Equip Type (+)
```

The Account dimension for these applications usually contains a portion of your Balance Sheet:

```
⊟ BalanceSheet (~) (Alias: Balance Sheet)
  ⊟ 100000 (+) (Alias: Total Assets)
    ⊟ 150000 (+) (Alias: Fixed Assets)
      ⊟ 151000 (+) (Alias: Gross PPE)
          ─ 151100 (+) (Alias: Construction in Progress)
          ─ 151200 (+) (Alias: Land)
          ─ 151300 (+) (Alias: Buildings)
          ─ 151400 (+) (Alias: Leasehold Improvements)
          ─ 151500 (+) (Alias: Mfg Mach and Equip)
          ─ 151600 (+) (Alias: Office Furn and Fixtures)
          ─ 151700 (+) (Alias: Computer Equipment)
          ─ 151800 (+) (Alias: Computer Software)
          ─ 151900 (+) (Alias: Vehicles)
        ─ 152000 (+) (Alias: Accumulated Depreciation)
```

Other metrics that tend to show up in the Measures dimension include quantities, charges, months in service, asset life, and other drivers related to capital equipment.

Generally, CapEx applications are loaded from the Fixed Asset module from your ERP, but it is not uncommon for plan data for capital expenditures to be entered directly into Essbase (or via Hyperion Planning's Capital Expenditure model available in System 9.3).

BUDGETING, PLANNING, AND FORECASTING

With highly sophisticated write back capabilities, Essbase provides an excellent solution for budgeting, planning, and forecasting systems. Hyperion Planning was built on top of Essbase specifically to take advantage of Essbase's sublime ability to not only be used for reporting of data, but also multi-user submission of data.

Back in the days before Hyperion Planning was invented, many companies built Essbase cubes for budgeting purposes. They sent their data in via the Essbase Add-In and they were happy. Essbase security limited the dimensions and members for which data could be entered by users and calc scripts were used to calculate data if necessary.

If Essbase is perfect for budgeting, why was Planning created? The answer is simply due to the needs of planners and budgeters expanding beyond the abilities of Essbase. Modern forecasters require things like audit trails, integrated workflow, and web-based data entry. While Essbase can meet straight-forward budget needs, it doesn't have the built-in functionality that you get when you pay for Hyperion Planning.

Budgeting and forecasting applications written in Essbase (or built in Essbase via Hyperion Planning) will tend to look very similar to your reporting and analysis applications. For example, you may have a budgeting application to capture budget for income statement items, another application for capital equipment planning, and another application for salary planning. Though these applications will be similar to your reporting and analysis applications, they often do not contain the same level of detail. In general, budget data is not as granular as actual data.

In the example below, budget is captured at the reporting line level of Market while actual data is captured by GL account:

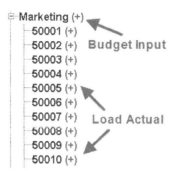

So...can we just capture budget and forecast information in our reporting and analysis applications? Yes, but there are some things to consider. First, understand the level of detail. If you are capturing budget at a higher level, you have to think carefully about how consolidations will take place in Essbase. If you enter data at an upper level and then run an aggregation, you could easily erase the data that was entered by users at the higher points in the dimension. There are ways to prevent this but the traditional work around is to use "dummy" members (see page below).

Second, we need to think about the dimensionality required for each purpose. In your reporting and analysis databases, you may want to analyze actual data by more dimensions or slices than you would for budget data. Too many dimensions can overly complicate the budgeting and planning process.

Third, you may also want to think about splitting reporting and budgeting for backup reasons. You'll want to backup your budgeting and planning applications more often as data changes far more frequently.

HOW I ALMOST KILLED A MAN – A CONCLUSION

Now that I had learned everything about Smart View (and how to handle a crazy boss like Lumberght) from that best-selling Smart View and Essbase book, I raced to the Smart View menu and within minutes had resubmitted my budgets, consolidated them, and performed some pretty amazing analysis. I finished everything just in time to sing along with Ode to Joy in gleeful gibberish German.

I must have fallen asleep, because the next thing I knew, my boss was standing at the entrance to my cubicle wearing golf attire.

Doctor's appointment? Yeah, right. He spoke as I wiped the drool from the corner of my mouth.

"Wow, that outfit looks great on you. It looks even better on you today than it did yesterday. Say, what happened to your cat poster?"

It was balled up in my trash can at the moment, but I knew just where he should stuff it. I started to suggest it when he said, "I got the analysis you sent me at 4AM. I don't know how you got it done in time. It was wonderful."

Clearing thoughts from my head of relocating my poster into one of his orifices, I managed to eke out, "Thank you?"

He smiled and put his hand warmly on my shoulder. I didn't immediately try to break his wrist, which meant that my thoughts of death by mind/coffee were gone only to be replaced (momentarily) with thoughts of a sexual harassment lawsuit.

"While I'd love to take the credit, Mr. Deadman, I have to say that I couldn't have done it without Essbase and Smart View. It saved my life last night," and yours too, I didn't add out loud.

He smiled from sunburned ear to sunburned ear. "Well, I always knew that buying Essbase was a good idea. I guess this proves it. You owe me one!"

He skipped off as I grabbed my copy of *Look Smarter Than You Are with Smart View and Essbase 11.1.2: An End User's Guide* and threw it at his head.

Note that the authors of this book do not condone in any way killing people with your thoughts, your latte, or your copy of this book. While the story above is fiction, similar situations occur all the time. We hope that you learn from this book so that you don't do something you might regret after enduring your 5-10 years of hard labor. Don't wait until 3AM to recall your Essbase teachings. Read this book, learn how to use Smart View and Essbase to your advantage, and please, get a good night's sleep.

Appendix:
GENERAL NOTES

Don't stop reading now. The Appendix has some helpful notes and knowledge to keep in your Smart View and Essbase toolbox.

NOTE ON THIS BOOK

Our objective is to teach you Smart View for Essbase data sources. Because Hyperion Planning stores data in Essbase, 100% of this book is applicable to Planning databases. About 75% of the content in this book is also applicable to analyzing and reporting against Financial Management sources. Future versions of the book will include Planning and HFM specific details.

We've tried to be as detailed as possible but if we described every single click or button, you'd be 100 years old before you were ready to use Essbase (and at that point, Hyperion would probably not even be an independent company but rather bought by some totally awesome firm like Oracle and Hyperion's CEO would be replaced with a really great guy like Larry Ellison, who if he's looking for an heir apparent should contact me at eroske@interrel.com). So we don't mention the fairly obvious tasks and buttons. For example, if there is a Close button, we probably skipped defining what this button does. Cancel means Cancel (doesn't save anything that you just did). Nothing tricky there.

WHY IS THIS OPTION GREYED OUT?

Smart View is the single add in for all of the Oracle EPM System and BI products. With that said, a number of options are specific to a product like Planning or Financial Management and are not available for Essbase connections. Keep this in mind if you find an option that is unavailable. With the new data source specific ribbons in 11.1.2.102 and 11.1.2.2, you will run into this less often.

Appendix:

MOVE FROM ESSBASE SPREADSHEET ADD-IN TO SMART VIEW

We'd like to thank Shubhomoy for writing this appendix to help further convince you Excel Add-in die hards that now is the time to switch to Smart View!

Author: Shubhomoy Bhattacharya
July, 2012

SMART VIEW USAGE SCENARIOS

The Office environment is one of the predominant interfaces that power EPM and BI users. Smart View usage can be classified as described below.

Ad Hoc Analysis

Ad hoc analysis lets Excel users interactively investigate the data contained in the source(s), where they "slice and dice" the data. They may start with templates (such as East > Cola > Sales) or a blank sheet where they begin shaping and altering the grids of data as they work. Typically, users retrieve the data from Oracle EPM sources—such as Essbase, Planning, Profitability or Financial Management—using mouse clicks or drag-and-drop. Free form analysis is a variant of ad hoc analysis where users can type in member names from a dimension directly on a spreadsheet and refresh the data.

Pre-defined Form Interaction

EPM application users who execute predefined input or reporting forms find Smart View a convenient way of completing tasks within Office. Such users are planners, consolidators and others who want to work in Excel for a consistent experience compared to a web application or to tie other spreadsheet-based models into their process. For example, customers use Smart View for Planning to incorporate data that is still housed in spreadsheet- and workbook-based models.

Pre-created Content Access

Another area of use is for importing pre-created content—for example, charts or grids— from Reporting & Analysis products to PowerPoint, Word, or Excel. The imported content can be refreshed from the Office environment.

Reporting

Reporting is another dimension of Smart View usage which leverages the capabilities of EPM and Oracle® BI data retrievals. Once the data is available within Office, you can create reports as needed based on a combination of data sources. For example, Planning and Financial Management data could be used to compare actual to budget. The ability to compare multiple scenarios, for different periods, products, locations, etc., enables more complex reports. The power of Office can be used to create Reports in the Office environment, which can be refreshed as needed.

Functions

Users can customize and automate common tasks by using Visual Basic for Applications (VBA) functions in Smart View. Functions are meant for advanced users who know exactly what they need (for example, Actual profit for month of January for Eastern Region for all products) and want to create custom applications. These users typically build VB Applications and incorporate Smart View functions to get relevant information. Functions also allow combining multiple data sources on a single grid. For example, it is possible to display Essbase and Planning data on the same worksheet using functions.

Outlined above were the general capabilities of Smart View. The next few sections specifically focus on various aspects of moving from the Essbase Spreadsheet Add-in to Smart View.

REASONS TO MOVE TO SMART VIEW

Smart View is the Strategic Office Add-in for Oracle EPM and Oracle® BI products including Oracle® Essbase. Smart View is vastly improved from the Oracle® Essbase Spreadsheet Add-in many ways. Here are some reasons to consider for moving from Essbase Spreadsheet Add-in to Smart View:

- Improved feature functionality over Essbase Spreadsheet Add-in
- Single add-in for multiple products as opposed to only Essbase
- Rich functionality specific to the data source (Essbase, Planning etc.)
- Support for Word and PowerPoint
- 64-bit Office support
- Support for newer versions of Office and Windows O/S's

STATEMENT OF DIRECTION – ESSBASE SPREADSHEET ADD-IN

Essbase Spreadsheet Add-in will be in maintenance mode starting January, 2013. As such, platform updates for Essbase Spreadsheet Add-in will no longer be done, which means newer versions of Office or Windows will not be supported. New features will only be added to Smart View and not the Essbase Spreadsheet add-in. Releases prior to 1st January, 2013 should be considered terminal releases for the Essbase Spreadsheet Add-in.

Official Oracle® Essbase Spreadsheet Add-in statement of direction:
https://support.us.oracle.com/oip/faces/secure/km/Document Display.jspx?id=1466700.1

PLANNING FOR THE MOVE

Moving from Essbase Spreadsheet Add-in to Smart View involves some planning. There are various aspects to consider in order to make this a successful transition. Outlined below are the areas that you will need to be informed about or implement prior to the move.

Platform Support

Smart View is supported for Microsoft® Office 2007 and 2010. At the time of writing this paper Release 11.1.2.2.000 of Smart View is available and it supports the 64-bit version of Microsoft® Office. For exact version support and related details, please refer to the support matrix.
http://www.oracle.com/technetwork/middleware/bi-foundation/hyperion-supported-platforms-085957.html

Essbase and Provider Services

In order to take advantage of the new features added to Smart View 11.1.2.1.102 (and higher), it is required that Essbase (Essbase Server) and Oracle® Hyperion Provider Services also be release 11.1.2.1.102 (or higher). Please make sure that necessary upgrades to the new version have been completed by the Essbase administrator before trying out the new features using Smart View. While Smart View can connect to older versions of Essbase (9.3.3 and up), most of the features introduced in 11.1.2.1.102 will not be available unless Essbase and Hyperion Provider Services are upgraded as well.

Note: Smart View accesses Essbase data sources, via a middle tier. Hyperion Provider Services is commonly referred to as a provider or as APS (Analytic Provider Services).

Understanding the New Features

Understanding the new features is very important in order to either use Smart View or guide others who are moving from Essbase Spreadsheet Add-in. The new features are explained throughout this book and in a detailed whitepaper that I have written, posted here:

http://www.oracle.com/technetwork/middleware/smart-view-for-office/overview/sv-wp-oracle-toc-revrec-2012-ea-1722850.pdf.

Re-using Essbase Spreadsheet Add-in Content (without VBA)

By and large, workbooks created in Essbase Spreadsheet Add-in should be usable in Smart View without any changes. The spreadsheet needs to be connected to the right data source and refreshed. Thereafter, any Smart View operations should be possible on those workbooks. Remember, the appropriate sheet options should be applied as they will not be applied automatically in Smart View. While there is no way to test all combinations and spread sheets, 99% of spreadsheets (without VBA) can be refreshed in Smart View without any changes on the grid itself. It is possible that the spreadsheet has some grid combinations rarely used (most users are unaware of those), which may have to be re-created in Smart View based on supported features or functionality.

Converting Essbase Spreadsheet Add-in VBA

It is common for Essbase Spreadsheet Add-in users to create and use Visual Basic Applications. This will involve redesign and rewrite of functions or applications to work with Smart View. Prior to going down that path, an evaluation will be needed. This is to identify if the custom code has been replaced with a feature in Smart View, calls that have been deprecated, and more. To help in this process, you can use the Smart View VBA Conversion Tool:

http://www.oracle.com/technetwork/middleware/smart-view-for-office/downloads/index-088403.html

This will assist in the conversion of Legacy (Classic) Add-In VBA code to equivalent Smart View VBA code. Please be aware that Oracle® Technology Network (OTN) Developer License Terms apply. You can read the OTN License agreement prior to download. Also, keep in mind that Oracle's technical support organization will not provide technical support, phone support, or updates to you for the Smart View VBA Conversion Tool. It is intended for providing guidance to developers who are otherwise adept in building Visual Basic Applications. Useful Link:

http://essbaselabs.blogspot.com/2010/07/converting-legacy-add-in-vba-to-smart.html

For more information, please see my complete whitepaper, Moving from Essbase Spreadsheet Add-in to Oracle® Hyperion Smart View for Office, Fusion Edition at http://www.oracle.com/technetwork/middleware/smart-view-for-office/overview/sv-wp-oracle-toc-revrec-2012-ea-1722850.pdf.

Appendix:

WHAT'S NEW IN SMART VIEW?

NOTE ON SMART VIEW VERSIONS

Smart View was introduced pre-System 9 for Essbase but it wasn't the full product we know and love. The full product was introduced in System 9, though it has changed through the different versions 9.0 to 9.2, 9.3 and finally, 11x. While we love Smart View, various features will work in certain versions but not necessarily in other versions. The steps to perform tasks also change. This book is based on version **11.1.2.1.102 and 11.1.2.2**. We mention the **.102** because there is are some big differences between 11.1.2.0 and 11.1.2.1.102 forward.

WHAT'S NEW IN 11.1.2.1.102?

By Glenn Schwartzberg, Oracle ACE Director and interRel Sr. Architect.

Smart View 11.1.2.1.102 was released in fall of 2011 as a patch set on Support.oracle.com. Big deal, you say, it's just another patch! Oh how wrong you are my friends. This is the patch of all patches. The patch we have been waiting our collective lives for. Why? Because it makes Smart View act and behave like the Essbase add-in (among other things).

The first thing that I consider a fix is that you can now do a submit data without first refreshing the sheet if you make changes to it. Second, we have all checked the "Use Excel formatting" option only to find the formatting disappears if we zoom in or pivot. Well, now it really does work, and it works in two ways. If checked, it leaves the Excel formatting completely alone. For example, if you highlight cell C3 as red, and you pivot a page member to a row, cell C3 will still be red. But the Smart View team has figured how to set it so that, if you zoom in, the formatting will get carried along with the zoom in. Very nice!

But that is just the beginning. Here are a few of my favorite new things.

Full Parity

1. You can select multiple members on which to do Ad Hoc operations at one time (zoom in, zoom out, keep only, remove only). This is not limited to just row or column member, you can select both at the same time.

2. Support for LROs and Linked Partitions.

3. Aliases. There are two items here. First, you can have both the member name and aliases on rows in the report. Second and one of my favorites, if you use an alias from an alias table that is not active, Smart View now understands it and returns the member name or alias for the active alias table (depending on what you have your options set to).

4. **SHEET LEVEL OPTIONS are back!** All options are defined as sheet level options and are stored with the sheet. That means you no longer have to worry about what happens if you change options and then do a retrieve on a different sheet. Also there is now a dropdown on the options dialog, so when you change your options, you can set a default set. This default set is used when new sheets are created.

5. All of the zoom options that you know and love in the add-in are now available. They are also on the ribbon bar as a dropdown on zoom in so you can select the zoom level/type you want to do.

6. Formula preservation and Formula fill are working like they should and then some. If you pivoted in the add-in you would lose the formulas. In this release, in most cases, the formulas are preserved. They may no longer be accurate, depending on what you did, but they will be there.

7. While the new features document does not talk about it, I believe range retrievals are back. You can highlight an area of a report and, as long as all of the dimensions are represented, you can retrieve just that part of the report.

New and Enhanced Features

While the above items allow for Parity, the Smart View team was not satisfied with just making things the same. In a number of areas, they went miles beyond what the Excel add-in could do.

1. You can have multiple grids on a single sheet. Remember the old message "Multiple grids on a single sheet are not supported at this time"? Well, the time has come, and that message can now be archived forever. You can set up multiple connections to the same or different databases and do a refresh and they all update. I had 4 different reports on a single sheet and they all pulled data properly.

2. Butterfly and reverse formatted reports are now available. A butterfly report is where member names are in the middle with number on each side. (As shown below. Note, the numbers are not from sample basic. I made then up to show a report sample):

	A	B	C	D
1		Jan	Market	sales
2	actual		budget	
3		500 100-10	400	
4		300 100-20	400	
5		200 100-30	150	
6		250 100-40	100	
7				

You can also do a reverse report where the member names follow the data values:

	A	B	C	D
1		Jan	Market	sales
2	actual	budget		
3	500	400 100-10		
4	300	400 100-20		
5	200	150 100-30		
6	250	100 100-40		
7				

3. In the 11.1.2.1.102 version, you actually are not hiding POV but putting it onto the sheet. In this new version, the POV members are stored on the sheet in row 1 (or wherever you designate them to be). When you enable the POV, it hides the row on the sheet. Changing the member names on the sheet or in the POV bar affects both locations. Another nice feature with the POV is that you can type in member names directly if you know them. (It was actually introduced in 11.1.2.1.)

4. A Member information button has been added to the ribbon bar. From this you can get almost all of the information about a member, such as generation and level, consolidation properties, aliases, attribute associations, formulas, comments and UDAs.

5. Within the Smart View connection information dialog, new functionality has been included. For multiple grids on a single

sheet, you can delete the connection info (currently the only way to reset multiple connections) and also copy off the connection into a sheet to send to someone if you are having issues with your retrievals so they know what you are connected to.

6. A host of new VBA toolkit functions have been added. The development team asked what APIs people were using and turned most of them into toolkit macros. This is very handy because you don't need to code to the API any more; you can do it all with macros.

Considerations

As with any release, there are disclaimers and this is no exception. Per the Oracle documentation, unless otherwise noted, the features described here are available only in Smart View 11.1.2.1.102 connected to Oracle Essbase 11.1.2.1.102 through Oracle Hyperion Provider Services 11.1.2.1.102. They are not available in other releases of Smart View, Essbase, or Provider Services. They are not available in data providers other than Essbase.

This means that you have to install the patches for Smart View, APS and Essbase to take advantage of the features. You can use this version of Smart View with older versions of APS but won't have the new features available.

As for upgrades, here is what the support matrix says: You can upgrade to Smart View Release 11.1.2.1.102 from the following releases:

Release Upgrade Path From	To
11.1.2.1.x	11.1.2.1.102
11.1.2.1.102	11.1.2.1.102
11.1.1.3.x	11.1.2.1.102
9.3.3.x	11.1.2.1.102

I am truly excited about this release. It gives us things we have been asking for in the add-in for a long time and now puts Smart View ahead of the add-in in functionality.

For more fun reading by Glenn, check out his blog: http://glennschwartzbergs-essbase-blog.blogspot.com.

WHAT'S NEW IN 11.1.2.2?

The big changes for Smart View were seen in 11.1.2.102 but version 11.1.2.2 does have some cool new features that are covered in this book.

A new query tool, Smart Query, allows users to build reusable complex queries against Essbase data sources. Users can create and save multiple member sets and filters for advanced analysis. The member sets and filters can be joined together in a Smart Query and used and reused for analysis.

Move on Formatting on Operations will apply Excel formatting on zoom and pivot operations. You can now Cascade to different workbooks.

Two new logging levels were introduced to provide more detail when troubleshooting and debugging query issues with Smart View: Extended Info and Profile.

The Panel and Connection buttons were split into two separate icons on the Smart View ribbon to make it easier and more intuitive to connect to data sources and access the Smart View panel.

Several new VBA functions were released (e.g. HypGetMemberInformationEx, HypGetActiveMember, HypGetMmembers).

Smart View now supports 64 Microsoft Office and has two new extensions for Hyperion Strategic Finance (HSF) and Predictive Planning.

WHAT'S NEW IN 11.1.2.2.300?

The most recent patch of 11.1.2.2.300 introduces a few handy new features. My favorite is the new cell based POV feature. Now you can access the POV drop down from a cell within Excel (in addition to the floating POV). You can either select a member from the drop down box in the POV cell or type the member name directly in the cell:

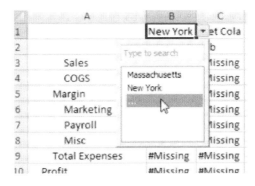

By selecting the ellipses (...) you can launch the member selector to select lists of members to display in the drop down. All of the member selector functions are available like Children or Descendants.

A new Function Builder is introduced in 11.1.2.2.300 that now follows the way Microsoft builds functions. The new function builder is much easier to use, providing a guided wizard interface that even a nontechnical person can use:

Ever had someone send you a document that had a number of linked cells or references that were broken when you opened the spreadsheet? The new Fix Links option on the main Smart View menu will go through the worksheet automatically and clean up the references.

And finally users now see a status bar when long queries are run:

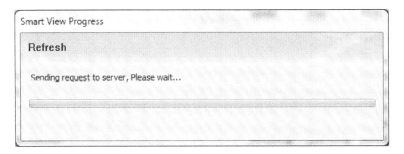

This is important to help users understand that their query is still running (so they don't just try and relaunch the same really big query multiple times). To see the status bar, you must select the "Show progress information after (seconds)" option with a recommended setting of 5. Note if you are using functions in Smart View, you must set the Show progress information to zero in 11.1.2.2.300.

EXCEL ADD-IN VS. SMART VIEW ADD-IN 11.1.2.2

	Excel Add-in 11.1.1	*Smart View for Essbase 11.1.2.2*
Drill Capabilities	Yes	Yes
Keep only, Remove Only	Yes	Yes
Member Selection	Yes	Yes
Member Selection Filtering Options	Yes	Yes
Find in Member Selection	Yes	Yes
Advanced Member Selection by Subsets	Yes	Yes (Smart Query)
Query Designer	Yes	Yes (different)
Smart Query	No	Yes
Suppress Missing Rows	Yes	Yes

	Excel Add-in 11.1.1	*Smart View for Essbase 11.1.2.2*
Suppress Missing Columns	Yes	Yes for Planning and HFM; Coming soon for Essbase
Display Member Name and Alias	Yes	Yes
Retain Formulas	Yes	Yes
Formula Fill on Zooms	Yes	Yes
Formula Fill on POV Change	Yes	Yes
Butterfly Reports	No	Yes
Formatted Reports	Yes	Yes
Cell Text / LROs	Yes	Yes
Adjust function	No	Yes
DTS	Yes	Yes
Substitution Variables	Yes	**Yes**
Member name referenced in a linked formula	Yes	Yes
Cascade	Yes	**Yes but way better**
Ancestor Position	Yes	No
Use Excel Formatting & Cell Styles	Yes	Yes
Flashback / Undo	Yes – One Undo	Yes – Multiple Undo's
View Connection Information	*Options >> Styles tab*	Sheet Info
Define Default Starting POV	No	**Yes with Smart Slices**
Multi-Source Grids / Reports	Yes	Yes
Alias Table defaults to Default	Yes	Yes
Alias Table Selection Remembered	Yes	Yes (sheet level option)

	Excel Add-in 11.1.1	*Smart View for Essbase 11.1.2.2*
Submit Data to Essbase	Yes	Yes
MDX vs. Rpt Script	Rpt Script	MDX
Copy / Paste Data Points	No	Yes
Visualize in Excel	No	Yes
Support for Word	No	Yes
Support for PowerPoint	No	Yes

POV MANAGER

We know you are asking, "Why is this an appendix"? Smart View provides the ability to utilize point of views across spreadsheets using Point of View manager (sort of). A point of view is the default starting point for each dimension for a database connection. POVs are used primarily with default starting points for ad hoc analysis and in the background for data points.

You've used the POV Manager in this book to change the POV for data points created with the *Copy Data points* feature. You can also use the POV Manager to set a POV for a new spreadsheet. We've moved this to an appendix because POV Manager can be unpredictable or buggy at times and you have better alternatives available to you with Smart View ad hoc functionality and the POV toggle on/off feature, Smart Slices and Report Designer.

But just in case you'd like to take the longer, difficult, unpredictable path, here are the steps.

If you are performing ad hoc analysis and want to leverage a saved POV, you must open an unconnected worksheet. You can copy a saved POV to a blank worksheet. Select *Refresh* and the POV will be applied to the query. You can copy POVs to different spreadsheets, but for those that already have queried grids the POV will have no effect. Once you start using the grid, you can no longer make changes with the POV Manager.

For example, say you are the sales manager for the East region for Diet Cola products, so you might want your POV to be the following:

Market: East
Scenario: Actual

Products: Diet Colas

Accounts: Sales

Do you have to reference every dimension in your POV? No. You can pick and choose the dimensions that are applicable for your POV. Can you reference more than one member for a single dimension in a POV? Again no; you can only choose one member for each dimension.

By default the POV will reference the top member of every dimension. To edit a POV, select *Functions>>Manage POV* on the Smart View ribbon:

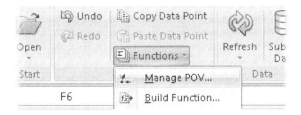

The POV Manager will display:

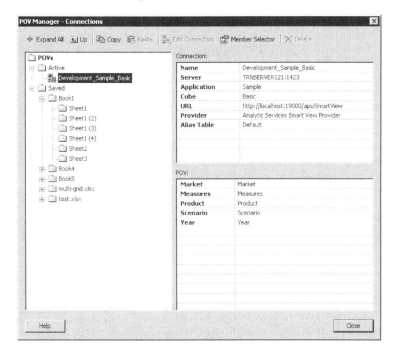

Note!

A POV is tied to a database connection.

Tip!

Make sure the Query Designer is closed when you want to work with the POV Manager. If the Query Designer is open, the POV Manager option is grayed out.

Let's edit the POV for our East sales manager. Select the dimension by double clicking in each dimension in the POV Manager and the Member Selection window will display. Choose the desired members for each dimension (in our case, East, Diet Colas, and Sales).

Now refresh your existing report or query. Nothing happened, right? Yes, unfortunately once you've retrieved data the POV becomes useless in ad hoc analysis or existing grids in Excel. POVs provide the real value in starting point analysis (and in the use of data points, covered in just a bit).

Let's copy this POV to a blank worksheet. To copy and paste a point of view, select *Functions >> Manage POV*. From the Active folder, select the Active application connection. Select the members for the POV and save the workbook. Click *Copy:*

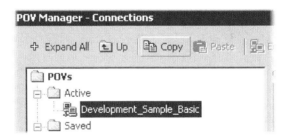

Expand the Saved folder to select the workbook and blank worksheet into which you want to paste the POV. Click *Paste:*

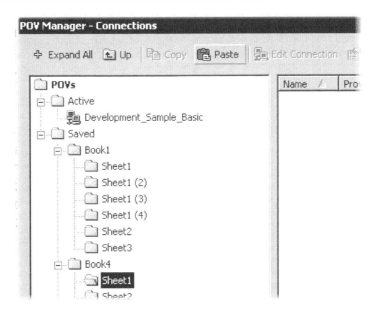

Tip!

You can also drag and drop POVs within the POV Manager.

Navigate to the worksheet. Activate the database connection if necessary. Select *Refresh* and you should see the query updated with the appropriate POV.

Optionally, to copy a saved POV from another workbook, open the workbook and select the saved POV. Copy and paste the source POV to the target worksheet in the Saved folder.

And so we conclude our Look Smarter Than You are with Smart View. You can thank us later from saving you from prison (no need to kill our bosses any longer). Happy analyzing!

INDEX

Made in the USA
Middletown, D'
03 October 2C